Depósito Legal: M-000763/2025

email: carl.mcbride@protonmail.ch
ORCiD: 0000-0003-2966-7530
LinkedIn: www.linkedin.com/in/carl-mcbride-ellis

ISBN 978-1-80808-131-6
Book GitHub: github.com/Carl-McBride-Ellis/TOBoML

Green edition, version 2.5.3 (3 June 2026)

Contents

This book is based on my five day course which I had the pleasure of teaching in the following Spanish cities: A Coruña, Algeciras, Alicante, Bilbao, Cáceres, Granada, Huesca, Jaén, Madrid, Málaga, Murcia, Sevilla, Valencia, Valladolid, and Zaragoza. I would like to take this opportunity to say a big thank you to all of my students *¡un gran placer!*

This 'Green' edition builds upon the material originally imparted in the aforementioned course. This book uses the `python` programming language largely in conjunction with the `scikit-learn` machine learning library, and `pandas` for data manipulation. All example notebooks use the Jupyter Notebook environment and many of the sample code snippets are also available as GitHub gist files.

Special thanks to: Carlos Ortega, Santiago Mota Herce, Norberto Malpica, Charles H. Martin, Roland Stevenson, Adrian Olszewski, Ambros Marzetta, Valeriy Manokhin, and everyone on Kaggle.

I would also very much like to thank Dr. Valeriy Manokhin and Miguel Pérez Michaus for their critical reading of prior versions of this book, as well as feedback from both Dr. David Holzmüller and Dr. Noah Hollmann particularly regarding Chapter 13.

For Cristina

1. Introduction

Statisticians torture their data to fit the model.
Data scientists torture their models to fit the data.

1.1 The $\hat{\beta}$ and the $\hat{y}$

A statistical model, primarily designed for explanatory or inference purposes, will use a simple predefined function (based on the assumption that the data can be modelled by a parametric distribution) and will then estimate the best parameters, $\hat{\beta}$, for said function. A non-parametric, *i.e.* making no assumptions about the distribution of the data, machine learning model forgoes explanatory power for predictive power, with the emphasis on producing the best possible predictions, $\hat{y}$, for previously unseen data (at the end of the day we are not interested in predicting the data that we already have!).

Equation: Fundamental assumption: our data is composed of signal + noise which is symmetrically distributed either side of the signal (*i.e.* $\mathbb{E}[\varepsilon] = 0$). In one dimension we can write this as

$$y = \underbrace{f(x)}_{signal} + \underbrace{\varepsilon}_{noise} \tag{1.1}$$

In multiple dimensions the signal $f(\mathbf{X})$ due to the data generating process will form a hypersurface. Our objective is to produce the best possible fit to this hypersurface. Suffice to say that in machine learning we do not know the original $f(\mathbf{X})$ and our challenge, somewhat akin to an inverse problem, is to find an approximation to $f(\mathbf{X})$ having been given a (sparse) smattering of (noisy) points on y. This short book is dedicated to introducing us to the essentials of a number of techniques for producing such a fit: this book is all about the $\hat{y}$.

1.2 Estimators and approximators

Generalized linear models such as linear regression and logistic regression are statistical estimators; their purpose is to estimate values of the parameters of a model, for example $\hat{\beta}_1$ and $\hat{\beta}_0$, that has been fitted to samples taken from a population that has a well defined distribution. On the other hand in approximation theory the target that one fits to is usually sampled via an evenly spread dense grid of points on the domain. Indeed both decision trees and artificial neural networks are universal approximators. However, in machine learning neither are we so much interested in the parameters of a model, but rather the predictions of said model, nor are we provided with a nice grid of points having noiseless targets; we work with the data that we are given. In some sense machine learning is situated somewhere between estimation and approximation. Perhaps for that reason the algorithms that we employ are sometimes known as *learners*, rather than as estimators or as approximators.

1.3 Transductive vs inductive models

A transductive model is one in which the data *is* the model; when one makes a prediction one consults the training data itself. Examples are the k-nearest neighbors regressor and classifier. On the other hand an inductive model has generalization in mind; it will distill the training data into a intermediate compact form and it is this compact representation that is used for prediction. An example would be linear regression; in the univariate case the form is a straight line, and any number of training data points become represented by just two values, namely β_1 and β_0. When making a prediction the training data is no longer relevant and one instead consults the model. The majority of this book is concerned with creating such inductive models.

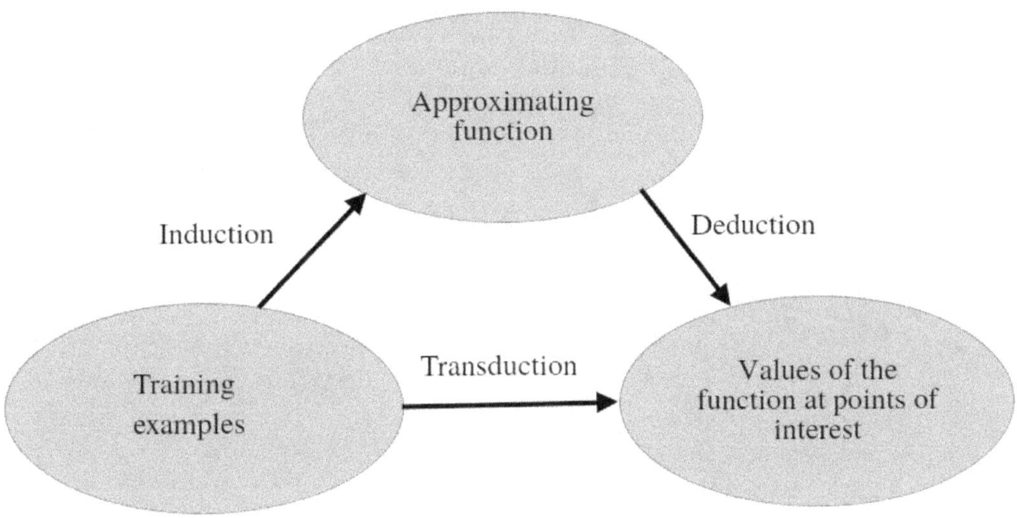

Figure 1.1: Different types of inference (adapted from the book "The Nature of Statistical Learning Theory" by Vladimir N. Vapnik).

1.4 Prediction vs forecast

The etymology of the verb *to predict* is *to say before*, but before exactly what is ill defined. To avoid getting embroiled in semantics I shall simply provide an example.

Say we use gradient descent as our **optimization algorithm** (or **solver**) to **learn** from our set of empirical data points (our **dataset**) in order to **estimate** the parameters $\hat{\beta}_1$ and $\hat{\beta}_0$ for the **model**

$$\hat{y}(x) = \hat{\beta}_1 x + \hat{\beta}_0$$

for the one-dimensional independent variable, x, whose data had a range $[a,b]$. If we now use this **hypothesis** or **fit** (model + parameters) to calculate the value $\hat{y}(x=c)$ where $a < c < b$ this is a (point) **prediction**. If $c < a$ or $c > b$ this is an **extrapolation**, and when the independent variable is time and $c > b$ this is called a (point) **forecast**.

1.5 Errors and residuals

The error is the difference between the observed value and the ideal value. For example, a chocolate bar may have the ideal value printed on the packet, say 100g. However, no chocolate bar has ever been made that weights *exactly* 100g, and the difference between the actual weight and ideal 100g is the error. On the other hand the residual is the difference between the predicted value and the observed value. Note however that in this text when we use the word error correctly speaking we should really use the word residual, and we do this simply because of the prevalence of the word error in the machine learning literature, for example the mean absolute error (MAE) or the root mean squared error (RMSE).

1.6 Sources of uncertainty: aleatoric and epistemic

Aleatoric, or stochastic, uncertainty is due to inherent random noise in a system/generating process. Epistemic, and Knightian, uncertainty is due to a lack of data or knowledge; for example having an incomplete dataset.

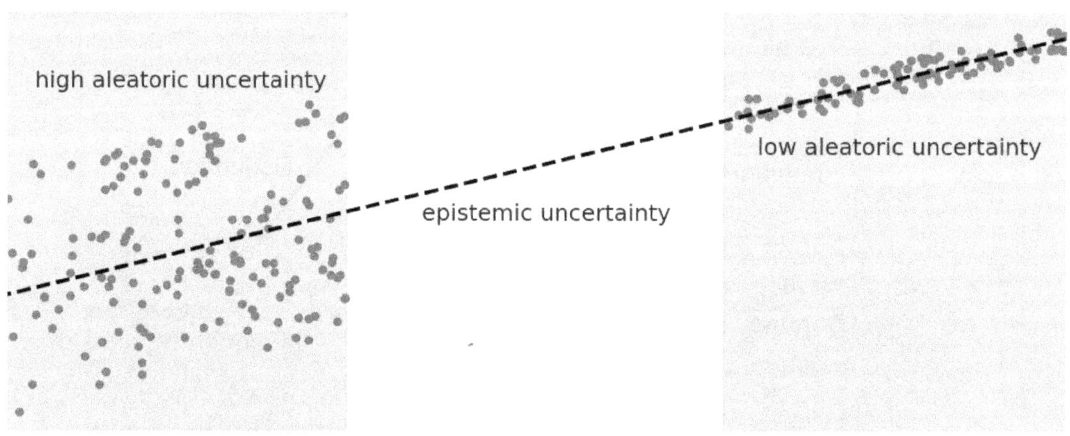

Figure 1.2: Aleatoric and epistemic uncertainty in a dataset.

Aleatoric uncertainty is considered to be irreducible, whereas epistemic uncertainty is reducible; one could fill gaps present in the data. Knightian uncertainty could take the form of invisible features that influence the target, but are either not provided, or whose collection was perhaps never even contemplated, or our data could have missing values. Knowing how the uncertainty is partitioned could indicate whether further data acquisition could lead to better predictions. However, in practice a neat decomposition into the aforementioned components is not empirically practicable.

1.7 Confidence and prediction intervals

Confidence intervals[1] quantify the uncertainty in the estimated parameters $\hat{\beta}$. Prediction intervals quantify the uncertainty in the estimated predictions $\hat{y}$. We shall see how to calculate regression confidence intervals in Section 7.3.4, and prediction intervals using conformal prediction in Section 7.17.

1.8 Explainability and interpretability

- Explainability: the ability to understand both the 'how' and the 'why' of a prediction
- Interpretability: the ability of understand the 'why' of a prediction

Explainability is the *forte* of statistical models; the 'how' is in-built from the very start by using simple models for the data. On the other hand the focus of machine learning (ML) is almost exclusively on prediction performance. Only the simplest ML models are interpretable; decisions trees are in principle very easy to explain and are often touted as being a 'white box' algorithm, but even at depth 3 (*i.e.* 8 leaves) and having several features then in reality their predictions quickly become very hard to interpret. There are packages such as SHAP (SHapley Additive exPlanations) and LIME (Local Interpretable Model-Agnostic Explanations) to facilitate post hoc interpretability. However, it has been seen that often even the data scientists themselves do not know how to use these packages properly[2]:

> *"...results indicate that data scientists over-trust and misuse interpretability tools. Furthermore, few of our participants were able to accurately describe the visualizations output by these tools".*

which does not bode well. To make matters worse of late some of the uses that people make of the SHAP technique, such as posing counterfactual questions, have been brought into question[3,4]. At the end of the day machine learning models are designed for performance, and generally interpretability takes a back seat. However, in many circumstances model interpretability is of paramount importance; indeed under the EU General Data Protection Regulation (GDPR) 2016/679 (Article 15 1h)

> *"The data subject shall have the right to obtain... the following information: the existence of automated decision-making... meaningful information about the logic involved, as well as the significance and the envisaged consequences of such processing for the data subject."*

With the ever increasing rôle that machine learning models play in modern society the creation of interpretability tools is an active area of development.

1.9 Correlation and causation

Caveat emptor: standard machine learning can only identify correlative patterns, but as the mantra goes *correlation does not imply causation.* A famous example is the purported correlation between ice cream sales and death by drowning. Indeed we could create a perfectly valid predictive model

$$\hat{y} = \hat{\beta}_1 x$$

where x is the number of ice creams sold, and $\hat{y}$ is our prediction for the number of drownings. However, suffice to say ice cream sales do not cause drownings. Here there is an invisible feature (known as a

[1] Morey *et al.* *"The fallacy of placing confidence in confidence intervals"*, Psychonomic Bulletin & Review **23** pp. 103-123 (2016)

[2] Kaur *et al.* *"Interpreting Interpretability: Understanding Data Scientists' Use of Interpretability Tools for Machine Learning"*, Proceedings of the 2020 CHI Conference on Human Factors in Computing Systems pp. 1-14 (2020)

[3] Huang, Marques-Silva *"The Inadequacy of Shapley Values for Explainability"*, arXiv:2302.08160 (2023)

[4] Bilodeau, Jaques, Wei Koh, Kim *"Impossibility Theorems for Feature Attribution"*, arXiv:2212.11870 (2024)

confounding factor) involved, namely temperature; when there is hot weather more people buy ice creams, and more people go swimming and unfortunately drown. We can see that in reality our interpretable model is highly misleading, and does not constitute an explanatory model.

Recommended reading

Papers

- Leo Breiman *"Statistical Modeling: The Two Cultures"*, Statistical Science **16** pp. 199-231 (2001)
- Galit Shmueli *"To Explain or to Predict?"*, Statistical Science **25** pp. 289-310 (2010)
- Hrushikesh N. Mhaskar, Efstratios Tsoukanis, Ameya D. Jagtap *"An Approximation Theory Perspective on Machine Learning"*, arXiv:2506.02168 (2025)
- Gruber *et al.* *"Sources of Uncertainty in Machine Learning - A Statisticians' View"*, arXiv:2305.16703 (2023)

Books

Explainability, interpretability, and trustworthiness

- Denis Rothman *"Hands-On Explainable AI (XAI) with Python"*, Packt Publishing Limited (2020)
- Serg Masís *"Interpretable Machine Learning with Python"*, Packt Publishing Limited (2023)
- Christoph Molnar *"Interpretable Machine Learning"*, (online book)
- Kush R. Varshney *"Trustworthy Machine Learning"*, (2022)
- Mucsányi, Kirchhof, Nguyen, Rubinstein, Oh *"Trustworthy Machine Learning"*, arXiv:2310.08215 (2023)

Causal analysis

- Matheus Facure *"Causal Inference in Python"*, O'Reilly Media, Inc. (2023)
- Aleksander Molak *"Causal Inference and Discovery in Python"*, Packt Publishing Limited (2023)

Packages

- SHAP
- SHAP-IQ - Shapley Interaction Quantification
- LIME
- ConformaSight Global Explainer Package (paper)
- EconML
- CausalML

2. Statistics

> 60% of the time, it works every time
>
> *Brian Fantana in 'Anchorman'*

In this chapter we briefly cover some essential statistical concepts that are useful when it comes to understanding our data and the workings of machine learning algorithms.

2.1 Centrality: mean, median, and mode

The mean and the median are measures of the central tendency, or *location*, of a distribution.

Equation: The Kolmogorov generalised mean is given by

$$M(x) := g^{-1}\left(\frac{1}{n}\sum_{i=1}^{n} g(x_i)\right) \tag{2.1}$$

If $g(x) = 1(x)$ we have the arithmetic mean of an additive sample of size n, given by

$$\bar{x} = \frac{1}{n}\sum_{i=1}^{n} x_i \tag{2.2}$$

The mean of the hypothetical population (*i.e.* the expectation value, $\mathbb{E}(x)$), from which the sample was supposedly obtained, is denoted by μ.

If $g(x) = \log(x)$ and where $x_i > 0$ we have the geometric mean, given by

$$\text{GM}(x) = \left(\prod_{i=1}^{n} x_i\right)^{\frac{1}{n}} \tag{2.3}$$

and is used for values that are combined multiplicatively.

If $g(x) = (1/x)$ and where $x_i > 0$ we have the harmonic mean, given by

$$\text{HM}(x) = \frac{n}{\sum_{i=1}^{n} \frac{1}{x_i}} \tag{2.4}$$

The median ($\tilde{x}$) of a set of values is a number such that half of the values are below the median value, and the other half are above the median value. The median is said to be a *robust* statistic in that it is less influenced by a few extreme or outlier values. For example here we calculate the mean and the median for an *array* of values using the python numpy library

```
import numpy as np
from scipy import stats

np.mean([1, 2, 3, 4, 5, 6, 1001]) # arithmetic mean
146.0

stats.gmean([1, 2, 3, 4, 5, 6, 1001]) # geometric mean
6.867897363489863

stats.hmean([1, 2, 3, 4, 5, 6, 1001]) # harmonic mean
2.855978316248548

np.median([1, 2, 3, 4, 5, 6, 1001])
4.0
```

The mode is the most frequently occurring value, and can be useful when working with a discrete distribution (such as count data), categorical features, or for quickly identifying a zero-inflated distribution.

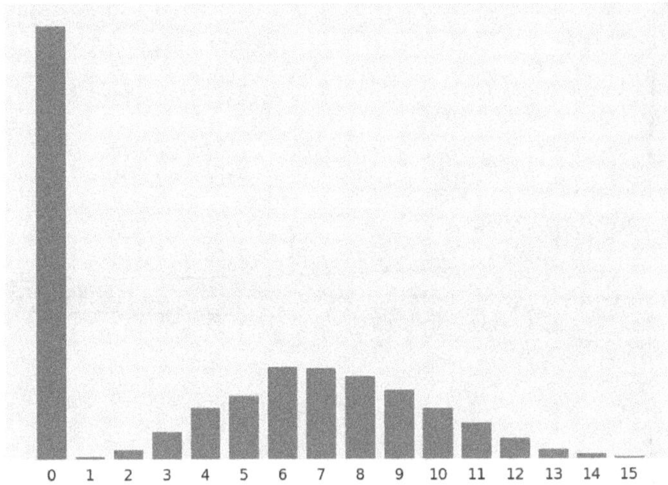

Figure 2.1: An example of zero-inflated count data.

An example of zero-inflated data would be the number of items purchased when visiting a web site; most visits result in no purchase.

> Remark: For our intents and purposes it is interesting to consider the mean, median, and mode not so much as simply being summary statistics, but rather to think of them as being elemental baseline models of a set of numbers having one degree of freedom.

2.1.1 Law of large numbers

The law of large numbers states that, as the number of samples (n) increases, the mean of the sample converges on the mean of the population that the samples were drawn from

$$\bar{x} \rightarrow \mu \quad \text{as } n \rightarrow \infty. \tag{2.5}$$

This has very important implications for our machine learning model; our model, if it was trained on a sufficiently large sample, should then be transferable (*i.e.* make just as good predictions) for a different sample taken from the same population. Transferability is an absolutely vital quality of a machine learning model as at the end of the day its sole function is to provide trustworthy predictions for data (*i.e.* $\mathbf{X}_{new}$) that it has never seen before.

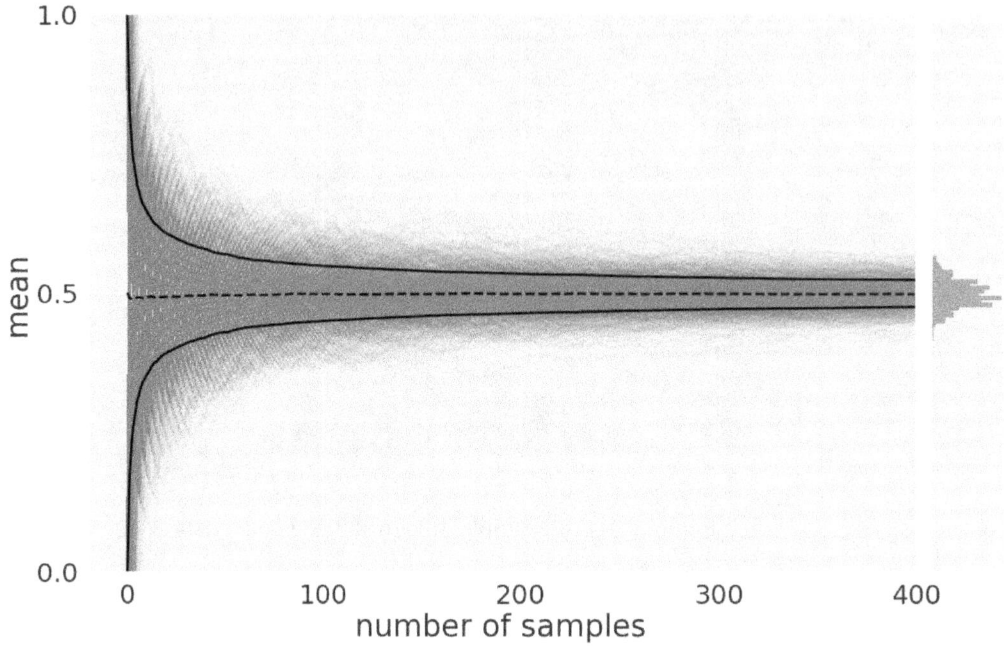

Figure 2.2: The results of 1,000 simulations (green lines) for the mean of flipping a fair coin for a total of 400 flips. The horizontal dashed black line represents the mean of the 1,000 trajectories at that step, and the upper and lower black curves represents the ± 1 standard deviation of the trajectories at that step. The (orange) histogram on the right is the distribution of the final mean value for each trajectory.

2.2 Dispersion: range, variance, MAD, and quartiles

In Figure 2.3 we have two distributions that have exactly the same mean value.

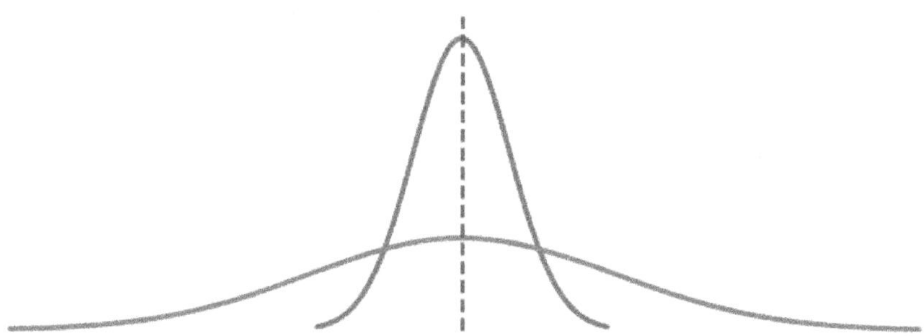

Figure 2.3: Two distributions with same central tendency.

We can see that centrality only tells part of the story and evidently we also need to be able to describe how spread out a distribution is as well. The range (R) of a distribution is simply the difference between the largest and smallest values, *i.e.*

$$R(x) = \max(x) - \min(x) \tag{2.6}$$

Equation: The variance, Var or σ^2, is given by

$$\sigma^2(x) := \frac{1}{n}\sum_{i=1}^{n}(x_i - \bar{x})^2 \tag{2.7}$$

and $\sqrt{Var}$, or σ, is known as the standard deviation.

Remark: When calculating the variance or standard deviation by default, unlike numpy, pandas applies the Bessel correction of $n-1$.

Equation: The sample covariance, between the ordered pair x and y, is given by

$$cov(x,y) = \frac{1}{(n-1)}\sum_{i=1}^{n}(x_i - \bar{x})(y_i - \bar{y}) \tag{2.8}$$

We have

$$Var(x+y) = Var(x) + Var(y) + 2cov(x,y) \tag{2.9}$$

In 2-dimensions we can now also construct a variance-covariance matrix:

$$\mathbf{K} = \begin{bmatrix} Var(x) & cov(x,y) \\ cov(y,x) & Var(y) \end{bmatrix} \tag{2.10}$$

(note that $cov(x,y) = cov(y,x)$ so this matrix is symmetric).

```
import numpy as np

K = np.cov(df, rowvar=False)
```

The median absolute deviation is the robust statistic for dispersion.

Equation: The median absolute deviation (MAD) is given by

$$\text{MAD}(x) := \text{median}(|x_i - \tilde{x}|) \tag{2.11}$$

2.2.1 Quantiles, quartiles and the interquartile range (IQR)

The median is a special case of a quantile and is often denoted as Q2. Two other quantiles of note are Q1, below which lies 25% of the values, and Q3, above which also lies 25% of the data. Suffice to say the other 50% of the data has values between Q1 and Q3 and is known as the interquartile range (IQR).

```
import numpy as np

values = [1,2,3,4,5,6,7,8,9,10,11,12]
np.quantile(values, 0.25) # Q1
3.75
np.quantile(values, 0.5)  # Q2
6.5
np.quantile(values, 0.75) # Q3
9.25
np.quantile(values, 0.75) - np.quantile(values, 0.25) # IQR
5.5
```

Quantiles are excellent for producing prediction intervals as we shall see later in quantile regression.

2.3 Statistical (and mechanical) moments

We can view our distribution of samples from a physical perspective in terms of moments[1] where a moment (m) is the product of the distance (x) to a point, raised to a power, r:

$$m_r = x^r$$

Let us imagine our data series as if it were a 1-dimensional physical object with each sample having a mass of 1. The total mass of this object composed of n points is given by the zeroth moment ($r = 0$)

$$\text{total mass} = x_1^0 + x_2^0 + ... + x_n^0 = \sum_{i=1}^{n} 1 = n$$

where x is the position of the point mass. If we normalize this with respect to the number of points (samples) we will obtain the density, which is 1.

$$\text{density} = \frac{x_1^0 + x_2^0 + ... + x_n^0}{n} = \frac{n}{n} = 1$$

If we set $r = 1$, the first moment, we can find the location of the centre of mass (CoM) of this object

$$\text{centre of mass (CoM)} = \frac{x_1^1 + x_2^1 + ... + x_n^1}{n} = \frac{1}{n}\sum_{i=1}^{n} x_i = \bar{x}$$

notice that this is the same as the equation of the arithmetic mean of a sample, $\bar{x}$. If we now set this CoM to be the new origin of our coordinate system (rather than 0) and calculate the second moment ($r = 2$) we obtain what is known in mechanics as the moment of inertia of this hypothetical body

$$\text{moment of inertia} = \frac{(x_1 - \text{CoM})^2 + (x_2 - \text{CoM})^2 + ... + (x_n - \text{CoM})^2}{n} = \frac{1}{n}\sum_{i=1}^{n} (x_i - \bar{x})^2$$

which we see is the same as the equation for the variance. The third (m_3) and fourth (m_4) moments are used in calculating the skewness and kurtosis of a distribution respectively.

2.4 Gaussian distribution: additive

[1] Karl Pearson *"Asymmetrical Frequency Curves"*, Nature **48** pp. 615-616 (1893)

Equation: The Gaussian probability density function (PDF) is given by

$$f(x;\mu,\sigma) = \frac{1}{\sigma\sqrt{2\pi}} e^{-\frac{1}{2}\left(\frac{x-\mu}{\sigma}\right)^2} \quad (2.12)$$

where μ is the mean and σ is the standard deviation, and is sometimes represented as $\mathcal{N}(\mu,\sigma^2)$.

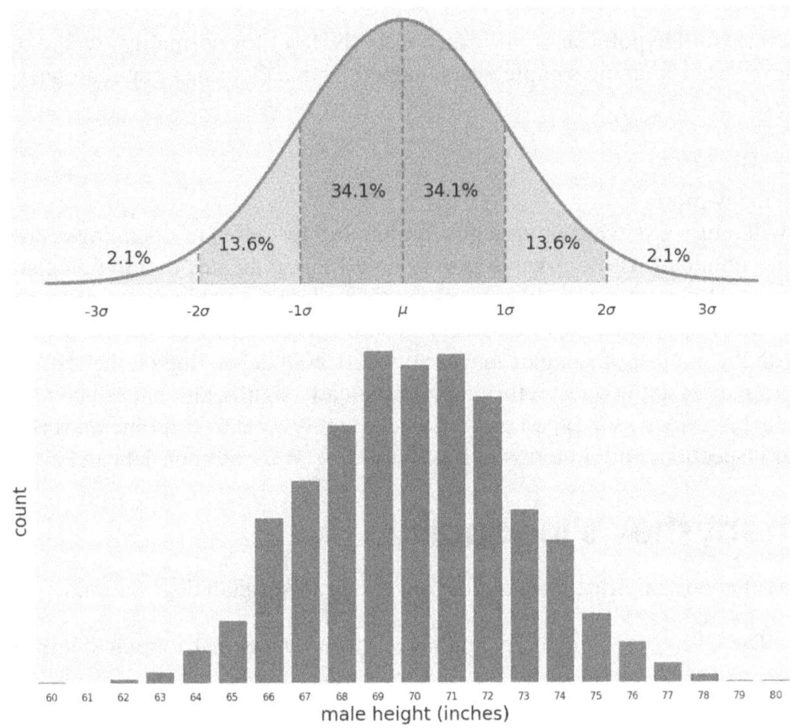

Figure 2.4: The Gaussian distribution, the percentages represent the relative areas under the curve (AUC) of each of the shaded regions. The lower plot is a countplot of 4082 adult male heights (Data source: ANSUR II).

Equation 2.12 leads to the easy to remember 68–95–99.7 rule for the percentage of data that lies between $\mu \pm 1\sigma$, $\mu \pm 2\sigma$, and $\mu \pm 3\sigma$ respectively. A Gaussian distribution can approximately be obtained as a result of a large number (say > 5000) of independent additive samples.

As alluded to in the introduction, it is entirely reasonable for the empirical errors in a measurement to be equally likely to lie either side of the signal (*i.e.* the true value) hence the assumption that the mean value of the error (ε) in repeated measures of a given vector will tend towards zero. However, it was the work of Gauss in 1802, published in 1809 and expanded upon by Laplace in 1810, in a somewhat cart before the horse manner showed that for ordinary least squares to return the most likely signal (in this case the signal was the orbit of the dwarf planet Ceres[2]) then the form of the distribution of the errors (the *error curve*) has to follow what we now know as the Gaussian distribution. Regarding the nomenclature 'normal' distribution Karl Pearson wrote:

[2]Saul Stahl *"The Evolution of the Normal Distribution"*, Mathematics Magazine **79** pp. 96-113 (2006)

"Many years ago I called the Laplace-Gaussian curve the normal curve, which name, while it avoids an international question of priority, has the disadvantage of leading people to believe that all other distributions of frequency are in one sense or another 'abnormal' That belief is, of course, not justifiable."[3]

N Jupyter Notebook: Animated histogram of the central limit theorem

2.4.1 Statistical tests for (non)-normality

There are several null hypothesis significance tests (NHST) for normality[4] where the null hypothesis (H_0) built into these tests is that the sample was obtained from a Gaussian population:

- Shapiro-Wilk
- D'Agostino
- Anderson-Darling
- many, many more...

These tests will return a statistic along with a probability (p-value) of obtaining a statistic at least as extreme as the statistic obtained. If the p-value is very small this indicates that the data is incompatible with the null hypothesis. However, it should be stressed that a large p-value does not imply evidence *for* the null hypothesis; other hypotheses may be equally or more consistent with the observed data[5]. Normality tests work best with the number of samples in the range $[20, 200]$ depending on the test. Be aware that having too many samples may result in a test returning a statistically significant, but effectively trivial, deviation from normality, what is known as a Type I error. It is extremely wise to combine ones NHST of normality along with a visual inspection, both in terms of plotting a histogram of your data and a quantile-quantile plot.

2.5 Chebyshev's inequality

Suffice to say that our empirical data almost never has a Gaussian distribution.

Equation: The Chebyshev inequality applies to virtually any distribution and is given by

$$p(|x-\mu| \geq k\sigma) \leq \frac{1}{k^2} \tag{2.13}$$

where p represents the probability.

Some of the results of this inequality are shown graphically in Figure 2.5 and listed in Table 2.1.

[3]Karl Pearson "*Notes on the history of correlation*", Biometrika **13** pp. 25-45 (1920)

[4]B. W. Yap, C. H. Sim "*Comparisons of various types of normality tests*", Journal of Statistical Computation and Simulation **81** pp. 2141-2155 (2011)

[5]Wasserstein, Lazar "*The ASA Statement on p-Values: Context, Process, and Purpose*", The American Statistician **70** pp. 129-133 (2016)

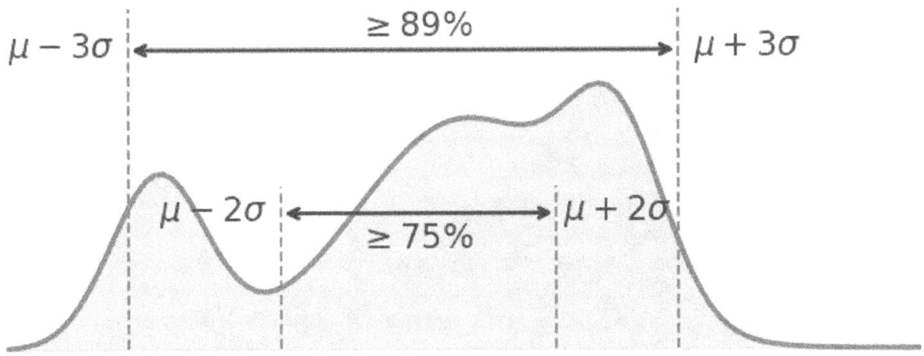

Figure 2.5: Chebyshev's inequality.

range	Gaussian	Chebyshev
$\mu \pm 2\sigma$	95.45%	75%
$\mu \pm 3\sigma$	99.73%	88.88%
$\mu \pm 5\sigma$	99.99994%	96%
$\mu \pm 6\sigma$	99.9999998%	97.22%
$\mu \pm 8\sigma$	99.99999999999987%	98.44%

Table 2.1: Comparison between the Gaussian distribution and the Chebyshev lower bound results for the percentage of values that lie within the given range.

We can see from the above table that if we step back from the, dare I say dogma, of the Gaussian distribution, so-called 'virtually impossible' 8-sigma events can actually have up to a 1.5% probability of occurring.

2.6 Galton distribution: multiplicative

The Galton, or log-normal, distribution is frequently seen in real datasets[6].

[6] Eckhard Limpert, Werner A. Stahel, Markus Abbt *"Log-normal Distributions across the Sciences: Keys and Clues"*, BioScience **51** pp. 341-352 (2001)

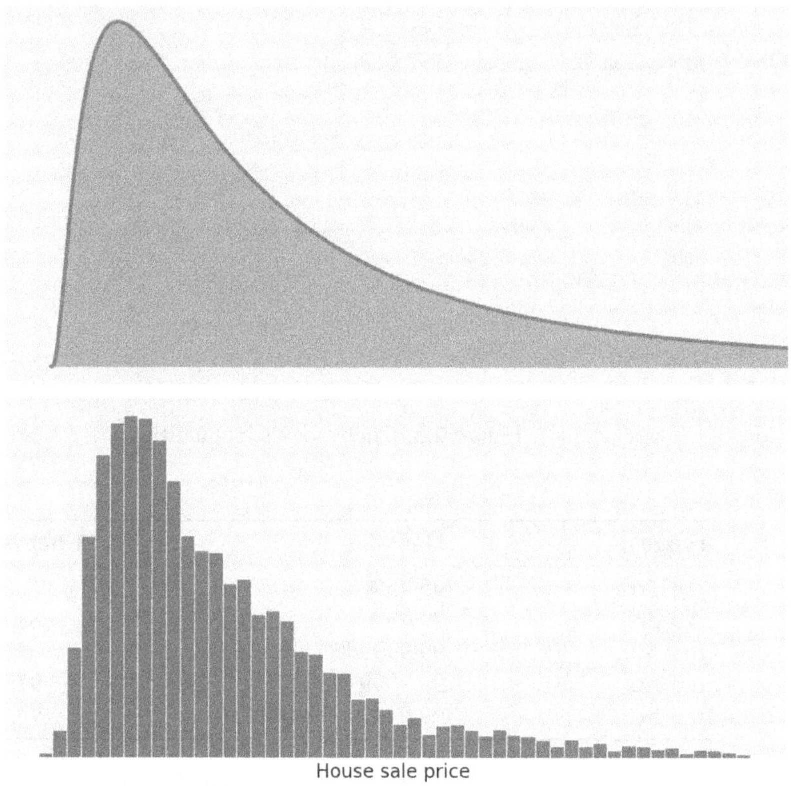

Figure 2.6: Galton or log-normal distribution. The lower plot is a histogram of house sale prices (Data source: King County home sales data).

If one were to take the logarithm of the independent variable one would obtain a Gaussian distribution. A Galton distribution can approximately be obtained as a result of a large number of independent multiplicative samples (see also Gibrat's law).

N Jupyter Notebook: Simulating a Galton distribution

2.7 Power-law and exponential distributions

Equation: A power-law distribution is given by

$$f(x;\alpha) = \frac{\alpha-1}{x_{\min}}\left(\frac{x}{x_{\min}}\right)^{-\alpha}, \qquad \alpha > 1;\ x > x_{\min} \tag{2.14}$$

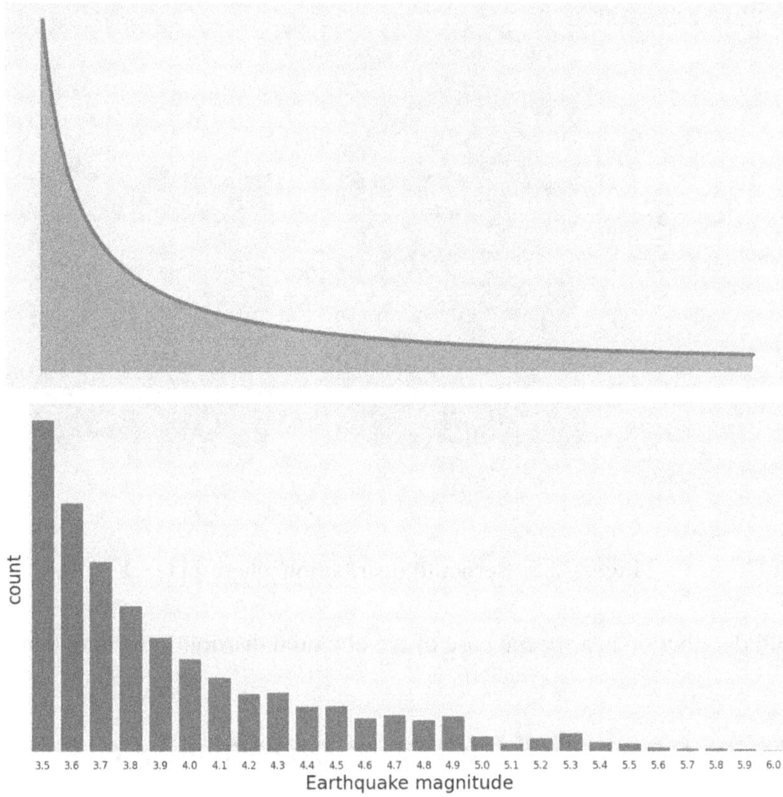

Figure 2.7: Power law distribution. The lower plot is a countplot of earthquake magnitudes in Turkey.

A well-known example of a power-law is the Pareto distribution.

Equation: The exponential probability density function is given by

$$f(x;\lambda) = \lambda \exp(-\lambda x), \qquad x \geq 0 \tag{2.15}$$

The exponential distribution is a special case of the gamma distribution where the shape parameter set to 1.

2.8 Bernoulli distribution

The Bernoulli distribution has the discrete binary support $\{0, 1\}$ and where $p(x = 0) = 1 - p(x = 1)$, *i.e.*

$$\begin{aligned} f(x;p) &= p^x(1-p)^{1-x} \qquad\qquad x \in [0,1] \qquad (2.16)\\ &\equiv \exp\left(x.\log\left(\frac{p}{1-p}\right) + \log(1-p)\right) \end{aligned}$$

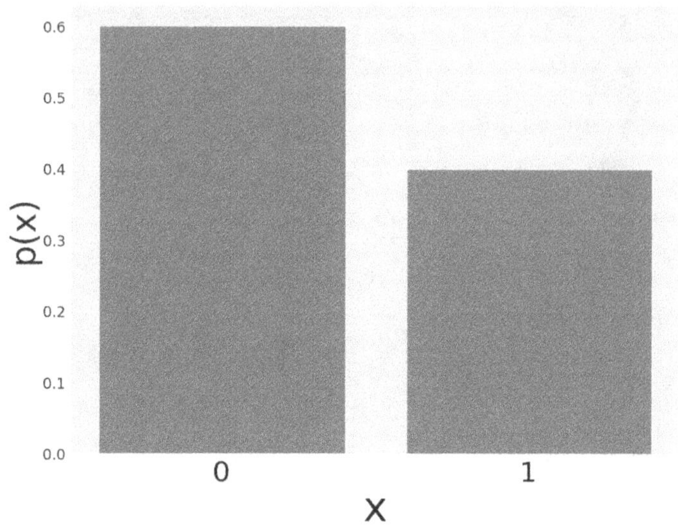

Figure 2.8: Bernoulli distribution where $p(x = 1) = 0.4$.

The Bernoulli distribution is a special case of the binomial distribution where there are only two possible outcomes.

2.9 The exponential family of probability distributions

Members of the exponential family of probability distributions can be expressed in the following canonical form

$$f(x;\boldsymbol{\theta}) = g(\boldsymbol{\theta})h(x)\exp\left(a(x)b(\boldsymbol{\theta})\right) \tag{2.17}$$

$$\equiv \exp\left(a(x)b(\boldsymbol{\theta}) + c(\boldsymbol{\theta}) + d(x)\right) \tag{2.18}$$

where $\boldsymbol{\theta}$ represents the set of parameters, a represents the sufficient statistic(s), b is known as the natural parameter(s), c is the (log) normalization term, and d is the carrier measure. For example:

distribution	$\boldsymbol{a(x)}$	$\boldsymbol{b(\theta)}$	$\boldsymbol{c(\theta)}$	$\boldsymbol{d(x)}$
Gaussian	(x, x^2)	$\left(\frac{\mu}{\sigma^2}, -\frac{1}{2\sigma^2}\right)$	$-\log(\sigma) - \frac{\mu^2}{2\sigma^2}$	$-\frac{1}{2}\log(2\pi)$
Galton	$(\log(x), (\log(x))^2)$	$\left(\frac{\mu}{\sigma^2}, -\frac{1}{2\sigma^2}\right)$	$-\log(\sigma) - \frac{\mu^2}{2\sigma^2}$	$-\frac{1}{2}\log(2\pi)$
exponential (special case of gamma)	x	$-\lambda$	$\log(\lambda)$	0
Bernoulli (special case of binomial)	x	$\log\left(\frac{p}{1-p}\right)$	$\log(1-p)$	0

For more members of the family see Frank Nielsen, Vincent Garcia *"Statistical exponential families: A digest with flash cards"*, arXiv:0911.4863.

2.10 Skewness and kurtosis

Skewness is a measure of distribution asymmetry. The Galton distribution is an example of a distribution having positive skew. Unlike the symmetric Gaussian distribution with similar tails on either side, here the long tail is located on the right hand side (RHS). For negative skew the long tail is on the left hand side (LHS). The sample `skew` is calculated from

$$\text{skew} = \frac{m_3}{m_2^{3/2}} \tag{2.19}$$

where m_2 and m_3 are the second and third moments respectively. One can perform an NHST test for skewness with respect to a Gaussian distribution using the `scipy.stats.skewtest`.

> Remark: Be wary of detecting skewness simply in terms of the relative locations of the mean and the median, especially for discrete distributions often seen in real data.

Kurtosis is a measure of tail thickness (not peakedness[7]), and `kurtosis` is calculated from the fourth moment via

$$\text{kurtosis} = \frac{m_4}{m_2^2} - 3 \tag{2.20}$$

Notice the adjustment factor of 3, which corresponds to the kurtosis of a Gaussian distribution, leading to the following nomenclature

- leptokurtic (kurtosis > 0): a distribution that has a fatter tail than a Gaussian
- mesokurtic (kurtosis $= 0$): Gaussian-like
- platykurtic (kurtosis < 0): a distribution that has a thinner tail than a Gaussian

One can perform an NHST test for kurtosis with respect to a Gaussian distribution using `scipy.stats.kurtosistest`.

Sample code

```
from scipy.stats import skew
print( skew( df["feature"] ) )

from scipy.stats import kurtosis
print( kurtosis( df["feature"] ) )
```

Recommended reading

Books

- Hans Fischer *"A History of the Central Limit Theorem"*, Springer (2011)
- Carlos Fernandez-Granda *"Probability and Statistics for Data Science"*

Packages

- NumPy
- SciPy

[7] Peter H. Westfall *"Kurtosis as Peakedness, 1905–2014. R.I.P."*, The American Statistician **68** pp. 191-195 (2014)

3. Exploratory data analysis (EDA)

> A computer should make both calculations and graphs. Both sorts of output should be studied; each will contribute to understanding.
>
> *Anscombe (1973)*

> garbage in, garbage out (GIGO)
>
> *unknown (1950's)*

The primary objectives of exploratory data analysis (EDA) in the context of predictive modeling are:

- to become familiar with the data we shall be working with
- awareness of any potential data quality issues
- obtain ideas for feature engineering

3.1 Data quality

In an insightful paper by Carlos Mougan *et al.*[1] they discuss five dimensions of data that lead to a project being able to leverage the most out of machine learning:

- Appropriateness: is the data actually relevant to the data question(s) posed?
- Readiness: is the data analysis-ready?
- Reliability: how biased is the data? Biases include historical, representation, measurement and aggregation.

[1] Mougan, Plant, Teng, Bazzi, Cabrejas-Egea, Sze-Yin Chan, Salvador Jasin, Stoffel, Jane Whitaker, Manser *"How to Data in Datathons"*, NeurIPS 2023 **458** pp. 10440-10456 (2023)

- Sensitivity: how sensitive is the data? Does it contain personal information or data which carries legal, reputational, or political risks?
- Sufficiency: how much data is enough data?

	Insufficient	Developing	Functional	Optimal
Appropriateness	Data unrelated to the research question(s)	Target variable is inappropriate for research question	Features are not entirely appropriate for question	Clear relation between features and target
Readiness	No data has been collected yet	Some data has been collected	Data collected, but needs merging, unifying, and cleaning	Data collected and cleaned
Reliability	Data has strong biases	Source of bias not determined	Source(s) of bias has been determined	Little or no bias
Sensitivity	Highly sensitive data	Requires extensive security measures	Data has little risk, but may be confidentail	Low risk dataset
Sufficiency	Prior experience shows low success rate	Does not meet the level of previous successful projects	Similar projects have been successful	Excess of data

Figure 3.1: Data assessment matrix. (Image adapted from: Mougan, Plant, Teng, Bazzi, Cabrejas-Egea, Sze-Yin Chan, Salvador Jasin, Stoffel, Jane Whitaker, Manser *"How to Data in Datathons"*, NeurIPS 2023 **458** pp. 10440-10456 (2023))

Assessing and addressing each of these dimensions forms part of the process of exploratory data analysis.

3.1.1 Synthetic and syncretic data

Synthetic data can indeed be useful from a software engineering/MLOps perspective; it can quickly produce as much data as needed similar to the real data that one expects to see in production thus can be used to stress test ML workflows and data pipelines. However, such data should never be used for model building purposes; since the synthetic data was the output produced by a model one will simply end up creating an inferior 2nd generation model.

Syncretic data is real training data that has been 'upsampled' or augmented with synthetic data

> *Some people, when confronted with a small tabular dataset, think "I know, I'll use synthetic data." ...now they have two problems.*

If one has insufficient data for machine learning there is sometimes a temptation to perform synthetic data augmentation, for example by using a pair of artificial neural networks known as a generative adversarial network (GAN), a prime example being `CTGAN` which can be found as part of the Synthetic Data Vault. For the same reasons that neural networks struggle to model tabular data, leads them to also fail to synthesize effective tabular data. Another synthetic data augmentation technique is SMOTE, designed to solve the purported imbalanced data 'problem'. At the end of the day there exists a synthetic tabular data augmentation paradox: when creating a predictive model of ones real dataset let us suppose one will want to use the best available machine learning algorithm. If one wished to further improve performance by the adding of new synthetic datapoints one would need to generate this new data using a model whose performance is even better than that of the machine learning algorithm one intends to use. However, one is *already* using the the best available machine learning algorithm, therefore improving model performance via synthetic tabular data augmentation is not possible.

It is worth mentioning that filling missing values using imputation is also a form of synthetic data augmentation, and is only beneficial if the gains associated with recovering the feature coefficients or feature vectors that sport `NaN` values outweighs the cost of completely ignoring (*i.e.* dropping) said columns or rows of data.

3.2 Getting to know your dataframe

Dataframes are 2-dimensional objects akin to tables in a relational database. There are many excellent packages for manipulating dataframes such as Polars, PySpark, Ibis, *etc.* Here we shall assume you have read in your dataset as a pandas dataframe, be it from a file stored in the popular `csv` format (for example with `pd.read_csv()`), in the highly efficient `parquet` format (`pd.read_parquet()`), or directly from a database via an SQL query, for example using something like `.to_dataframe()`. The following pandas methods are great for very quickly getting to know your dataframe `df`:

- `df.shape` - returns the number of rows and columns of the `df`
- `df.head(n)` - print out the first n rows
- `df.tail(n)` - print out the last n rows
- `df.dtypes` - print the data types of each column (float, integer, object, *etc.*)
- `df.describe()` - descriptive statistics for each column

Some useful `pandas` settings are

```
pd.set_option('display.max_columns', None)
pd.set_option('display.max_rows', 32)
pd.set_option('display.max_colwidth', 16)
```

The very first thing to do when working with a new dataset is to know how much data one is working with. `df.shape` will tell us the number of rows (*'feature vectors'*) and columns (*'features'*) we have in the problem.

> Remark: In older statistics literature one may happen across the *one in ten rule*, *i.e.* suggesting an events-per-variable ratio of 10. Regarding machine learning this value is way too low; when performing regression to be effective one should have `n_rows` $> 100 \times$ `n_columns`. This also applies to the number of minority class samples in classification. In order to estimate the amount of data required for a given model one should undertake a learning curve analysis.

We can also have too much data; the more data we have evidently the better the model we can make. But training a model on a very large dataset is computationally expensive, and for rapidly creating prototype models we may find it convenient to extract a subsample of the dataset to work with. For example we may like to use a randomly sampled subset of 25K rows of data (note that it is important to take a random sample of the data, and not simply the first 25K rows):

```
sample_df = df.sample(n=25_000, random_state=42)
```

where the `random_state` option permits the creation of a reproducible sample.

> Remark: Python very helpfully allows the insertion of underscores within numbers. These are discarded at run-time, but are a great visual aid. (PEP 515)

Once we are happy with our choice of estimator and hyperparameters we can then proceed to train our final model on the full dataset.

3.2.1 The curse of dimensionality

The curse of dimensionality, a wonderfully florid term by Richard Bellman, is due to having too many columns of data. One can very well imagine each column of data as an axes in an n_c dimensional vector space. As the volume of this space increases the datapoints rapidly become sparse. For example, say we wish to describe the average person. If our only characteristic, or *feature*, is their height then we could do this rather well. Now say we add more features, such as hair color, eye colour, age, weight, *etc*. Eventually with enough features we would find that every single person becomes unique, and the term average no longer has any meaning. Sparse data leaves plenty of room for epistemic uncertainty and is easily overfitted, and overfitting is the bane of machine learning.

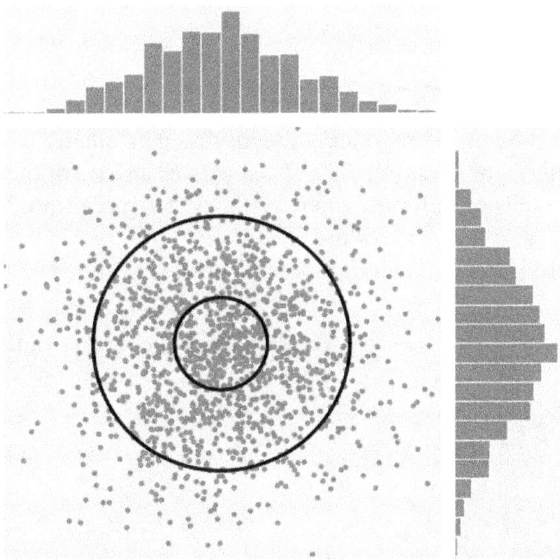

Figure 3.2: The curse of dimensionality in 2-dimensions. The inner circle contains 45% of the points, the outer circle contains 90% of the points.

In the following example we have hypothetical features that each have the same Gaussian distribution (*i.e.* we have a multivariate Gaussian distribution). In one dimension 45% of the data is located roughly between $\pm 0.60\sigma$, and 90% of the data between $\pm 1.64\sigma$, in other words the inner 45% lies along a line of length 1.2, and the outer 45% along a line of length 2.1. The ratio between the outer length and the inner length is 1.75 so on average in one dimension the inner 45% of the data is almost twice as dense as the outer 45%.

dimension	ratio
1	1.75
2	6.6
3	20
4	56
5	157
6	432
7	1191
8	3277
9	9018
10	24810

Table 3.1: Ratios of the volumes of an n-shell to an n-ball for $l_1 = 1$ and $l_2 = 2.75$.

From Table 3.1 we can see that for ten dimensions (*i.e.* 10 features) the outer 45% of the data is almost 25 thousand times more sparse than the central 45%. This is why it is very important in machine learning to have a very large number of rows of data.

3.2.2 Descriptive statistics

Descriptive statistics can be useful in quickly identifying data quality issues, for example perhaps the `Age` column has negative values, or ages over 120. It can give us an idea of the scale of the columns; `sales` may be of the order of thousands or millions, whereas maybe `temperature` has a scale of a few degrees. Here is the output of a `df.describe().T` for the Titanic dataset

	count	mean	std	min	25%	50%	75%	max
PassengerId	891.000000	446.000000	257.353842	1.000000	223.500000	446.000000	668.500000	891.000000
Survived	891.000000	0.383838	0.486592	0.000000	0.000000	0.000000	1.000000	1.000000
Pclass	891.000000	2.308642	0.836071	1.000000	2.000000	3.000000	3.000000	3.000000
Age	714.000000	29.699118	14.526497	0.420000	20.125000	28.000000	38.000000	80.000000
SibSp	891.000000	0.523008	1.102743	0.000000	0.000000	0.000000	1.000000	8.000000
Parch	891.000000	0.381594	0.806057	0.000000	0.000000	0.000000	0.000000	6.000000
Fare	891.000000	32.204208	49.693429	0.000000	7.910400	14.454200	31.000000	512.329200

Figure 3.3: pandas `describe().T` for the Titanic dataset

It reports centrality in the form of the mean and the median (*i.e.* the 50% column), and dispersion in the form of the standard deviation, the IQR (*i.e.* 75%-25%), and the range (*i.e.* $max - min$).

> **Remark:** When using `pandas describe()` it is perhaps preferable to print the transpose (`.T`), especially if the dataset has a lot of features. This then makes for a long table as opposed to a wide table.

3.2.3 Pivot and contingency tables

Another useful exploration tool, especially for classification tasks where the target column consists of labels (here `"Survived"`) is the pandas `pivot_table`

```
pd.set_option('display.max_columns', None)

df = dataset.select_dtypes(include='number')
pd.pivot_table(df, index=["Survived"], aggfunc="mean").round(2)
```

	Age	Fare	Parch	PassengerId	Pclass	SibSp
Survived						
0	30.63	22.12	0.33	447.02	2.53	0.55
1	28.34	48.40	0.46	444.37	1.95	0.47

Figure 3.4: A pandas `pivot_table` for the Titanic dataset

One can calculate a contingency table using the pandas `crosstab`

```
pd.crosstab(index    = [dataset["Survived"], dataset["SibSp"]],
            columns = [dataset["Pclass"], dataset["Sex"]])
```

	Pclass	**1**		**2**		**3**	
	Sex	**female**	**male**	**female**	**male**	**female**	**male**
Survived	**SibSp**						
0	**0**	1	59	3	67	33	235
	1	2	16	3	20	21	35
	2	0	1	0	4	3	7
	3	0	1	0	0	7	4
	4	0	0	0	0	4	11
	5	0	0	0	0	1	4
	8	0	0	0	0	3	4
1	**0**	48	29	41	9	48	35
	1	38	15	25	7	17	10
	2	3	1	3	1	4	1
	3	2	0	1	0	1	0
	4	0	0	0	0	2	1

Figure 3.5: A pandas `crosstab` example.

3.2.4 pandas groupby

The pandas groupby can be used, for example, to obtain category-wise descriptive statistics for (here) the target column:

```
df.groupby(by=["cat_col"])[['target']].count() # count rows in group
df.groupby(by=["cat_col"])[['target']].mean()
df.groupby(by=["cat_col"])[['target']].std()
df.groupby(by=["cat_col"])[['target']].min()
df.groupby(by=["cat_col"])[['target']].quantile(q=0.25)
df.groupby(by=["cat_col"])[['target']].median()
df.groupby(by=["cat_col"])[['target']].quantile(q=0.75)
df.groupby(by=["cat_col"])[['target']].max()
```

Examples of some other functions that can be applied are the sem (standard error of the mean), var, sum, and skew.

> Remark: One can also apply a bespoke user defined function. However, in terms of performance this can be excruciatingly slow in pandas and I would suggest using the highly efficient polars library instead.

3.3 Outliers, inliers and extreme values

Firstly is is very important to differentiate between outliers and extreme values. Extreme values are not bad values at all and should definitely be kept (they also help to expand the convex hull of the training data). Possible causes of outliers:

- human error when inputting data
- measurement error (broken device *etc*)
- ...

For example

- in a dataset containing peoples heights we discover someone who is 6 meters tall: this could well be due to someone recording data in feet rather than in meters. Here we can correct this error and keep this datapoint.
- a remote sensing device in the middle of the Sahara desert constantly returns a temperature of -150 degrees: the device is malfunctioning and this data should be discarded

A traditional method for detecting outliers is the z-score

> Equation: The z-score of a point x is given by
>
> $$z\text{--score} = \frac{x - \bar{x}}{\sigma} \tag{3.1}$$
>
> where $\bar{x}$ is the sample mean. For the Gaussian distribution one can make use of the relation MAD $\approx 0.67449\sigma$ to create the robust z-score
>
> $$z\text{--score} = \frac{0.67449(x - \tilde{x})}{\text{MAD}} \tag{3.2}$$
>
> where $\tilde{x}$ is the sample median, and MAD is the median absolute deviation.

In python one can use

```
from scipy.stats import zscore

df_z = df.apply(zscore)
```

where values $> |3|$ are beyond the $\pm 3\sigma$ (99.7%) of the rest of the data as per the Gaussian distribution. However, this is predicated on our data actually having a unimodal Gaussian distribution in the first place, which for real data is very rarely the case. Indeed, as we have seen with Chebyshev's inequality in general up to 11% of the data can lie outside the range $\pm 3\sigma$. Furthermore, the z-score is completely oblivious to *inliers*; potentially bad data that is situated within the bulk of the distribution.

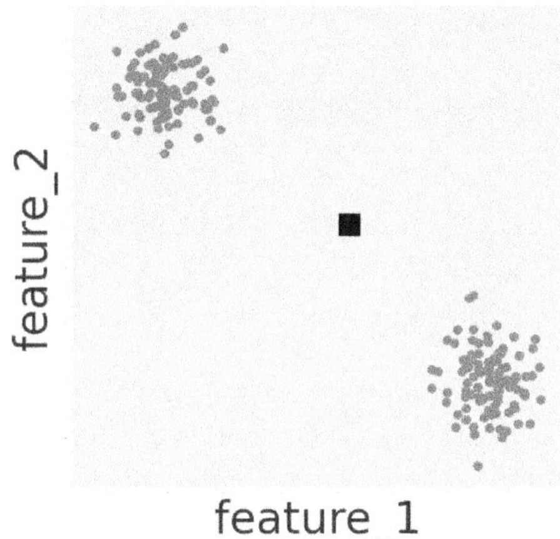

Figure 3.6: An outlier point (black square) that is actually an inlier, and will not be found from a z-score analysis.

We can also have multi-dimensional outliers; for example we have a weather dataset that has a temperature column, and also a snowfall column. A univariate analysis of each of these columns may appear to be completely reasonable. However, there could be a row of data that has both a temperature of 35 degrees Celsius and at the very same time a snowfall of 3cm, which is evidently incongruous. In a large dataset, due to the curse of dimensionality it is very difficult to detect such inliers because if there are a large number of features, all datapoints become 'unusual' (see also the isolation forest technique).

Remark: The Mahalanobis distance is the multivariate generalization of the z-score and is given by

$$z_M = \sqrt{(\mathbf{x}-\mu)^\mathsf{T}\mathbf{K}^{-1}(\mathbf{x}-\mu)} \tag{3.3}$$

where **K** is the variance-covariance matrix.

Sample code

Here is some sample code to calculate the Mahalanobis distance for a numeric dataframe (`gist`)

```
import numpy as np

def Mahalanobis(x, df):
    RHS = x - np.mean(df, axis=0)
```

```
    K = np.cov(df, rowvar=False)
    LHS = RHS.T
    Mahalanobis = np.sqrt(LHS @ np.linalg.inv(K) @ RHS)
    return Mahalanobis

df['Mahalanobis'] = df.apply(lambda x: Mahalanobis(x, df), axis=1)
```

3.4 Correlation coefficients

Pearson (number-number)

Equation: The Pearson correlation coefficient, r_{xy}, measures linear correlation between two sets of data, x and y:

$$r_{xy} = \frac{\sum_{i=1}^{n}(x_i - \bar{x})(y_i - \bar{y})}{\sqrt{\sum_{i=1}^{n}(x_i - \bar{x})^2}\sqrt{\sum_{i=1}^{n}(y_i - \bar{y})^2}} = \frac{cov(x,y)}{\sigma_x \sigma_y} \qquad \in [-1,1] \tag{3.4}$$

where cov is the covariance and σ is the standard deviation.

In Figure 3.7 are some values of the Pearson correlation coefficient for various datasets

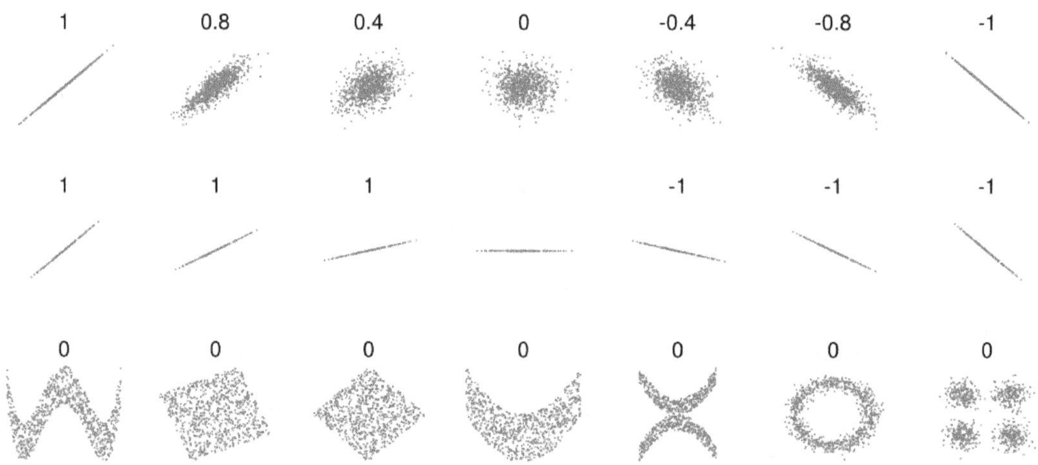

Figure 3.7: Some scatter plots and their corresponding Pearson correlation coefficients (Image credit: Wikimedia Commons).

The following is an example of a *correlation matrix*. Note that the main diagonal values are always 1, and that the matrix is symmetric ($A = A^\mathsf{T}$).

	PassengerId	Survived	Pclass	Age	SibSp	Parch	Fare
PassengerId	1.00	-0.01	-0.04	0.04	-0.06	-0.00	0.01
Survived	-0.01	1.00	-0.34	-0.08	-0.04	0.08	0.26
Pclass	-0.04	-0.34	1.00	-0.37	0.08	0.02	-0.55
Age	0.04	-0.08	-0.37	1.00	-0.31	-0.19	0.10
SibSp	-0.06	-0.04	0.08	-0.31	1.00	0.41	0.16
Parch	-0.00	0.08	0.02	-0.19	0.41	1.00	0.22
Fare	0.01	0.26	-0.55	0.10	0.16	0.22	1.00

Figure 3.8: Example of a Pearson correlation matrix (data: Titanic dataset).

Highly correlated features (columns) are not considered to be a good thing to have in our model as such features can complicate the interpretation of a fit. Each independent variable is assumed to be just that; independent of each other. However, if they are highly correlated, there exists the possibility that they are not actually independent. There is even a good chance that two very highly correlated features are simply different ways of representing the very same thing, leading to perfect multicollinearity. For example there may be a column with the speed of a car in *km/h* and another column in *mph*. If this is the case it is convenient to remove (`drop`) one of the offending features:

```
df = df.drop(["mph"], axis=1)
```

N Jupyter Notebook: Explainability, collinearity and the variance inflation factor (VIF)

Sample code

To create a correlation matrix using pandas `corr` (note the use of a background style to add colours as a function of the value, which is a very useful aid to the eye).

```
df.corr(method='pearson', numeric_only=True) \
    .style.background_gradient(cmap="coolwarm", vmin=-1, vmax=1) \
    .format(precision=2)
```

Here is some code to create a sortable list of the Pearson correlations between columns of a dataframe (`gist`)

```
import itertools

columns_list = df.select_dtypes(include='number').columns.tolist()
pairs = itertools.combinations(columns_list, 2)
correlation_list = []

for pair in (pairs):
    correlation_list.append([pair[0], pair[1],
                            df[pair[0]].corr(df[pair[1]])] )
```

```
correlation_df = pd.DataFrame(correlation_list)
print(correlation_df.sort_values(by=[2], ascending=False))
```

Spearman (number-number)

Equation: The Spearman rank correlation coefficient measures monotonic correlation between the ranks (R) of two sets of data, x and y both of size n:

$$r_{xy} = 1 - \frac{6\sum(R(x_i) - R(y_i))^2}{n(n^2-1)} \quad \in [-1,1] \tag{3.5}$$

Pandas: `df.corr(method='spearman')`

We shall now compare these correlation coefficients with the linear regression coefficient β_1 for the toy dataset illustrated in Figure 3.9 the results of which are in Table 3.2.

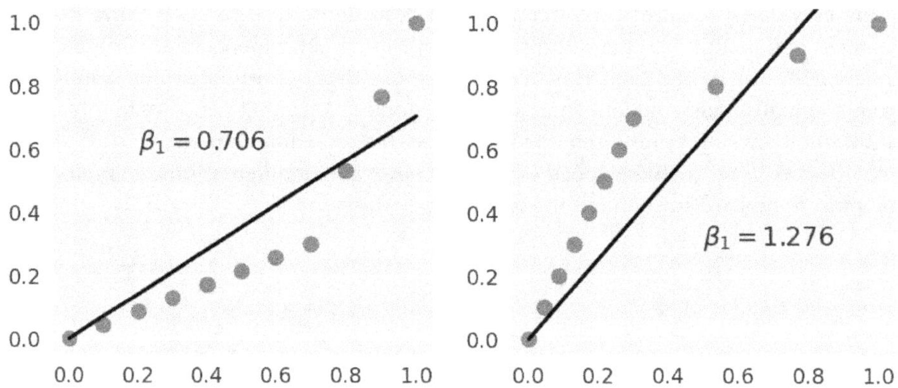

Figure 3.9: Toy dataset.

$\text{Pearson}(x,y) = \text{Pearson}(y,x)$	0.915
$\text{Spearman}(x,y) = \text{Spearman}(y,x)$	1.000
$y = \beta_1 x$	$\beta_1 = 0.706$
$x = \beta_1 y$	$\beta_1 = 1.276$

Table 3.2: Correlation coefficient results for the toy dataset in Figure 3.9.

We have a linear Pearson correlation coefficient of 0.915. The non-parametric Spearman correlation, based on rank, where in this example each x, y pair has a greater value than the last is thus a perfect 1. The linear regression coefficient β_1 for $y = \beta_1 x$ is 0.706, and if we swap the variables then for $x = \beta_1 y$ it becomes 1.276. However, if we standardize both x and y then in both cases β_1 becomes 0.915, *i.e.* the same as the Pearson coefficient.

3.4.1 Uncertainty coefficient: Theil's U (category-category)

Theil's U is used for calculating the correlation between discrete (categorical) features

Equation:

$$U(x|y) = \frac{H(x) - H(x|y)}{H(x)} \quad \in [0,1] \tag{3.6}$$

where H is the conditional entropy. Note that Theil's U is not symmetric, $U(x|y) \neq U(y|x)$.

Sample code

(gist)

```
df = dataset.select_dtypes(include='category')
columns_list = df.columns.tolist()

# convert dataframe to pyTorch tensor
import torch
matrix = torch.tensor(df.values)

from torchmetrics.functional.nominal import theils_u_matrix
corr_matrix = pd.DataFrame(theils_u_matrix(matrix).numpy(),
                           columns=columns_list)
corr_matrix.index = columns_list

# plot heatmap
fig, ax = plt.subplots(figsize=(15, 15))
ax = sns.heatmap(corr_matrix, linewidth=1, annot=True, fmt=".3f")
plt.show()
```

3.4.2 Φ_K (universal)

The Φ_K is a correlation coefficient between categorical, ordinal and interval variables with Pearson characteristics which can be installed from the dedicated phik python package

```
pip install phik
import phik

df.phik_matrix()
```

3.4.3 Mutual information (MI)

Both of the datasets plotted in Figure 3.10 have Pearson correlation coefficients of zero as it only picks up on linear relations. However, intuitively we can see that there is indeed a relation between the two axes (for the LHS example for a circle $x^2 + y^2 = r^2$).

Equation: The mutual information between two discrete variables, X and Y, is given by

$$I(X;Y) := \sum_{i,j} p(x_i,y_j) \ln \frac{p(x_i,y_j)}{p(x_i)p(y_j)} \tag{3.7}$$

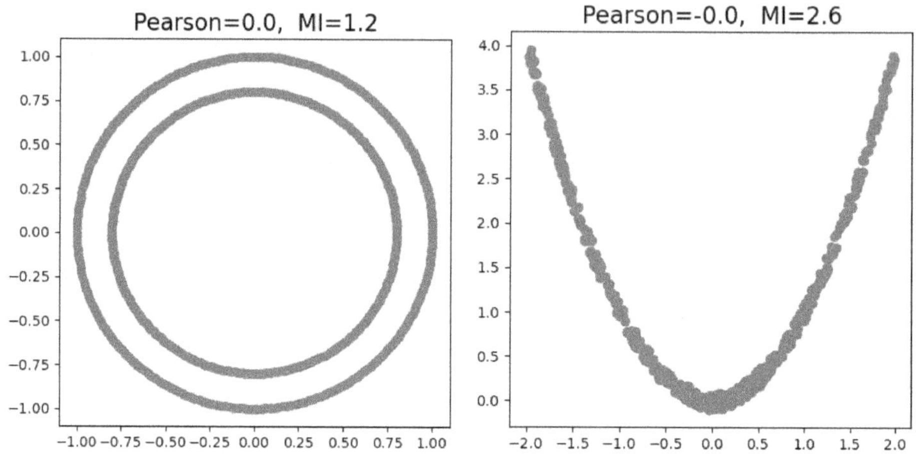

Figure 3.10: Example Pearson correlation and mutual information scores.

The mutual information[2] can be calculated via:

```
from sklearn.feature_selection import mutual_info_regression

mutual_info_regression(X, Y)
```

N Jupyter Notebook: Pearson correlation coefficient, mutual information (MI) and Predictive Power Score (PPS)

3.5 Why visualize data? Anscombe's quintet

Anscombe's quartet was invented by Frank J. Anscombe in 1973[3] and consists of four very carefully crafted datasets (here called A, B, C, and D). A fifth dataset (E) was added in 2025[4].

[2]Kraskov, Stögbauer, Grassberger *"Estimating mutual information"*, Physical Review E **83** 019903 (2011)
[3]F. J. Anscombe *"Graphs in Statistical Analysis"*, The American Statistician **27** pp. 17-21 (1973)
[4]C. McBride Ellis *"Anscombe dataset No. 5: Simpson's paradox"*, Zenodo (2025)

Statistic	A	B	C	D	E
$\bar{x}$	9.0	9.0	9.0	9.0	9.0
$\bar{y}$	7.5	7.5	7.5	7.5	7.5
$\sigma(x)$	3.317	3.317	3.317	3.317	3.317
$\sigma(y)$	2.032	2.032	2.030	2.031	2.031
β_1	0.5	0.5	0.5	0.5	0.5
β_0	3.0	3.0	3.0	3.0	3.0
$\sum(x-\bar{x})^2$	110.0	110.0	110.0	110.0	110.0
RSS	13.76	13.78	13.76	13.74	13.76
R^2	0.667	0.666	0.666	0.667	0.666
regression sum of squares	27.51	27.50	27.47	27.49	27.48
standard error of β_1	0.118	0.118	0.118	0.118	0.118
Pearson r_{xy}	0.816	0.816	0.816	0.817	0.816

Table 3.3: Descriptive statistics for Anscombe's quintet.

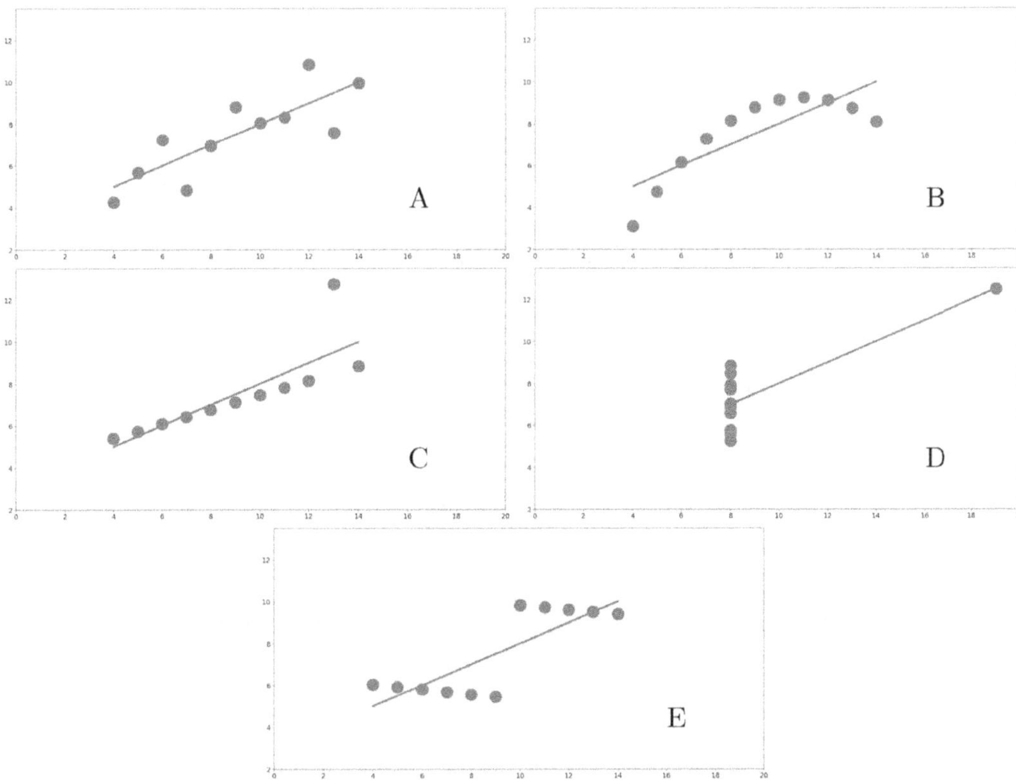

Figure 3.11: Anscombe's quintet

In Table 3.3 we can see that each of the five datasets have almost exactly the same descriptive statistics, but in Figure 3.11 when we visualize the data in a scatter plot we can see they are really rather different:

- in A we seem to have a good fit using linear regression

- in B here we are underfitting, and fitting a polynomial would be much better
- in C there seems to be an outlier point, whose removal would lead to a better fit
- in D we have a zero variance feature along with a 'leverage' point
- in E we have an example of Simpson's paradox; an extreme case of aggregation bias

The message is clear; it is very important to visualize ones data; descriptive statistics alone are simply not sufficient.

> Remark: There is a modern incarnation of Anscombe's quartet in the form of The Datasaurus Dozen whose animation is well worth watching.

3.6 Univariate visualisation: histograms and the eCDF

Histograms are fantastic for visualizing the distribution of continuous variables; to see whether a feature is unimodal, bimodal, or multimodal, or for visually detecting skewness or kurtosis. However, they have a potentially major drawback in that the information conveyed can change considerably depending on the choice of bin width. In Figure 3.12 both of the plots are for the very same dataset. On the other hand the empirical cumulative distribution function (eCDF) is independent of the width of the bins.

> Remark: In `seaborn` one can set `cumulative=True` or use the `seaborn.ecdfplot`.

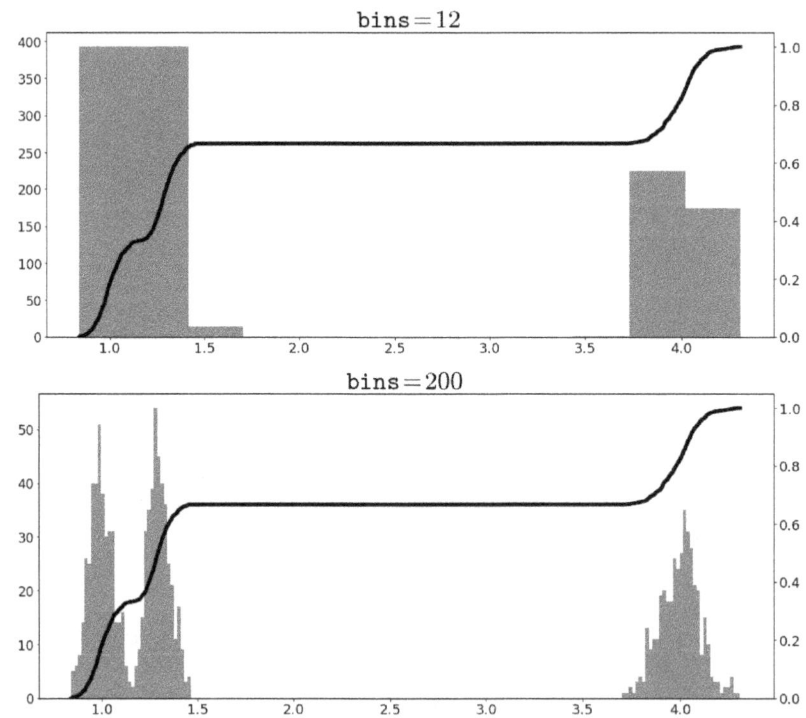

Figure 3.12: Histograms (green) with eCDF (black). The upper histogram has 12 bins as suggested by Sturges's rule. The lower histogram has 200 bins.

The main thing we are looking out for are plateaux on the eCDF; we can see a small plateau on the LHS due to the lack of data between the LHS bimodal peaks, whilst this bimodality is not seen at all in the upper histogram in the figure thus observing such a plateau in the eCDF is a warning that our bins are too wide and we should make them narrower. At the other extreme if there are too many bins then each datapoint will have its very own bin and we learn very little.

Equation: Sturges's rule suggests that a reasonable estimate for the number of bins for a series is given by

$$\texttt{n\_bins} = \lceil 1 + 3.322 \log_{10}(N) \rceil \tag{3.8}$$

where N is the number of samples. However, this rule assumes the data is from a unimodal Gaussian distribution, which is frequently not the case and Sturges's rule will under-estimate the number of bins.

Sample code

One can calculate the eCDF data via

```
import numpy as np

x_eCDF = np.sort(data)
y_eCDF = np.arange(1, len(data)+1 ) / len(data)
```

and to then plot both the histogram and the eCDF together via

```
import matplotlib.pyplot as plt

fig, ax1 = plt.subplots(figsize=(15, 7))
twin = ax1.twinx()
ax1.hist(data, bins=10, density=False)
twin.plot(x_eCDF, y_eCDF, linewidth=5, color="red")
twin.set_ylim(bottom=0, top=None)
plt.show();
```

Remark: By default the `matplotlib` `hist` plot will use `bins=10`.

3.6.1 Box, violin, and raincloud plots

For completeness here we shall mention box, violin, and raincloud plots. However, it should be said that I am not entirely sure what contribution they make above and beyond what can be achieved by using a histogram + eCDF plot. The first ever box plot was produced by Mary Spear in her 1952 book *"Charting Statistics"*. In Figure 3.13 we draw a box plot as per both matplotlib `boxplot` and pandas `boxplot`, where the box ranges from $Q1$ to $Q3$. We also have the 'Tukey fences', here at $Q1 - 1.5\text{IQR}$ and $Q3 + 1.5\text{IQR}$. Data beyond these fences are deemed to be outliers and are plotted as points. The whiskers then extend to the smallest and largest non-outlier points.

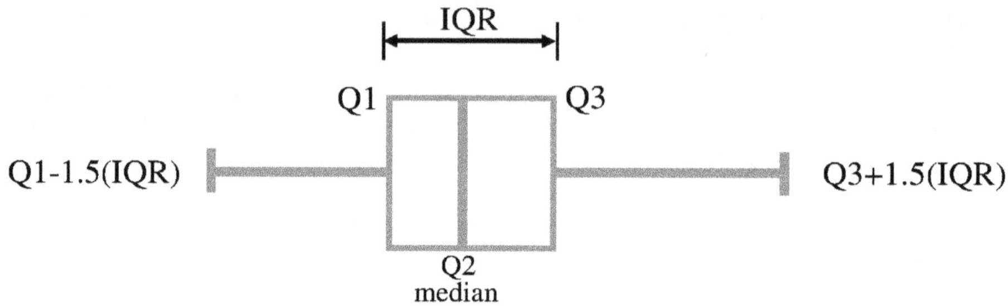

Figure 3.13: Anatomy of a box plot.

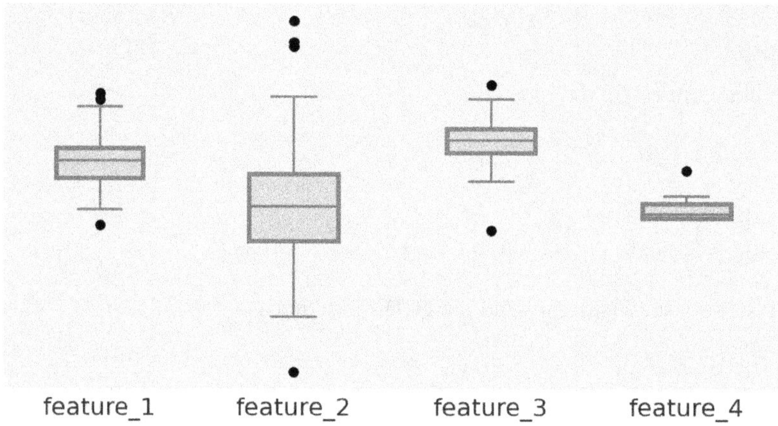

Figure 3.14: A typical box plot in action.

However, I would suggesting reading a wonderful article by Nick Desbarats *"I've Stopped Using Box Plots. Should You?"* highlighting the shortcomings of this venerable technique. In Figure 3.15 is an example of a violin plot

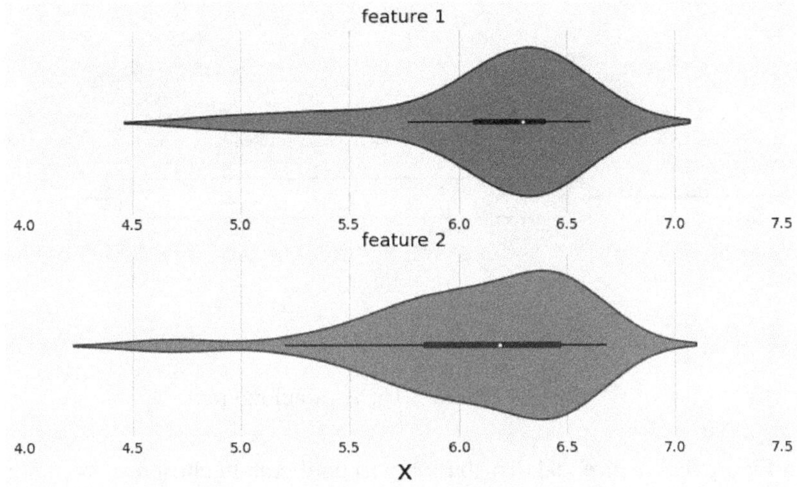

Figure 3.15: A violin plot.

which was produced using `seaborn.violinplot`.

Sample code

```
features = ["feature_1", "feature_2", "feature_3"]

# vertical stack of horizontal violin plots
fig, axes = plt.subplots(len(features),1,
                         figsize=(15, 4*len(features)))

for i, feature in enumerate(features):
    sns.violinplot(x=df[feature], ax=axes[i])
```

Finally, in Figure 3.16 a raincloud plot[5] is a combination of the upper half of a violin plot, a scatter plot, as well as a traditional box plot for good measure, created using the `PtitPrince` package.

[5] Micah Allen *et al.* *"Raincloud plots: a multi-platform tool for robust data visualization"*, Wellcome Open Research **4** 63 (2021)

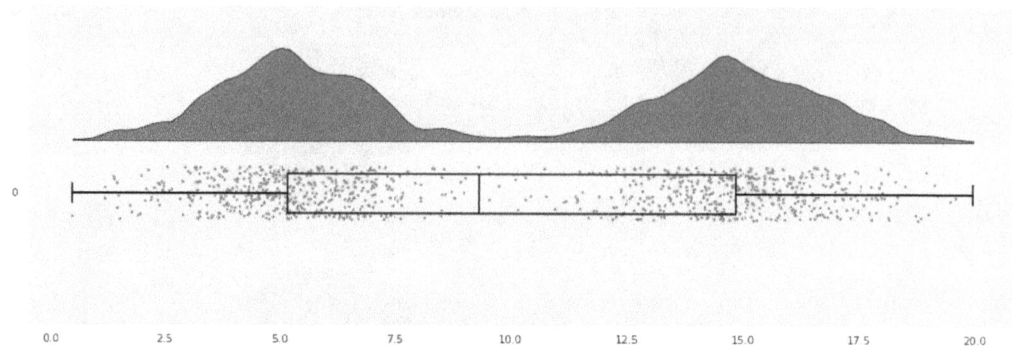

Figure 3.16: A raincloud plot

Note that in Figure 3.16 a bimodal distribution was deliberately chosen so as to highlight the problem of looking at box plots in isolation.

N Jupyter Notebook: Box + strip + violin = raincloud plot

3.6.2 Discrete (categorical) data: countplots

Countplots can be used to inspect count data or categorical features

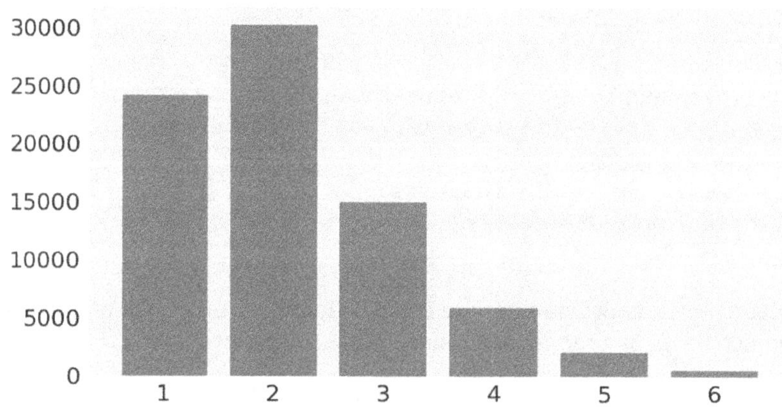

Figure 3.17: Example of a count plot.

```
# using matplotlib
import matplotlib.pyplot as plt
value_count = df["feature"].value_counts()
plt.bar(value_count.index, value_count.values)
plt.show()

# using seaborn
import seaborn as sns
```

```
sns.countplot(x="feature", data=df)
plt.show()
```

> Remark: **Warning**: Both of the above plots completely ignore any missing (`NaN`) values present in the `feature` column, even if using `.value_counts(dropna=False)`

3.7 Bivariate visualisation: scatter plot

I would suggest that the scatter plot is one of the most useful tools when it comes to visual inspection of bivariate data, *i.e.* comparing two numerical features with each other.

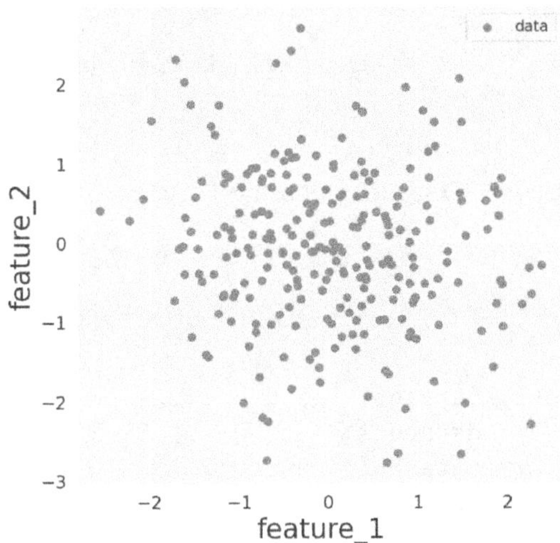

Figure 3.18: Scatter plot

> Remark: If one intends to later apply feature scaling it may not be a bad idea to visualize scatter plots using an aspect ratio of 1:1.

One can also produce interactive 3D scatter plots

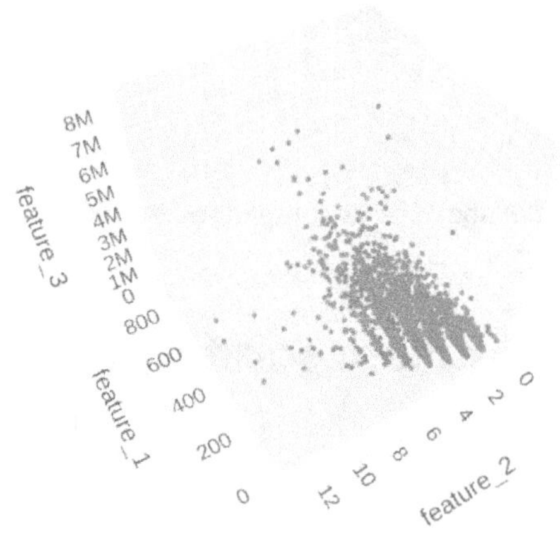

Figure 3.19: 3D Scatter plot

Sample code

Code to produce an interactive 3D scatter plot using `plotly.express`

```
import plotly.express as px
import plotly.graph_objects as go

fig = go.Figure()
fig = px.scatter_3d(x= dataset["feature_1"],
                    y= dataset["feature_2"],
                    z= dataset["feature_3"],
                    title="3D scatter plot",
                    labels={"x": "feature_1",
                            "y": "feature_2",
                            "z": "feature_3"}
                   )
fig.update_traces(marker=dict(size=1.5))
fig.show()
```

3.7.1 Pairplots (or perhaps not)

The seaborn `pairplot`, or the pandas `scatter_matrix`, ostensibly combines in one neat graphic arguably the two most useful data visualization tools at our disposal; for univariate data, *i.e.* for inspecting individual features, the histogram (+ eCDF), and for bivariate data, *i.e.* visualizing potential interactions between pairs of features, the scatter plot. However, in practice pairplots are only really useful if one likes penguins or is interested in varieties of iris flowers, but soon become impracticable if there are say more than 10 features as this will lead to a 10×10 grid of tiny and basically useless figures.

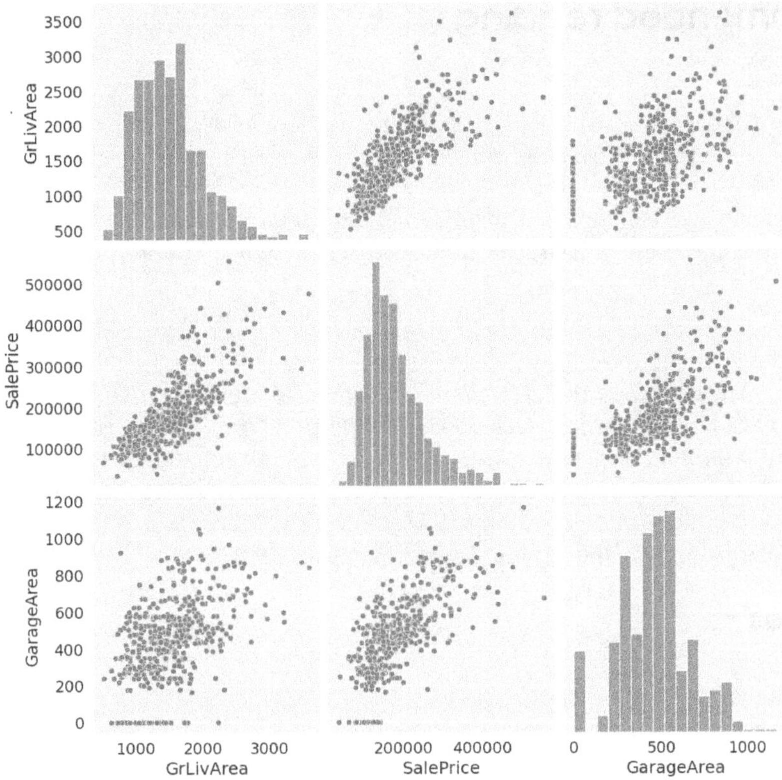

Figure 3.20: An example pairplot.

Sample code

If one has more than 10 features I would suggest, although not in the least bit elegant, printing out the scatter plots one after the other in a column to aid detailed visual inspection. (gist):

> Remark: If one has n numerical features there will be $(n^2 - n)/2$ unique scatter plots

```
import seaborn as sns
import itertools

df = dataset.select_dtypes(include='number')
numeric_features = df.columns.tolist()
pairs = itertools.combinations(numeric_features, 2)
for pair in (pairs):
    sns.lmplot(data=df, x=pair[0], y=pair[1],
               line_kws={'color': 'black'},
               aspect=1 )
    plt.show();
```

Recommended reading

Papers

- Charu C. Aggarwal, Alexander Hinneburg, and Daniel A. Keim *"On the Surprising Behavior of Distance Metrics in High Dimensional Space"*, Lecture Notes in Computer Science **1973** pp. 420-434 (2001)
- H. Aguinis, R. K. Gottfredson, and H. Joo *"Best-Practice Recommendations for Defining, Identifying, and Handling Outliers"*, Organizational Research Methods **16** pp. 270-301 (2013)

Books

- John W. Tukey *"Exploratory Data Analysis"*, Pearson (1977)
- Boris Iglewicz, David Hoaglin *"How to Detect and Handle Outliers"*, ASQC Basic References in Quality Control: Statistical Techniques **16** (1993)
- Leland Wilkinson *"The Grammar of Graphics"* (2nd Ed.), Springer-Verlag New York (2005)
- Nick Desbarats *"Practical Charts: The Essential Guide to Creating Clear, Compelling Charts for Reports and Presentations"*, Practical Reporting Inc. (2023)
- Matt Harrison *"Effective Visualization"*, MetaSnake (2024)

Packages

- Pandas
- matplotlib
- seaborn
- Plotly
- Vega-Altair
- PtitPrince by Davide Poggiali
- ydata-profiling

Other

- PyViz: lists of libraries for visualizing data in Python
- ISO/IEC 25012:2008 general data quality model
- ISO/IEC 25024:2015 measurement of data quality

4. Data cleaning

> ...the tasks of exploratory data mining and data cleaning constitute 80% of the effort that determines 80% of the value of the ultimate data mining results.
>
> *"Exploratory Data Mining and Data Cleaning" by Tamraparni Dasu and Theodore Johnson*

Machine learning is a numerical technique and as such can only be performed on a complete dataset, composed entirely of numbers. Indeed we will not be far wrong if we start thinking of our dataset as being a two dimensional augmented coefficient matrix $(\mathbf{X}|\mathbf{y})$. However, within the data that we have been provided there may often be missing values or columns (features) that are text encoded, which will have to be 'cleaned'. One may also have to address issues found during EDA, for example one may have encountered negative values in an `age` column that defy common sense, or duplicated entries.

4.1 Missing values: `NULL` or `NaN`

It is far from unusual for there to be missing values in a dataset, for many reasons including the merging of distinct tables. These missing values are represented by a placeholder, such as `NULL` or by `NaN` (**N**ot **a** **N**umber).

> Remark: There may well be non-missing missing values in your dataset. For example when the data was originally collated there may have been a pre-assigned value for missing data, such as `999` for a missing `age`. It is also entirely possible that you are not the first person to work with this data, and your predecessor filled missing values with an indicator value. For the purposes of imputation with a view to creating a machine learning model it is a good idea to re-set these values to become `NaN`, for example via:

```
df["age"] = df["age"].replace(999, np.NaN)
```

4.1.1 Visualization of NaN with missingno

A great visual tool to get an overall idea as to how much data is missing, and where, is the missingno package.

```
import missingno as msno

msno.matrix(df, sparkline=False);
```

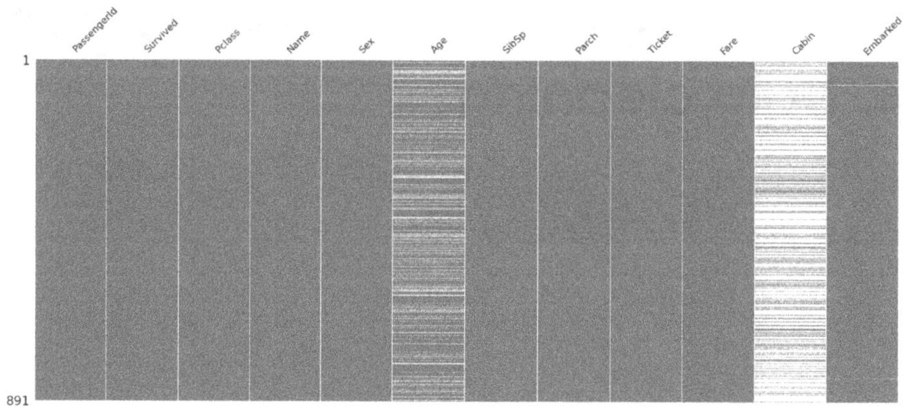

Figure 4.1: missingno for the Titanic data

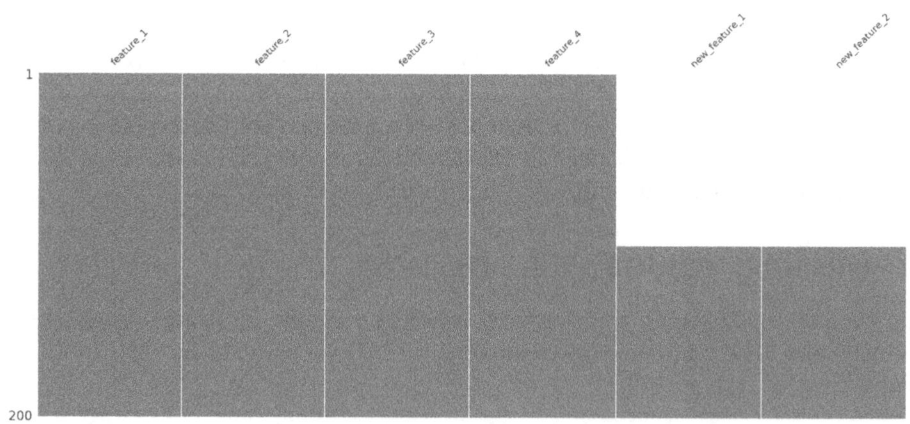

Figure 4.2: missingno of two dataframes that have been concatenated: the lower df had two new features, leading to NaN values in the upper df.

and to perform a quantitative analysis using pandas:

- df.isna().sum() - count the number of missing numbers in each column

- `df.isna().mean().sort_values(ascending=False)*100`
  - percentage of missing numbers in each column
- `df.isna().sum().sum()` - the total number of missing numbers in the `df`.

To inspect the all the rows that have a `NaN` in a given column

- `df[np.isnan(df["column"])]`

> Remark: The pandas method `df.isnull()` can be used too, as it is an alias for `df.isna()`. (I am not sure why the latter method was not more intuitively named `df.isnan()`).

What are some of the options we have to deal with missing values? Imputation:

- deletion of `NaN`
- replace ('fill') `NaN` with a constant value
- replace `NaN` with an average value
- ...

4.1.2 Types of missing: MCAR, MAR, and MNAR

Donald Rubin created a taxonomy for different types of missing data in a feature, depending on how the data came to be missing in the first place:

- **MCAR (missing completely at random)** whether a value is missing or not has absolutely nothing to do with any of the data itself.
- **MAR (missing at random)** the probability of a value in this feature being missing is a function of values in other feature(s) but not the feature itself.
  For example, imagine a questionnaire where first the respondent is asked whether they are concerned about data privacy or not, to which they reply. The very next question asks the respondent for their personal telephone number. It is easy to imagine that the telephone number field is more likely to be missing if the respondent replied 'Yes' to being concerned about their privacy. However, the probability of the telephone number being missing has absolutely nothing to do with the telephone number itself.
- **MNAR (missing not at random)** the probability of a value in this feature being missing is a function of the missing value itself.
  For example, in a questionnaire asking the respondent to say how many chocolate bars they ate yesterday, perhaps people who know they ate way too many may be somewhat less inclined to respond to that question. Thus in this case large values are more likely to be missing than small values.

Knowing if there is potential reason for the data being missing can help in directing ones effort to remediate these missing values.

4.1.3 Global delete

Suffice to say this is not a good idea at all, but to get going quickly on a project the easiest thing to do is to simply delete all of the NaN values, *i.e.* remove all incomplete cases. To delete all the columns that contain even just one missing value:

```
df = df.dropna()
```

To delete all of the rows that have one or more missing values:

```
df = df.dropna(axis='columns')
```

One can also set a threshold (`thresh`) for deletion. For example to delete columns in which more than 80% of the data in said column is missing:

```
df.dropna(thresh= int(0.2*df.shape[0]))
```

Be aware that if the data is MNAR then row-wise (listwise) deletion can introduce a bias in the resulting model.

4.1.4 Global fill

Another somewhat drastic quick fix, and again ill advisable in the long run, is to replace all of the NaN with a single value, say for example with zero:
`df = df.fillna(0)`

4.1.5 Univariate imputation with an average value

A very commonly used approach is to fill the missing values in a column with the average of said column, be it the mean, median, or mode, whilst paying no heed to the values of any of the other features in the dataset. This is how to fill all of the `NaN` in the dataframe with the mean of each column using pandas:
`df = df.fillna(df.mean())`
For example

```
X_train = X_train.fillna( X_train.mean() )
X_validation = X_validation.fillna( X_train.mean() )
X_test = X_test.fillna( X_train.mean() )
```

Notice how we fill the `NaN` in the validation and test sets using the means that were obtained from the train data so as to avoid data leakage.
How to fill `NaN` with the mode:
`df["col"] = df["col"].fillna(df["col"].mode(dropna=True)[0])`
which is particularly useful for imputing integer columns, or numerically encoded ordinal categorical features. Note that this operation is a little more elaborate because the most frequent value is not necessarily unique. Watch out for columns that have many missing values; the mode might turn out to actually be `NaN`, hence the `dropna=True`.

> Remark: Mean, median, and mode imputation is essentially equivalent to filling the missing values with the predictions obtained by fitting a baseline model (which is invariant to row permutation) to the column in question; mean imputation corresponds to using the regression baseline model for the $L2$ loss, or the median in conjunction with the $L1$ loss, and mode imputation is equivalent to the majority class baseline in classification.

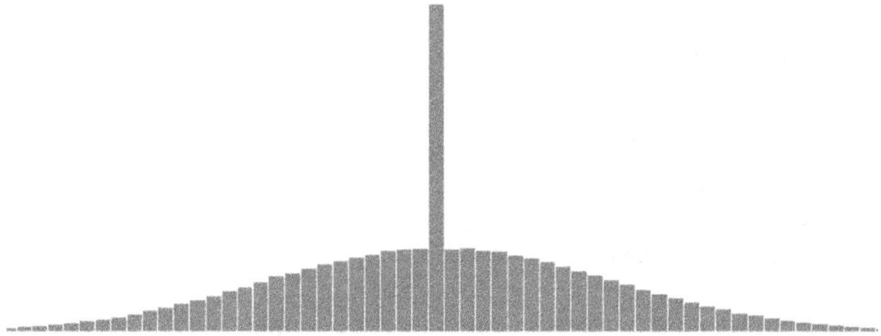

Figure 4.3: The aftereffect of mean imputation (for 10% missing) on data that follows a Gaussian distribution.

It is worth mentioning that mean imputation is less deleterious for predictive models than it is for inferential models[1].

> Remark: Pandas cannot deal with infinite values (produced for example by the division by zero[a]). The trick is to first replace them with NaN values
> `df = df.replace([np.inf, -np.inf], np.nan)`
>
> [a]Miguel de Carvalho *"R, Python, and Calculus: Are They on the Same Page?"*, CHANCE **38** pp. 71-72 (2025)

4.1.6 Multiple imputation

Multiple imputation methods, multivariate imputation by chained equations (MICE) being a well known example, involve treating a column with missing values as the target column and predicts the missing values using the other features. This is repeated for all of the columns that have missing data. This whole process is then repeated multiple times.

```
from sklearn.experimental import enable_iterative_imputer
from sklearn.impute import IterativeImputer

imputer = IterativeImputer(random_state=42, max_iter=10)
imputer.fit(dataset)
dataset = imputer.transform(dataset)
```

By default the `IterativeImputer` uses the `BayesianRidge` estimator.

4.1.7 Do nothing!

For tree based estimators such as XGBoost, LightGBM and CatBoost it is entirely possible that the best thing to do is absolutely nothing and leave them to the algorithm. In fact if ones dataset has a pre-defined value for missing data, it is actually a good idea to deliberately replace such indicator values with `NaN`. For example, if the indicator value was, say -1, then do a `df.replace(-1, np.nan)`, which is basically what XGBoost actually does under the hood if the `missing` parameter has been set with a value other than `NaN`. Indeed it has been found that

> *"Native support for missing values in supervised machine learning predicts better than state-of-the-art imputation with much less computational cost"*.[2]

4.1.8 Binary indicator column

Especially when data is MNAR, and even when it is MCAR[3] adding a new binary 'dummy' feature flagging where data was missing before having performed imputation can become a very informative feature. For example, missing financial data could turn out to be a good indicator of fraud.

```
df["col_is_NaN"] = np.where(np.isnan(df["col"].values), 1, 0)
```

creates a new `col_is_NaN` feature

[1]Josse, Chen, Prost, Scornet, Varoquaux *"On the consistency of supervised learning with missing values"*, arXiv:1902.06931 (2024)

[2]Perez-Lebel, Varoquaux, Le Morvan, Josse, Poline *"Benchmarking missing-values approaches for predictive models on health databases"*, GigaScience **11** giac013 (2022)

[3]Le Morvan, Varoquaux *"Imputation for prediction: beware of diminishing returns"*, arXiv:2407.19804 (2024)

col
2.3
NaN
4.9
NaN
NaN
1.6
2.6

col	col_is_NaN
2.3	0
2.85	1
4.9	0
2.85	1
2.85	1
1.6	0
2.6	0

before after

4.2 Outlier and inlier removal

4.2.1 Univariate outliers

If we are decided that we have unwelcome outlier values in a feature there are two basic options:

deletion (truncation)

Example of deleting rows whose value in the age column `Age` are below 0 or above 120 from the dataframe

```
df = df[ (df["Age"] >= 0) & (df["Age"] <= 120) ]
```

or a less drastic option is to replace the offending values with a `NaN` to then be imputed afterwards; here we replace all values below 0 in the column `col` with `NaN`:

```
df["col"] = np.where(df["col"] < 0, np.nan, df["col"])
```

clipping (Winsorizing)

Another option is to clip values below and/or above a given value to be said value (this is also known as Winsorizing, named after Charles Paine Winsor).
For example here all values below 0 become 0, and all values above 120 become 120:

```
df["col"] = df["col"].clip(lower=0, upper=120)
```

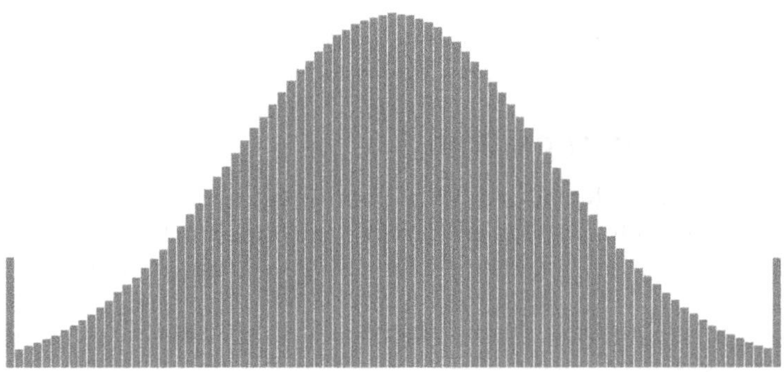

Figure 4.4: The aftereffects of Winsorizing a Gaussian distribution at $\pm 2.5\sigma$.

Sample code

```
mean, SD = np.mean(df["col"]), np.std(df["col"])

# Gaussian deletion
df = df[(df["col"] >= (mean-3*SD) ) & (df["col"] <= (mean+3*SD) )]
# Gaussian clipping
df["col"] = df["col"].clip(lower=(mean-3*SD), upper=(mean+3*SD) )
```

```
Q1 = df["col"].quantile(0.25)
Q3 = df["col"].quantile(0.75)
IQR = Q3-Q1 # interquartile range

# Tukey deletion
df = df[(df["col"] >= (Q1-1.5*IQR) ) & (df["col"] <= (Q3+1.5*IQR) )]
# Tukey clipping
df["col"] = df["col"].clip(lower=(Q1-1.5*IQR), upper=(Q3+1.5*IQR) )
```

4.2.2 Cook's distance

Cook's distance (D_i) is designed for the detection of influential observation in linear regression. It is calculated from

$$D_i = \frac{\Sigma(\hat{y} - \hat{y}^i)^2}{n.\text{MSE}} \tag{4.1}$$

where $\hat{y}$ are the predictions of the full fit to all of the data, and $\hat{y}^i$ are the predictions of a fit that did not include observation i, MSE is the mean squared error of the model, and n is the number of parameters (including the intercept term). Individual values of D_i greater than $3\overline{D_i}$ are deemed potential outliers.

Sample code

```
import statsmodels.api as sm

X1 = sm.add_constant(X)
model = sm.OLS(y,X1).fit()
influence = model.get_influence()
Di = influence.cooks_distance[0]
```

4.2.3 Isolation forest

When it comes to inliers (as well as outliers) one option is to make use of the unsupervised classification (an area of machine learning not covered in this book) technique known as the `Isolation Forest`[4], designed for anomaly detection.

[4] Fei Tony Liu, Kai Ming Ting, Zhi-Hua Zhou "*Isolation-Based Anomaly Detection*", ACM Transactions on Knowledge Discovery from Data **6** pp. 1-39 (2012)

Sample code

(gist)

```
from sklearn.ensemble import IsolationForest

IF_classifier = IsolationForest(n_estimators   = 100,
                                contamination = 0.05,
                                random_state   = 42)

y_pred_IF = IF_classifier.fit_predict(X_train)

X_train_filtered, y_train_filtered = X_train[(y_pred_IF == 1)], \
                                     y_train[(y_pred_IF == 1)]
```

The contamination hyperparameter is the fraction of datapoints to identify as outliers, and subsequently delete these outlier rows from the dataset.

N Jupyter Notebook: Filtering outliers using the Isolation Forest

4.2.4 Removal using PCA

Another technique for outlier/inlier removal is to use principal component analysis (PCA); when performing PCA the component with the largest eigenvalue is known as the principal component, explaining most of the signal in the data. On the other hand smallest eigenvalue represents the component with the least explained variance and this 'inexplicable' component is often associated with the noise in the data. Dropping this corresponding component should, in principle, have very little influence on the quality of the reconstruction. However, if there are individual points that are indeed strongly impacted they are 'noisier than the rest of the noise', and potentially represent anomalous values or 'outliers'.

Sample code

Here we drop the PCA feature having the least covariance, revert the PCA process, then drop the rows of data that are found to have the largest reconstruction error, *i.e.* that have moved the farthest from their original location upon reversion (gist):

```
from sklearn.decomposition import PCA

# parameters
n_components_drop = 1 # least explained variance
quantile = 0.99

pca = PCA(X_train.shape[1]-n_components_drop)
pca.fit(X_train)
X_transformed = pca.transform(X_train)
X_reconstructed = pca.inverse_transform(X_transformed)
reconstruction_error = np.sum(np.square(X_train - X_reconstructed), axis=1)
threshold = np.quantile(reconstruction_error, quantile)
# keep dataset rows with low reconstruction_error
X_train_filtered, y_train_filtered = \
                  X_train[(reconstruction_error < threshold)], \
```

```
y_train[(reconstruction_error < threshold)]
```

Jupyter Notebook: Filtering outliers using (inverse) PCA

4.3 Duplicated rows

Duplicated rows can unduly bias a machine learning model, and can arise for example in a dataset created via an SQL `UNION ALL` command or a pandas `concat`. To count the number of duplicated rows in a dataset one can use

```
len(df) - len(df.drop_duplicates())
```

and to delete them

```
df = df.drop_duplicates(keep='first')
```

4.4 Duplicated columns

It is entirely possible that a dataframe can have columns with the same column names. One can test for the condition that there are duplicate column names via

```
df.columns.is_unique
```

One way to de-duplicate such a repeated column name is by using the column position (here the 12th column) via

```
df = df.rename(columns={df.columns[11]:"new_column_name"})
```

(remember that pandas uses zero-based indexing).
One can drop columns whose values are duplicated via transposing the dataframe

```
df = df.T.drop_duplicates().T
```

which is oblivious to the actual column names.

4.5 Boolean columns

To convert a Boolean column (`True` or `False`) into a binary column:

```
df["col"] = df["col"].astype("int")
```

4.6 Zero variance columns

As far as machine learning is concerned columns that have zero variance have no predictive power whatsoever and are best dropped. This can be done using

```
df = df.loc[:, df.var() != 0]
```

If there are categorical columns, where the variance is not defined, one could use:

```
df = df.drop(df.columns[df.nunique() == 1], axis=1)
```

Such a situation could occur if the dataset is the result of filtering. For example, say one had a dataset of global sales, but decided to create a model for the sales in Spain. Filtering the country column for Spain would naturally lead to zero variance for the country feature. Another reason to drop such columns is that the model is completely unprepared to produce a prediction if somehow a new value is encountered in the corresponding column in the test or production data.

> Remark: Scikit learn has a filter `sklearn.feature_selection.VarianceThreshold` although I would be hesitant to recommend it; zero variance columns can be removed with impunity, but even a slight variance in some features could be informative.

4.7 Feature scaling: standardization and normalization

From a numerical stability standpoint some solvers, such as gradient descent or L-BFGS-B used in logistic regression, work best when the data is either standardized or normalized.

Equation: Standardization (also known as z-score scaling) is when we set the mean to be zero and then scale to unit standard deviation or variance (*i.e.* $\sigma^2 = \sigma = 1$)

$$z = \frac{(x - \mu)}{\sigma} \tag{4.2}$$

Sample code

```
# fit
x_train_mean = x_train.mean()
x_train_std  = x_train.std()

# transform the training data
z_train = (x_train - x_train_mean) / x_train_std

# transform the test data
z_test = (x_test - x_train_mean) / x_train_std
```

Note that we fit the parameters μ and σ to the training data, and use the same parameters when transforming the test data. This is done to prevent data leakage.

Equation: Normalization scales the data to lie in the range $[0, 1]$

$$z = \frac{x - \min(x)}{\max(x) - \min(x)} \tag{4.3}$$

> **Remark:** Both standardization and especially normalization are very sensitive to the presence of outliers.

I would suggest the best scaler is the `sklearn.preprocessing.RobustScaler` which removes the median and scales the data according to the interquartile range (IQR).

Equation: Robust scaling

$$z = \frac{x - Q_2(x)}{Q_3(x) - Q_1(x)} \tag{4.4}$$

Sample code

```
from sklearn.preprocessing import RobustScaler
```

```
RS = RobustScaler().set_output(transform="pandas")

train_data = RS.fit_transform(train_data)
test_data  = RS.transform(test_data)
```

Feature scaling can easily be performed thanks to the following scikit-learn routines:

- sklearn.preprocessing.StandardScaler
- sklearn.preprocessing.MinMaxScaler
- sklearn.preprocessing.RobustScaler

4.8 Encoding categorical features

Categoricals are discrete features composed of values that belong to a set. They may be numerical or they may be strings (objects). There are two types of categorical features; ordinal and nominal.

- **ordinal**: have an order to them, *i.e.* small < medium < large
- **nominal**: nominated values, *i.e.* cat, dog, panda, badger

4.8.1 Ordinal features

An example of an ordinal feature would be a dataset of Olympic athlete performance where there is a `Medals` column, which may contain the values `Gold`, `Silver`, `Bronze`, and `none`. What do we do with this feature? We simply numerically re-code the column, for example via a dictionary

```
dictionary = {"Gold":3, "Silver":2, "Bronze":1, "none":0}
df["Medals"] = df["Medals"].replace( dictionary )
```

or via a mapping

```
df["Medals"] = df["Medals"].map( dictionary )
```

the difference being that `replace` will leave values not seen in the dictionary as they are (and the feature will remain of dtype object), whereas `map` will create a `NaN` entry. Note that when performing ordinal encoding, ideally semantic relationships should be preserved. For example we should encode `small`$\rightarrow$ 1, `medium`$\rightarrow$ 2, and `large`$\rightarrow$ 3, and not `small`$\rightarrow$ 1, `medium`$\rightarrow$ 3, and `large`$\rightarrow$ 2, even for tree-based models if one is to use monotonic constraints.

> Remark: **Warning**: Numerical encoding of ordinal features may not preserve the 'distance' between categories. For example, simply encoding `small`, `medium` and `HUGE` as 1, 2, and 3 implies that the difference between `small` and `medium` is equivalent to the difference between `medium` and `HUGE`, which may well not be the case.

If necessary one can easily revert the mapping and thus restore the dataframe to its original values by using a reverse dictionary

```
reverse_dictionary = dict( (value, key) for key, value in dictionary.items() )
df["Medals"] = df["Medals"].map( reverse_dictionary )
```

One can also use the scikit sklearn.preprocessing.OrdinalEncoder()

```
from sklearn.preprocessing import OrdinalEncoder
encoder = OrdinalEncoder()

ordinal_features = ["feature_3", "feature_7"]
encoder.fit(train[ordinal_features])
train[ordinal_features] = encoder.transform(train[ordinal_features])
test[ordinal_features] = encoder.transform(test[ordinal_features])
```

Remark: **Warning**: The scikit `OrdinalEncoder` encodes the columns based on the following sort of the categories therein: 0-9, A-Z, a-z, `NaN`, so for example the aforementioned encoded `Medals` values will become `Silver` > `Gold` > `Bronze`.

	number	ordinal encoding
0	one	4.0
1	two	9.0
2	three	8.0
3	four	2.0
4	five	1.0
5	six	6.0
6	seven	5.0
7	eight	0.0
8	nine	3.0
9	ten	7.0

Figure 4.5: Demonstration of how the scikit `OrdinalEncoder` would encode a feature that is composed of numbers in the form of text.

4.8.2 Nominal features

Nominal features contain 'nominated' values, a good example are post codes (ZIP codes). Although numerical in nature these are not actually meaningful as numbers in themselves.

One-hot encoding

What can we do with nominal features: perform *one-hot encoding*. For example, here the feature `pets` of type `object` has four distinct values:

pets
cat
dog
cat
panda
dog
badger

which is converted into four new orthogonal features having binary values (and delete the original feature):

pets_cat	pets_dog	pets_panda	pets_badger
1	0	0	0
0	1	0	0
1	0	0	0
0	0	1	0
0	1	0	0
0	0	0	1

This can be done via

- One-hot encoding creates a bit-mask leading to n new columns, where n is the number of distinct values seen in the feature that is being encoded `sklearn.preprocessing.OneHotEncoder()`
- One-hot encoding can also be performed using `pandas.get_dummies`

```
df = pd.get_dummies(df, columns=["feature_2", "feature_9"],
          drop_first=True, # only if using linear regression
          dummy_na=True, dtype="int")
```

where `dummy_na=True` will also create a missing value indicator column.

> Remark: Dummy Variable Trap: one-hot encoding will create perfect multicollinearity since each coefficient in a given column, say x_0, can be exactly obtained from $x_0 = 1 - \sum_{i=1,n} x_i$. This is potentially problematic for linear models, and the solution is to drop one of the columns, for example the very first column via `drop_first=True`. On the other hand for Decision Tree based models such as Random Forest, which use feature subsampling, it is better to keep all of the one-hot encoded columns.

Note that, for example, in Spain there are 11,752 post codes. One-hot encoding the post code feature could create up to 11751 columns of very sparse data. The post codes for Madrid all start with 28, whereas the post codes for Barcelona start with 08. Madrid is not 28 because it is more than Barcelona or vice versa; these codes were assigned alphabetically by province. One could drastically reduce the sparsity of the dataset by, for example, just using the first two digits of the post code as the features to be encoded, which in would lead to a much more manageable 52 columns of data.

Another option to prevent too much sparsity when one-hot encoding is to group infrequent categories into a new category prior to encoding. For example, say the vast majority of our pets are either cats or dogs, then every other pet we encounter becomes classed as 'other'

```
animals = ["cat", "dog"] # majority categories

df['pets'] = np.where(df['pets'].isin(animals), df['pets'], 'other')
```

This has the added advantage that if there are new pets present in the test data that were not previously seen in the training data our model will not raise an error.

pets
cat
panda
cat
dog
badger
dog
cat

before

pets
cat
other
cat
dog
other
dog
cat

after

Table 4.1: Grouping infrequent nominal categories as `other` before one-hot encoding to reduce column proliferation.

Frequency or count encoding

An alternative worth exploring which does not involve the creation of new columns is to use the frequency that we see a given category as the value that is encoded.

```
count_map = X_train["cat_col"].value_counts().to_dict()
X_train["cat_col"] = X_train["cat_col"].map(count_map)
X_test["cat_col"] = X_test["cat_col"].map(count_map)
```

Target encoding

Mean target encoding[5] is yet another option which avoids sparsity; in effect we replace each category with its mean baseline model, akin to the mean imputation of missing values:

```
target_mean = train.groupby(["cat_col"])["Target"].mean().to_dict()
train["cat_col"] = train["cat_col"].map(target_mean)
test["cat_col"] = test["cat_col"].map(target_mean)
```

When target encoding is used in the context of classification the value of the category becomes the conditional probability of seeing said category, and in regression, the expectation value of the target.

> Remark: **Warning**: When using target encoding in conjunction with cross-validation be *extremely* careful about data leakage, specifically target leakage, since infrequently seen, and especially the unique categories will essentially adopt the value of the target itself.

[5] Daniele Micci-Barreca "*A preprocessing scheme for high-cardinality categorical attributes in classification and prediction problems*", ACM SIGKDD Explorations Newsletter **3** pp. 27-32 (2001)

To reduce the possibility of overfitting one can blend the mean target encoding value ($\bar{e}_v$) with the overall baseline value ($\bar{y}$) where here λ acts as a regularization hyperparameter

$$e_v \leftarrow \lambda \bar{e}_v + (1-\lambda)\bar{y} \qquad \lambda \in [0,1] \tag{4.5}$$

This is implemented in the `sklearn.preprocessing.TargetEncoder`. When performed correctly target encoding has been found to be highly effective.[6]

Other encodings

Indeed the package Category Encoders has no less than 20 different encoders for transforming ones categorical data.

> **Remark:** GBDT estimators have native support for categorical features, see the section in Chapter 9.

4.8.3 Label encoding of classification targets

In classification problems the target column may contain the labels as strings, such as `planet` and `star`. These can be numerically encoded using the scikit `LabelEncoder`. However, the `LabelEncoder` encodes the column based on the following sort of the categories: 0-9, A-Z, a-z, `NaN`. If one wishes to follow the convention of the majority class becoming class 0 then one could use the following function

```
def label_encoder(df, target):
    counts = df[target].value_counts()
    mapping = {value: key for key, value in enumerate(counts.index)}
    df[target] = df[target].map(mapping)
```

4.9 Removing personally identifiable information

Removing personally identifiable information (PII), particularly what are known as direct identifiers such as peoples names, addresses, telephone numbers, or identity document details such as passport numbers is vitally important, especially if ones data is to be made publicly available. Indeed removing direct identifiers form published datasets is compulsory under the EU General Data Protection Regulation (GDPR) 2016/679. There exist a host of techniques to hide PII based for example on obfuscation or substitution, however there is always a potential re-identification risk. In an interesting study it was found that with just the following three features; gender, date of birth, and ZIP code that around 87% of US citizens were uniquely identifiable[7] so even after removing direct identifiers a degree of re-identification can still be possible. From a modeling perspective complete removal (irreversible anonymisation) is the best solution; a high-cardinality categorical feature composed of unique values will have very little predictive value, so dropping such data will not only aid in regulatory compliance, but will lead to a more robust machine learning model. For more on this subject see for example the review "*Anonymization Procedures for Tabular Data: An Explanatory Technical and Legal Synthesis*".

[6] Florian Pargent, Florian Pfisterer, Janek Thomas, Bernd Bischl *"Regularized target encoding outperforms traditional methods in supervised machine learning with high cardinality features"*, Computational Statistics **37** pp. 2671-2692 (2022)

[7] L. Sweeney *"Simple Demographics Often Identify People Uniquely"*, Carnegie Mellon University, Data Privacy Working Paper 3 (2000)

Recommended reading

Papers

- Yufeng Ding, Jeffrey S. Simonoff *"An Investigation of Missing Data Methods for Classification Trees Applied to Binary Response Data"*, Journal of Machine Learning Research **11** pp. 131-170 (2010)
- H. Aguinis, R. K. Gottfredson, H Joo *"Best-Practice Recommendations for Defining, Identifying, and Handling Outliers"*, Organizational Research Methods **16** pp. 270-301 (2013)
- Pierre-Olivier Côté, Amin Nikanjam, Nafisa Ahmed, Dmytro Humeniuk, Foutse Khomh *"Data Cleaning and Machine Learning: A Systematic Literature Review"*, arXiv:2310.01765 (2024)

Books

- "DAMA DMBOK2", Technics Publications (2017)
- Stef van Buuren *"Flexible Imputation of Missing Data"*, 2nd edition, CRC Press (2018)
- Brett Kennedy *"Outlier Detection in Python"*, Manning Publications (2024)

Packages

- scikit-learn
- missingno by Aleksey Bilogur
- Python Outlier Detection (PyOD)
- Category Encoders
- missingpy
- AWS Deequ
- Great Expectations

5. Cross-validation

> • `train` is `train`, and `test` is `test`, and never the twain shall meet.
> • Do unto `test` as you have done unto `train`.

Once we have explored our data and cleaned it up we are now ready to create our machine learning model. Perhaps the biggest difference between the statistical modeling ('$\hat{\beta}$') and the machine learning modeling ('$\hat{y}$') paradigms is how model quality is evaluated. In statistical modeling the emphasis is on in-sample 'goodness of fit' tests; ¿how well does the model fit to the data that it was fitted on? On the other hand, machine learning modeling tests how well the model does at predicting the target for out-of-sample data that has never seen before, responding to the question ¿is our model transferable to new data? In this sense machine learning modeling is more akin to the scientific method, and maybe the reason for the term 'data science'. In this chapter we see how our initial dataset is partitioned into a number of disjoint datasets for the purpose of model evaluation and selection.

5.1 Why out-of-sample evaluation?

In Fig. 5.1 we fit a linear regression model to an existing dataset that now has ever increasing numbers of uninformative random noise features, and then monitor both the corresponding in-sample and out-of-sample RMSE performance (note that the same will hold for the MAE). The in-sample RMSE decreases monotonically with each new noise feature. However, on the out-of-sample data we see the reality that the model will produce progressively worse predictions. Our model is making use of each additional parameter associated with each new feature to overfit to the training data, and this deleterious overfitting can only be detected by way of out-of-sample evaluation.

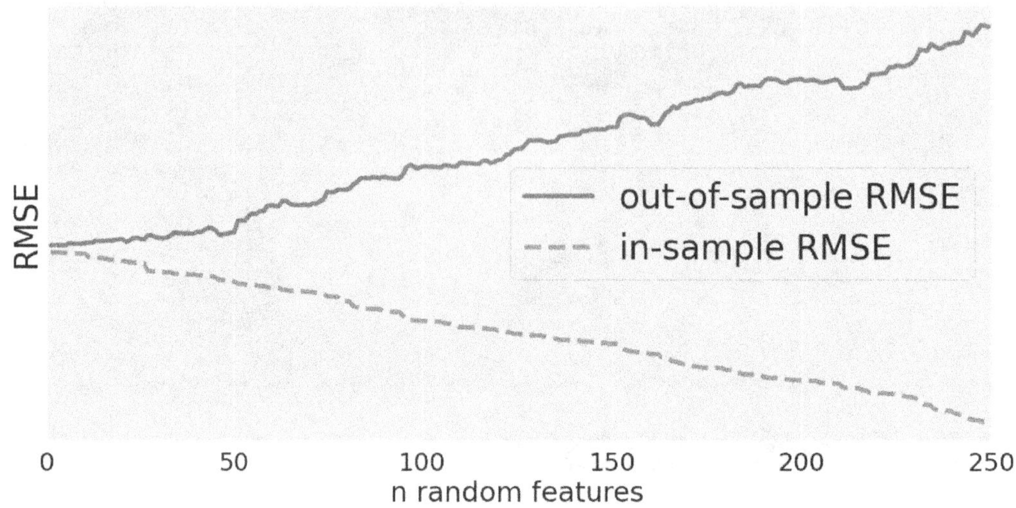

Figure 5.1: *Kitchen sink regression*: fitting to uninformative features leads to improved in-sample performance, but degrades the out-of-sample performance.

5.2 Three-way split: train, validation, and test

The very simplest incarnation of performing the three-way split or 'train-test split' is shown in Figure 5.2.

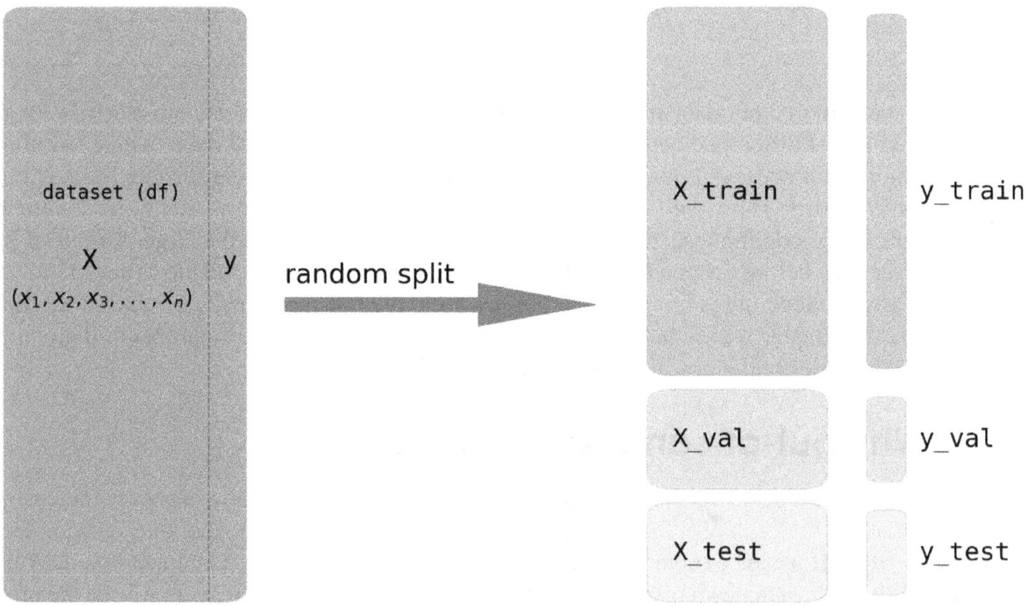

Figure 5.2: Splitting a dataset

Our first operation is to split the dataset (*i.e.* our augmented matrix) vertically, separating the feature columns from the target column. Thus we now have our coefficient matrix (**X**) and a column vector (**y**).

```
X = dataset
y = X.pop('Target')
```

Then we create (at least) three disjoint datasets, namely train, validation and test:

- train: the training data is used to find (or 'learn') the parameters of our model; this is the data that we fit to and will be the largest of the three sets
- validation: the validation dataset is used to find the best model with corresponding hyperparameters
- test: (or *hold-out*) is used as a final performance 'reality-check':

  "...the cautious statistician who sets aside a randomly selected part of his sample without looking at it and then plays without inhibition on what is left, confident in the knowledge that the set-aside data will deliver an unbiased judgment on the efficacy of his analysis." M. Stone[1] (1974)

A rough guide is to perform a 'Pareto' split: 80% of the data for training purposes, and the remaining 20% is used for the validation and the test sets, which should be around the same size (same number of rows) so as to have the same pessimistic bias. It is very important that each dataset should be representative of the whole (or be independent and identically distributed (i.i.d.) random variables in statistical parlance). A very simple way to achieve this is simply to randomly shuffle the rows before performing the splits. For the 'horizontal' splits scikit-learn provides a helpful routine to take care of this task for us, namely the train_test_split

```
from sklearn.model_selection import train_test_split

X_train, X_tmp, y_train, y_tmp = train_test_split(X, y,
                                                  test_size=0.2,
                                                  random_state=42)
X_val, X_test, y_val, y_test   = train_test_split(X_tmp, y_tmp,
                                                  test_size=0.5,
                                                  random_state=42)
del X_tmp, y_tmp
```

When performing classification, to ensure equal proportions of each class are assigned to each split one can use stratify=y. It is a good idea to also use random_state=42 in order to make the random split reproducible for testing purposes. This seed value can also be periodically changed to create 'fresh' datasets in order to prevent overfitting to a specific validation dataset.

5.3 Permutation invariance

Once we have our datasets, suffice to say our predictions should be invariant to the actual order of the rows and columns within said dataframes, *i.e.* the rows and columns are said to be exchangeable.

5.4 Cross-validation

Cross-validation is a clever technique designed to make the very most out of a small dataset where one may not be able to afford the luxury of holding out a sizable chunk of data for validation purposes. In cross-validation the training dataset also becomes the validation dataset. This is achieved by k-fold cross-validation, drawn schematically in Figure 5.3 using $k = 5$:

[1] M. Stone *"Cross-Validatory Choice and Assessment of Statistical Predictions"*, Journal of the Royal Statistical Society: Series B (Methodological) **36** pp. 111-133 (1974)

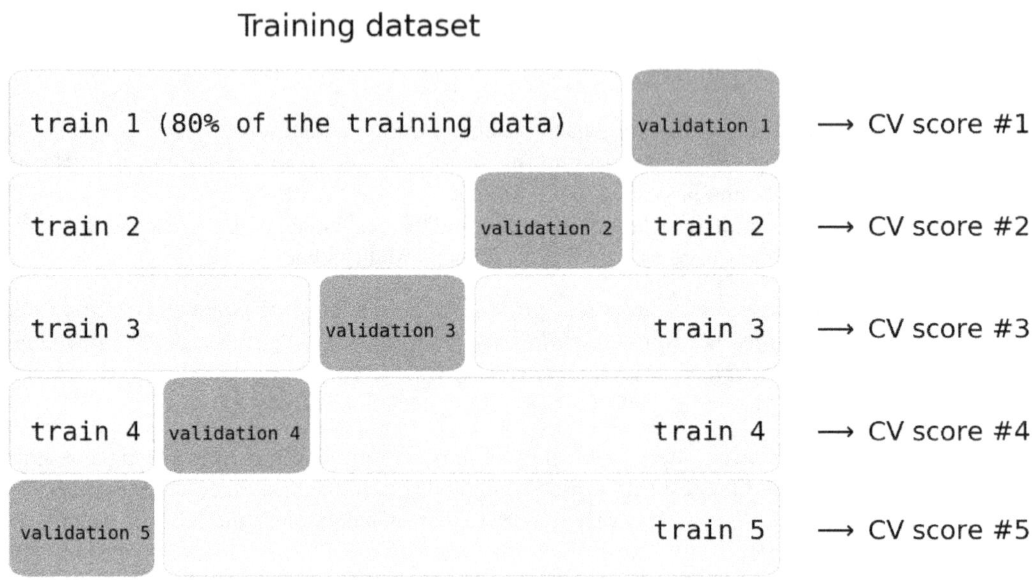

Figure 5.3: Schematic of 5-fold cross-validation

Taken to the extreme one can even perform *leave-one-out* CV (LOOCV), where each time the validation set consists of just a single row of the training data. However, this implies training our model as many times as there are rows of training data. For obvious reasons this is not an advisable strategy when using large datasets.

Sample code

Scikit-learn provides a `cross_val_score` routine

```
from sklearn.model_selection import cross_val_score, KFold
from sklearn.metrics import root_mean_squared_error
from sklearn.metrics import make_scorer

# Regression using the L2 loss
RMSE = make_scorer(root_mean_squared_error)
kf = KFold(n_splits=5, shuffle=True, random_state=42)
CV_scores = cross_val_score(regressor,
                            X, y,
                            cv=kf,
                            scoring=RMSE,
                            n_jobs=-1)

print("* CV scores: ", CV_scores)
print("* RMS of CV RMSE: ",round(np.sqrt(np.mean(np.square(CV_scores))),1))
print("* Std. dev of CV score: ",round(np.std(CV_scores),1))
```

where we estimate the average generalization error, and the standard deviation is indicative of the sampling uncertainty associated with these k scores. Suffice to say ideally we would like to know the true value of the generalization error, but this could only be obtained as the size of the training dataset tends to infinity.

And we would like to have as little dispersion as possible associated with this value, but this could only be obtained as the size of the validation dataset tends to infinity. The difference between the true generalization error and generalization error obtained from a finite number of training examples is known as the *estimation error*.

> Remark: Note that when using the RMSE metric one should not directly average over the k individual CV scores but rather
>
> $$RMSE = \sqrt{\frac{\sum(RMSE_i)^2}{k}}$$
>
> where it is assumed that there are equal numbers of samples in each split.

> Remark: Tip: One can inspect the complete list of available pre-defined scorers via:
> ```
> import sklearn
> sklearn.metrics.get_scorer_names()
> ```

Sample code

It is worth mentioning that the scikit-learn `cross_val_score` routine admits the possibility of data leakage. To avoid leakage here we provide an example of performing cross-validation where we can apply bespoke `cleaning` functions to the `X` data, such as fits and transformations to the `X_train` data, and apply the same corresponding transformations to the `X_validation` data (`gist`)

```
from sklearn.model_selection import KFold
from sklearn.metrics import mean_squared_error as metric

def cross_validation(X, y, estimator, metric, n=5, seed=42):
    kf = KFold(n_splits=n, random_state=seed, shuffle=True)
    OOF_predictions = [] # save predictions for each fold
    CV_scores = [] # save scores for each fold
    baseline_scores = [] # save the baseline scores for each fold

    for train_index, validation_index in kf.split(X, y):

        X_train = X.iloc[train_index]
        #X_train = cleaning_train(X_train)
        X_validation = X.iloc[validation_index]
        #X_validation = cleaning_validation(X_validation)

        y_train = y.iloc[train_index]
        y_validation = y.iloc[validation_index]

        # fit
        estimator.fit(X_train, y_train)

        # predict
        # for regression / classification:
        y_pred = estimator.predict(X_validation)
```

```
        # for probabilistic classification:
        #y_pred = estimator.predict_proba(X_validation)[:,1]

        # calculate the metric for this fold
        CV_score = metric(y_validation, y_pred)
        CV_scores.append( CV_score )

        # calculate the baseline score for this fold
        # for regression / probabilistic classification:
        y_baseline = np.full( len(y_validation), np.mean(y_train) )
        # for binary classification:
        #y_baseline = np.zeros( len(y_validation) )
        baseline_score = metric(y_validation, y_baseline)
        baseline_scores.append( baseline_score )

        # save the predictions for this fold
        preds_df = pd.DataFrame(validation_index, columns=["idx"])
        preds_df["y_pred"] = y_pred
        OOF_predictions.append( preds_df )

    # stitch all the OOF predictions together
    df_y_pred = pd.concat(OOF_predictions).sort_values(by=["idx"]).set_index("idx")
    return CV_scores, baseline_scores, df_y_pred


CV_scores, baseline_scores, df_y_pred = cross_validation(X, y, regressor, metric)
print(metric(y, df_y_pred["y_pred"]))
```

This routine is also useful for saving the out-of-fold (OOF) predictions of the model for later use in a stacking ensemble.

5.4.1 $\mathbb{E}$(CV): ...now change the `random_state`

Even though cross-validation returns an evaluation based on all of the training data, a different partition of the data found in each of the splits will lead to slightly different results. In view of this in the following example we estimate an expectation value for the CV score by repeating 5-fold CV ten times using ten different seed values, and when finished we then average the results:

```
from sklearn.model_selection import cross_val_score, KFold

CV_results = []
for seed in range(10):
    kf = KFold(n_splits=5, shuffle=True, random_state=seed)
    CV_scores = cross_val_score(regressor, X,y, cv=kf, scoring=RMSE)
    CV_results.append(CV_scores)

print(np.mean(CV_results))
```

or one could make use of the `sklearn.model_selection.RepeatedKFold` routine.

5.4.2 How many folds? Pessimistic bias

If we consistently either overestimate or underestimate a statistic then our estimates are said to be *biased*. If we make our validation set too large then we introduce a bias underestimating our model performance as it has only been trained on a small training set, and would surely be a better model if it were to be trained on more training data examples. On the other hand if we use a very small validation set, so as to train or model on as much data as possible, then there will be a large variance in estimate of the generalization error.

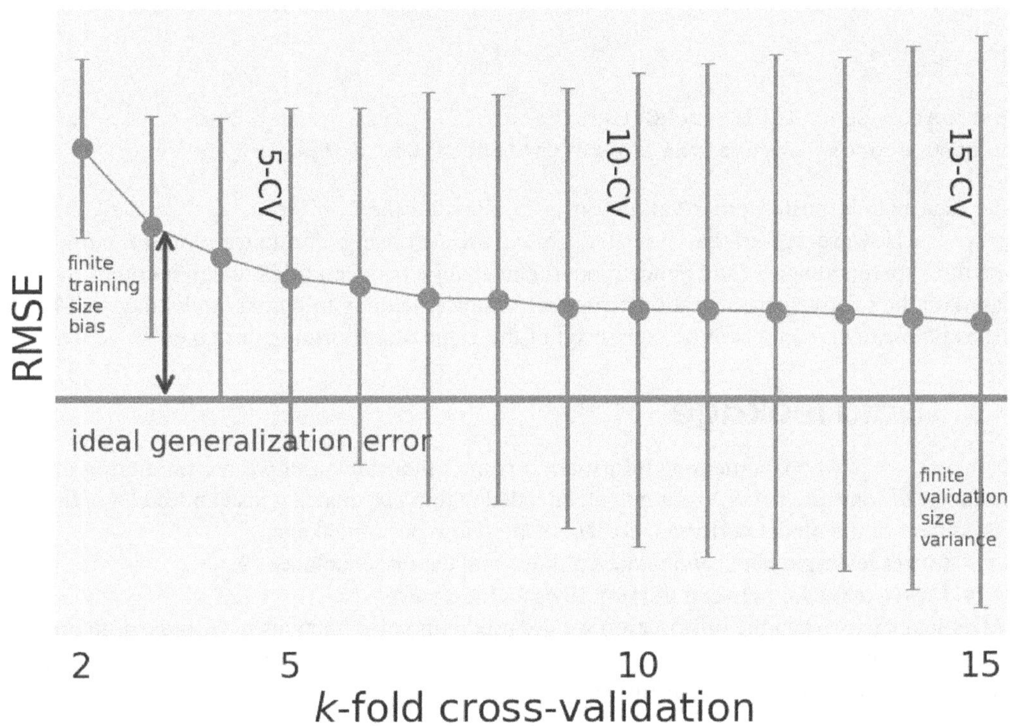

Figure 5.4: Pessimistic bias in k-fold cross-validation due to finite training dataset size (the ideal generalization error is estimated via a fit to extremely large training and test sets).

In Figure 5.4 we see the results of an empirical regression experiment where we vary the number of CV folds. In this experiment the ideal (population) generalization error was estimated by fitting a model to, and evaluating on, extremely large training and test sets. The most pessimistic bias is seen with 2-CV, which is only able to make use of 50% of the available training data. The limiting case of using LOOCV will result in an almost unbiased estimate of the generalization error, but will have the largest validation variance. The points in Figure 5.4 essentially trace out a learning curve.

We can see that cross-validation is great for model selection; where relative estimates of the generalization error are enough for us to choose the model with the lowest generalization error. However, one should be aware that it will provide a pessimistic estimate of the true generalization error that we can expect to see on a large quantity of new data.

5.5 Nested cross-validation

In nested (or 'double') cross-validation the inner loop is for model selection, where we find the optimal hyperparameters via for example a `GridSearchCV`, and the outer loop is for testing generalization using the `cross_val_score`. Thus here the model hyperparameters may vary in each CV fold, unlike in the un-nested CV where we are assessing the performance of one specific set of hyperparameters.

Sample code

```
param_grid  = {"max_depth": [3, 4, 5]}

estimator_GS = GridSearchCV(estimator=DT, param_grid=param_grid, cv=5)
nested_scores = cross_val_score(estimator_GS, X=X, y=y, cv=4)
```

The idea behind nested cross-validation is to alleviate the optimistic bias inherent in hyperparameter selection. However, given that in nested CV we are still using a finite training set, a finite validation set, and the hyperparameters (and hence model) can change between folds, when it comes to model selection based on the relative generalization error performance, leading to a final model that will be fitted to all of the available data, I am yet to be convinced of the value of performing nested cross-validation.

5.6 Data leakage

Data leakage is when, somehow, information from either the target we are predicting or the test dataset becomes, to some greater or lesser extent, encoded within our model. This can lead an optimistic bias in our assessment of the model performance. There are two types of leakage:

- **target leakage**: between feature columns and the target column
- **future leakage**: between training rows and test rows

Target leakage is when the information we are predicting also happens to be present in one or more of the features that we are using to predict the target. For example we are predicting the price of a house (€) and we have the features m^2 and €/m^2 in our dataset.

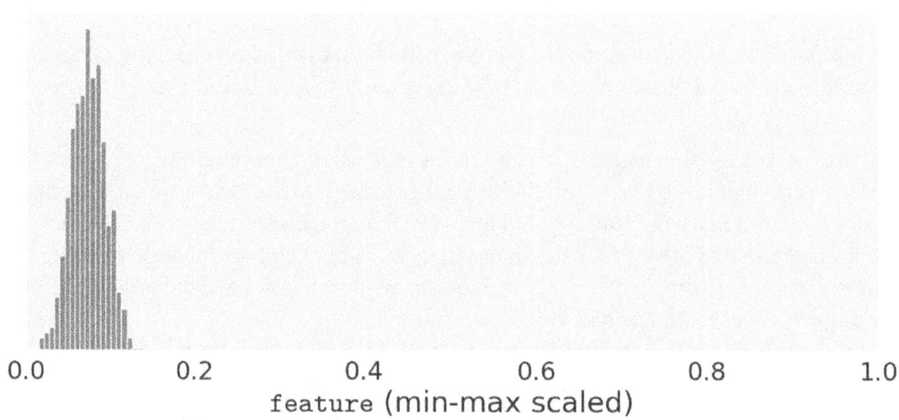

Figure 5.5: Future leakage: `X_train` after min-max scaling the whole dataset that has even just one large positive outlier in `X_test`.

Future leakage can be caused for example by transformations, such as scaling or mean imputation. If the train, validation and test sets are all i.i.d. then mean imputation should not be too serious (but still should be avoided). Non-robust scaling can be a disaster due to outlier values. In Figure 5.5 we see the effect of the presence of a single outlier value in the test dataset on the training dataset if min-max scaling ($[0,1]$) is performed on the whole dataset before the train-test split. Future leakage can also be caused by duplicated rows of data which become divided between the train and validation datasets. How can one avoid data

	feature	feature	feature
train	2.3	2.3	2.3
	NaN	714288	2.85
	4.9	4.9	4.9
	NaN	714288	2.85
	NaN	714288 ✗	2.85 ✓
	1.6	1.6	1.6
	2.6	2.6	2.6
test	3.6	3.6	3.6
	5000000	5000000	5000000
	NaN	714288	2.85
	1.9	1.9	1.9

Table 5.1: Future leakage: Here we see the effect of mean imputation incorrectly preformed before the train-test split (middle column).

leakage? By processing/cleaning each of our `X_train`, `X_validation`, and `X_test` datasets all in the same way, but each separately. For example, if we impute missing values in a feature using the mean in the `X_train` dataset, then missing values in the `X_validation`, and `X_test` datasets for that feature should be filled with the very same mean value calculated for the `X_train` data.

> Remark: The Scikit-learn `cross_val_score` routine does not process the train/test splits separately and thus has the potential to lead to overly optimistic results.

5.7 Covariate shift and Concept drift

A fundamental assumption in tabular machine learning is that the data we are predicting for has the very same hypersurface that we originally fitted to. However, new data seen in production may be subject to:
Covariate shift $P(X)$: when the distribution of some or all of the `x` in `X_train` is not similar to that of the `x` in `X_test`. This leads to a resulting change in the shape of the convex hull between the training and test data sets. For example, we modeled houses having an area in the range of 70m^2 to 120m^2 but we are then asked to make predictions for houses in the range 120m^2 to 170m^2.
Concept drift $P(y|X)$: when the `y` in `y_train` are not similar to the `y` in `y_test`.
For example we fit our model to house prices that were collected in 1980. The actual houses themselves (the `X`) have not changed at all since then, but prices today are very different from those in 1980. The concepts that have changed could be for example inflation, market demand, or a singular sudden 'intervention' event such as a currency change from Pesetas to Euros.

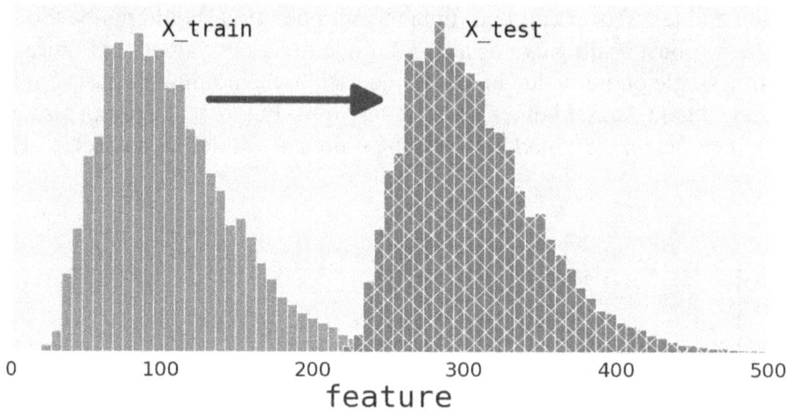

Figure 5.6: Covariate shift: Here the distribution of a feature (covariate) in the test data (right hand hashed green histogram) is significantly different from the distribution of said feature in the training data (left hand orange histogram).

> Remark: Performing a randomized `train_test_split` on ones data (*i.e.* having `shuffle=True`) before performing EDA or model fitting on the training portion may well serve to hide any concept drift that is already present in ones dataset. It could be a good idea to compare the target distributions from data sampled from the start of ones dataset with a sample from the end of the dataset beforehand.

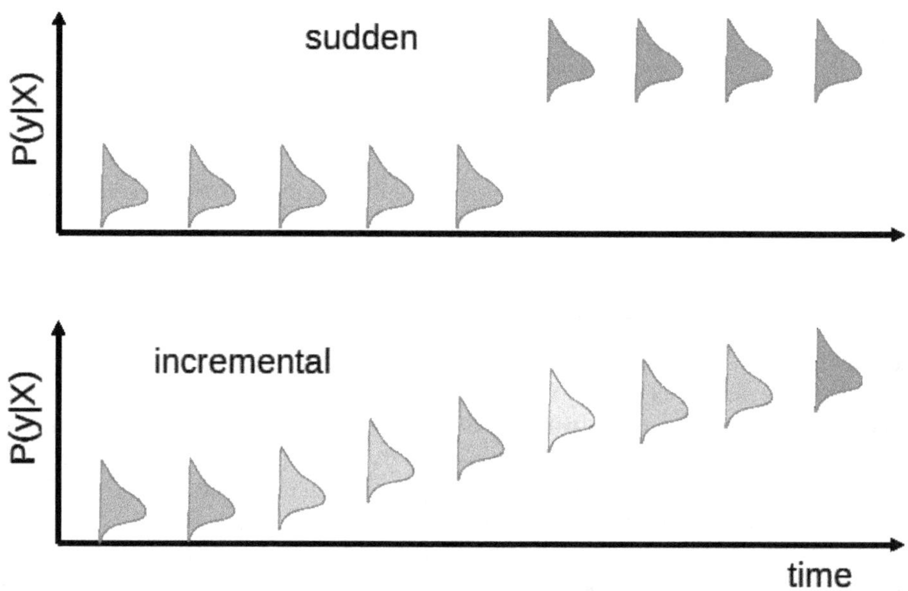

Figure 5.7: Sudden and incremental concept drift.

The easiest solution to both shift and drift is to re-fit our model using the new training data. This can be done either periodically when performance monitoring indicates that model degradation has passed an unacceptable limit, or can be done continuously via what is variously known as incremental, stream, or online learning[2].

5.7.1 Comparing univariate distributions: two-sample tests

Two-sample tests can be very useful in detecting if there is significant covariate shift (or concept drift if comparing the target columns) between the data the model was trained on and the data that the model is being asked to predict for. The simplest test is to compare the mean of each feature between the two samples, where we are assuming that they are i.i.d. samples both drawn from the same population. If the features, or target column, have a Gaussian distribution one can perform a two-sample Student's t-test, where the null hypothesis is that $\mu_1 = \mu_2$. Non-parametric tests, which make no assumptions regarding the distribution of the feature, are for example the Kolmogorov-Smirnov and the Cramér-von Mises tests. We can also perform visual inspections via quantile-quantile plots.

5.7.1.1 Kolmogorov-Smirnov test

The two-sample Kolmogorov-Smirnov test compares the eCDF for two distributions.

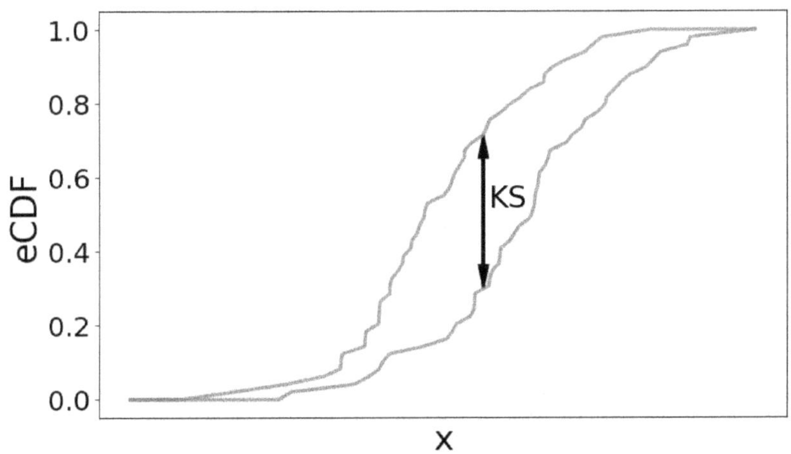

Figure 5.8: The two-sample Kolmogorov-Smirnov test.

It is based on finding the largest vertical distance between the two eCDF

$$\text{KS} = \sup_x |\text{eCDF}_A(x) - \text{eCDF}_B(x)| \tag{5.1}$$

and can be computed via

```
from scipy import stats

KS_test = stats.ks_2samp(eCDF_A, eCDF_B)
print("* distance:", KS_test.statistic)
print("* location:", KS_test.statistic_location)
print("* p_value:", KS_test.pvalue)
```

where the p-value is based on the null hypothesis (H_0) that the two distributions are identical.

[2]Hoi, Sahoo, Lu, Zhao "*Online Learning: A Comprehensive Survey*" arXiv:1802.02871 (2018)

5.7.1.2 Cramér-von Mises test

The two-sample Cramér-von Mises test, in the continuous case, calculates the square of the area between the two eCDF. When working with samples it is calculated in a point-wise fashion with a summation

$$\text{CvM} = \sum_{x} (\text{eCDF}_A(x) - \text{eCDF}_B(x))^2 \tag{5.2}$$

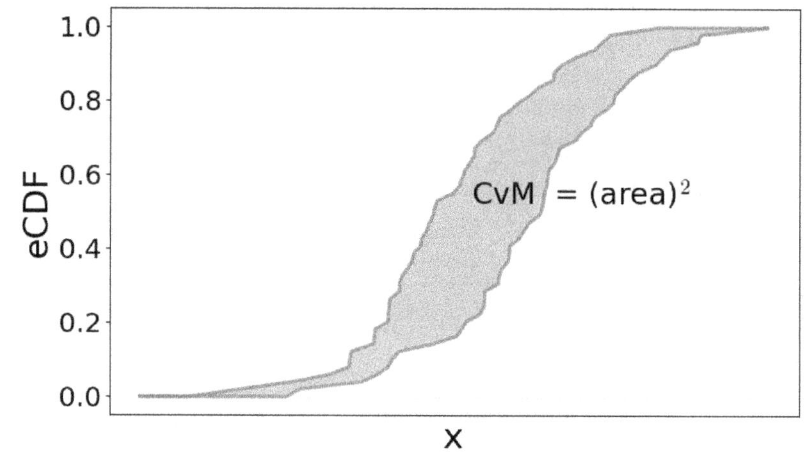

Figure 5.9: The two-sample Cramér-von Misess test.

```
from scipy import stats

CvM_test = stats.cramervonmises_2samp(eCDF_A, eCDF_B)
print("* squared area:", CvM_test.statistic)
print("* p_value:", CvM_test.pvalue)
```

where again the p-value is based on the null hypothesis (H_0) that the two distributions are identical.

5.7.1.3 Anderson-Darling test

The Anderson-Darling test is an extension of the Cramér-von Mises test

$$\text{AD} = \sum_{x} \frac{(\text{eCDF}_A(x) - \text{eCDF}_B(x))^2}{\text{eCDF}_B(x)(1 - \text{eCDF}_B(x))} \tag{5.3}$$

where here the denominator serves to add extra weight to both of the tail regions.

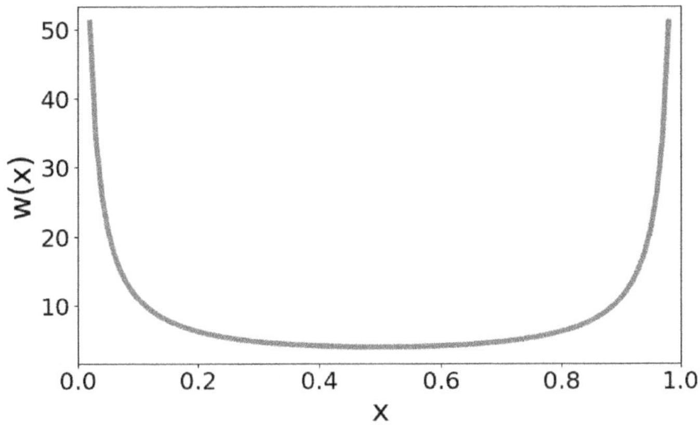

Figure 5.10: Plot of the Anderson-Darling weight function for $\mathrm{eCDF}_B(x) = x$.

```
from scipy import stats

AD_test = stats.anderson_ksamp([eCDF_A, eCDF_B])
print("* statistic:", AD_test.statistic)
print("* p_value:", AD_test.pvalue)
```

5.7.1.4 Quantile-quantile (Q-Q) plot

A quantile-quantile (Q-Q) plot is a technique for performing a bivariate visual comparison of the relative distributions of data samples, for example here comparing the distributions of a given univariate feature in the training and in the test datasets respectively. If the two samples are identical, in other words we have i.i.d. samples, all the points will lie along the identity line. However, deviations from the identity line will indicate that the distributions of the two samples differ, and we have a problem.

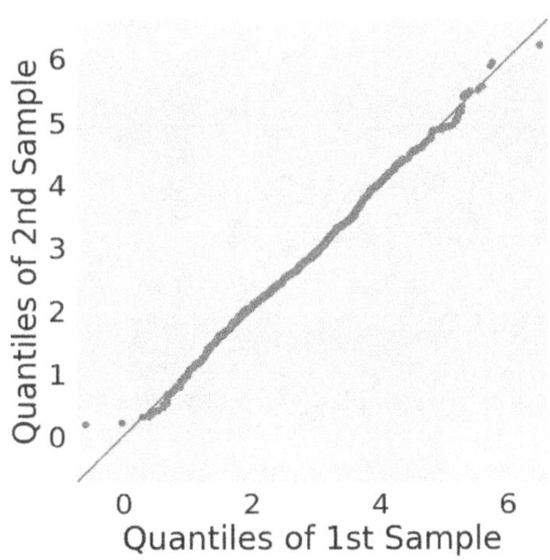

Figure 5.11: Example of a two-sample Q-Q plot for very similar distributions. We can see that the points lie roughly along the identity line, *i.e.* $\beta_0 = 0$ and $\beta_1 = 1$.

Centrality

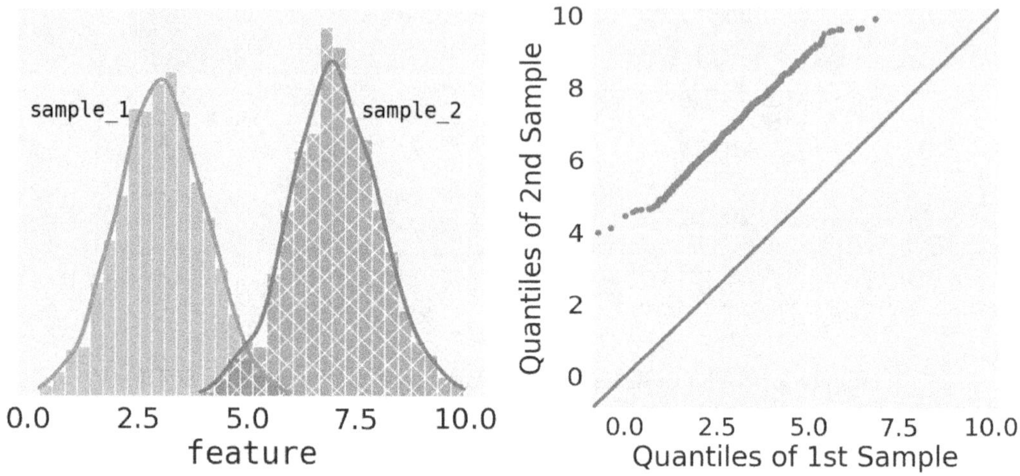

Figure 5.12: Example of a two-sample Q-Q plot where the median $\tilde{x}_2 > \tilde{x}_1$. We can see the points have shifted upwards by $\beta_0 \approx \tilde{x}_2 - \tilde{x}_1$.

Dispersion

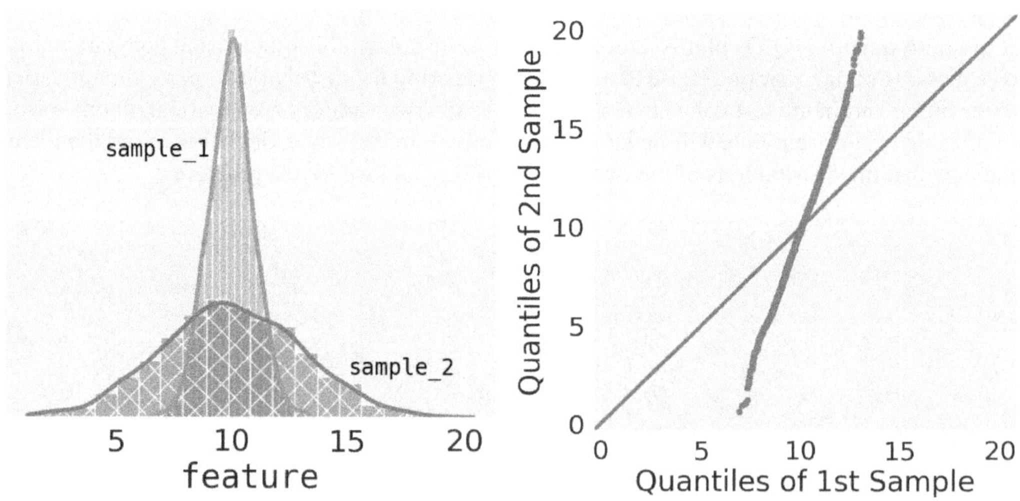

Figure 5.13: Example of a two-sample Q-Q plot where the range $R_2 > R_1$. The points now have slope of $\beta_1 \approx (R_2/R_1)$.

Sample code

Using the statsmodels package to create a two-sample Q-Q plot

```
import statsmodels.api as sm

sm.qqplot_2samples( sample_1, sample_2, line="45")
```

5.7.2 Comparing multivariate distributions: C2ST

In the case of multivariate distributions, *i.e.* now comparing whole datasets rather than individual features, Jerome Friedman proposed the clever use of a binary classifier[3]. To perform a classifier two-sample test (C2ST)[4] also known as 'adversarial validation', one proceeds as follows; we combine our train and test data, creating a new target column labeling them with say a 0 for the training data and a 1 for the test data, mix them up, then see if we are able to correctly re-identify them using a binary classifier, the null hypothesis being that the train and the test sets are i.i.d. samples. If we cannot correctly classify them, *i.e.* say we are using the area under the receiver operating characteristic curve (ROC) as our statistic, if we obtain a chance-level score of 0.5 then the two sets are indistinguishable, we accept the null hypothesis and we are good to go. However, if we can classify them (ROC > 0.5) then we have a problem, either with the whole dataset or more likely with some features in particular, which potentially have different distributions in the test and train datasets. If we have a problem, we can look at the feature(s) that was most out of place using the aforementioned univariate tests.

Sample code

Here is some sample code to set up our data for a C2ST test

```
# create the new train/test labels
X_train["C2ST_label"] = 0
X_test["C2ST_label"]  = 1

# create one unified dataset
all_data = pd.concat([X_train, X_test], axis=0, ignore_index=True)

# now randomly shuffle
all_data_shuffled = all_data.sample(frac=1)
```

N Jupyter Notebook: What is Adversarial Validation?

[3]Jerome H. Friedman *"On multivariate goodness of fit and two sample testing"*, SLAC-PUB-10325 (2003)
[4]David Lopez-Paz, Maxime Oquab *"Revisiting Classifier Two-Sample Tests"*, arXiv:1610.06545 (2016)

Recommended reading

Papers

- S. Kaufman, S. Rosset, C. Perlich, O. Stitelman *"Leakage in data mining: Formulation, detection, and avoidance"*, ACM Transactions on Knowledge Discovery from Data (TKDD) **6** Article 15 (2012)
- Mervyn Stone *"Cross-Validatory Choice and Assessment of Statistical Predictions"*, Journal of the Royal Statistical Society: Series B (Methodological) **36** pp. 111-133 (1974)
- Sudhir Varma, Richard Simon *"Bias in error estimation when using cross-validation for model selection"*, BMC Bioinformatics **7** 91 (2006)
- Gavin C. Cawley, Nicola L. C. Talbot *"On Over-fitting in Model Selection and Subsequent Selection Bias in Performance Evaluation"*, The Journal of Machine Learning Research **11** pp. 2079-2107 (2010)
- Sebastian Raschka *"Model Evaluation, Model Selection, and Algorithm Selection in Machine Learning"*, arXiv:1811.12808 (2020)
- Stephen Bates, Trevor Hastie, Robert Tibshirani *"Cross-validation: what does it estimate and how well does it do it?"*, Journal of the American Statistical Association **119** pp. 1434-1445 (2024) (arXiv copy)
- Lu, Liu, Dong, Gu, Gama, Zhang *"Learning under Concept Drift: A Review"*, IEEE Transactions on Knowledge and Data Engineering **31** pp. 2346-2363 (2018)
- Jakub Białek, Juhani Kivimäki, Wojtek Kuberski, Nikolaos Perrakis *"Estimating Model Performance Under Covariate Shift Without Labels"*, arXiv:2401.08348 (2024)

Other

- Scikit-learn: *"Cross-validation: evaluating estimator performance"*

6. Interpolation and smoothing

All models are wrong, but some are useful[1].

George E. P. Box

Interpolation is the fancy mathematical name for the century old pastime of *connect-the-dots*. Interpolation passes through every single data point, whereas in general curve fitting does not have to do this. Indeed to some great extent machine learning can be thought of as little more than glorified curve fitting. Ideally we fit a curve to all of the signal, and to none of the noise. If it were not for noise, potentially leading for example to y being multi-valued, then interpolation would have done the job just fine from a $\hat{y}$ point of view (but would be useless from a $\hat{\beta}$ viewpoint).

6.1 Interpolation

6.1.1 k-nearest neighbors (k-NN) regression

Here we look at the k-nearest neighbors (k-NN) algorithm, which can be implemented via the `sklearn KNeighborsRegressor`.

[1]George E. P. Box *"Science and Statistics"*, Journal of the American Statistical Association **71** pp. 791-799 (1974)

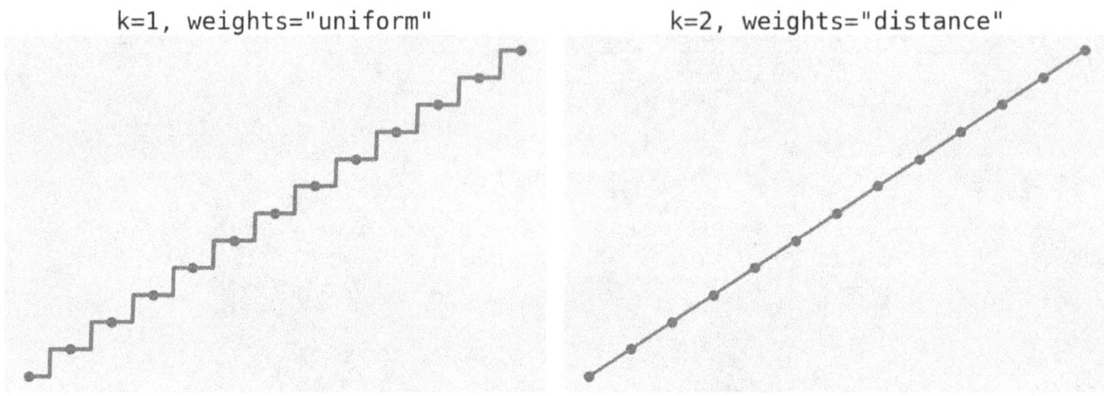

Figure 6.1: k-NN interpolation using (LHS) uniform weights, and (RHS) weighted by inverse distance

In Figure 6.1 we have a series of datapoints (for simplicity's sake generated via the function $y = x$). On the LHS of the figure we perform *proximal* interpolation (by setting $k = 1$ and `weights="uniform"`) where the interpolated value is exactly the same as that of the nearest datapoint to the value we wish to predict. On the RHS we perform linear interpolation (also known as *lerp*) by setting $k = 2$ and `weights="distance"`. This time we are joining each pair of neighbouring datapoints by a straight line. Given the linear nature of the ground truth function, and the absence of any noise component, this can be considered to be a perfect fit to our data. In Figure 6.2 we now add some curvature to the datapoints ($y = \sin(x)$) and again perform linear interpolation. We can now see that the interpolations is still not too bad, although is somewhat less reliable where the curvature is greatest.

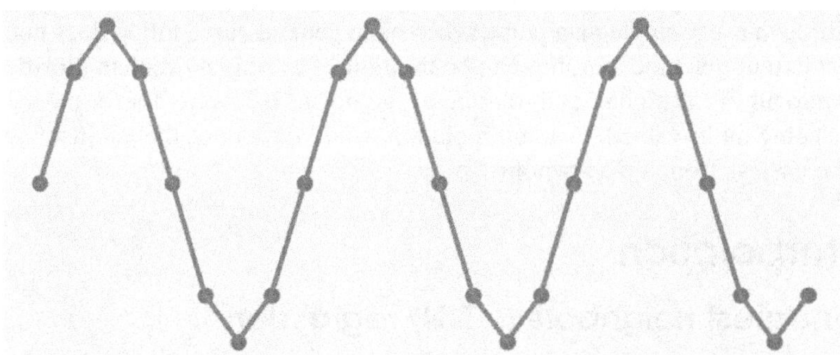

Figure 6.2: Linear interpolation of points sampled from a sine wave

Finally, in Figure 6.3, we shall perform linear interpolation for a dataset that has noise (this is actually the Anscombe 'A' dataset).

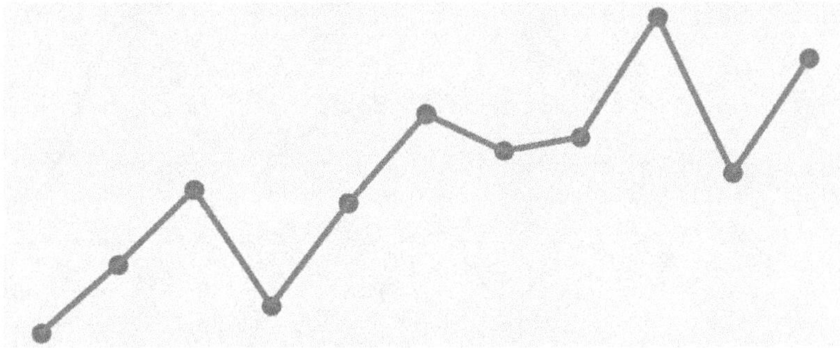

Figure 6.3: Linear interpolation of noisy data

We can now see the principal shortcoming of interpolation; there is no underlying concept of signal and noise, all points are treated as pure signal points.

Sample code

```
from sklearn.neighbors import KNeighborsRegressor

interpolation = KNeighborsRegressor(n_neighbors= 2,
                                    weights= "distance")
interpolation.fit(X,y)
y_pred = interpolation.predict(X)
```

6.1.2 Splines: piece-wise polynomials

Another popular interpolation technique is, rather than fitting (*i.e.* connecting) a straight line to two points, is to fit a cubic polynomial to four points. Remember, one can perfectly fit $n+1$ points by using a polynomial of degree n, so with $n=3$ we are (almost) guaranteed to pass through all four points. An additional boundary constraint is to require that overall the final interpolation is smooth. These are known as cubic splines. In Figures 6.4 and 6.5 we can see the results of a cubic spline fitted to sine wave samples, and to the noisy Anscombe 'A' dataset.

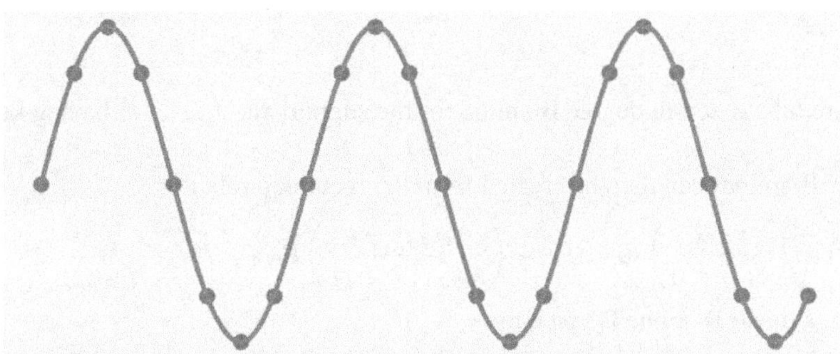

Figure 6.4: A cubic spline ($k=3$) fitted to points sampled from a sine wave

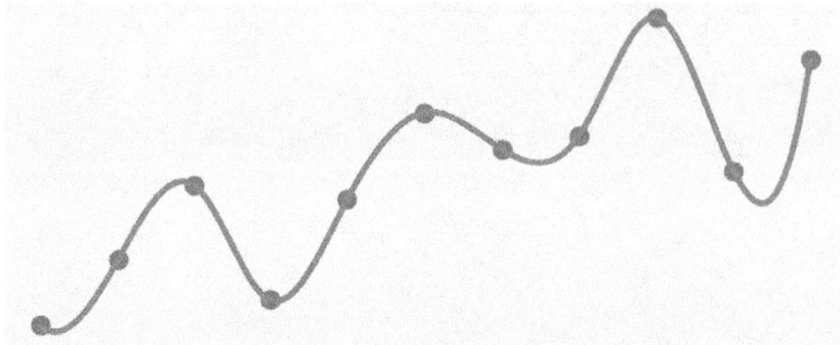

Figure 6.5: A cubic spline fitted to noisy data

We see that the fit to the sine wave is really rather good, but in the Anscombe case it is still clear that this technique is oblivious to the concept of noise.

6.1.3 B-spline basis functions

One can express a curve as a linear combination of basis functions in the form B-splines. A zeroth degree B-spline is defined as

$$B_{i,0}(x) := \begin{cases} 1 & \text{if } x_i \leq x < x_{i+1}, \\ 0 & \text{otherwise.} \end{cases} \tag{6.1}$$

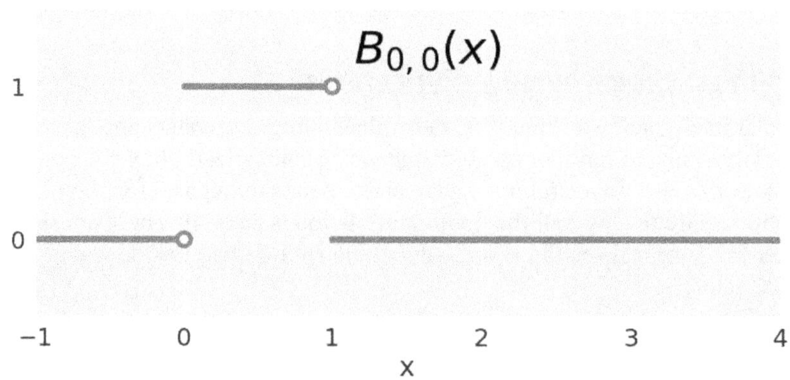

Figure 6.6: A zeroth degree B-spline for the support $x \in [0, 1)$, *i.e.* having knots at 0 and 1.

Higher order B-splines can then be created from the recursion relation

$$B_{i,j}(x) = \left(\frac{x - x_i}{x_{i+j} - x_i}\right) B_{i,j-1}(x) + \left(\frac{x_{i+j+1} - x}{x_{i+j+1} - x_{i+1}}\right) B_{i+1,j-1}(x) \tag{6.2}$$

For example, a linear B-spline is given by

$$B_{i,1}(x) := \begin{cases} \frac{x - x_i}{x_{i+1} - x_i} & \text{if } x_i \leq x < x_{i+1}, \\ \frac{x_{i+2} - x}{x_{i+2} - x_{i+1}} & \text{if } x_{i+1} \leq x < x_{i+2} \\ 0 & \text{otherwise.} \end{cases} \tag{6.3}$$

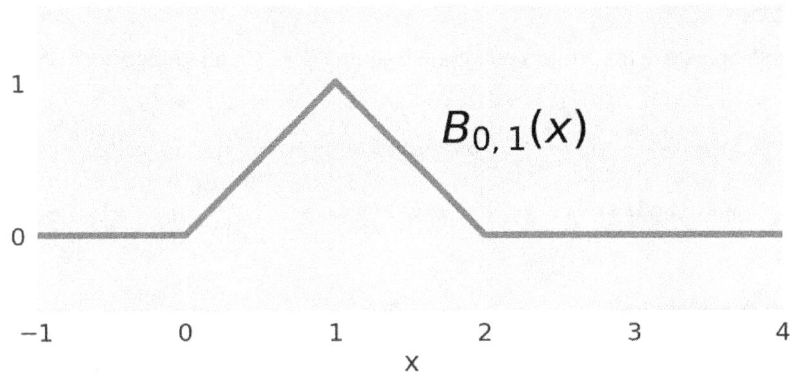

Figure 6.7: A first degree (linear) B-spline, having knots at $x = 0$, 1, and 2.

and a quadratic B-spline is given by

$$B_{i,2}(x) := \begin{cases} \frac{(x-x_i)^2}{(x_{i+2}-x_i)(x_{i+1}-x_i)} & \text{if } x_i \leq x < x_{i+1}, \\ \frac{(x-x_i)(x_{i+2}-x)}{(x_{i+2}-x_i)(x_{i+2}-x_{i+1})} + \frac{(x_{i+3}-x)(x-x_{i+1})}{(x_{i+3}-x_{i+1})(x_{i+2}-x_{i+1})} & \text{if } x_i \leq x_{i+1} < x_{i+2}, \\ \frac{(x_{i+3}-x)^2}{(x_{i+3}-x_{i+1})(x_{i+3}-x_{i+2})} & \text{if } x_i \leq x_{i+2} < x_{i+3}, \\ 0 & \text{otherwise.} \end{cases} \tag{6.4}$$

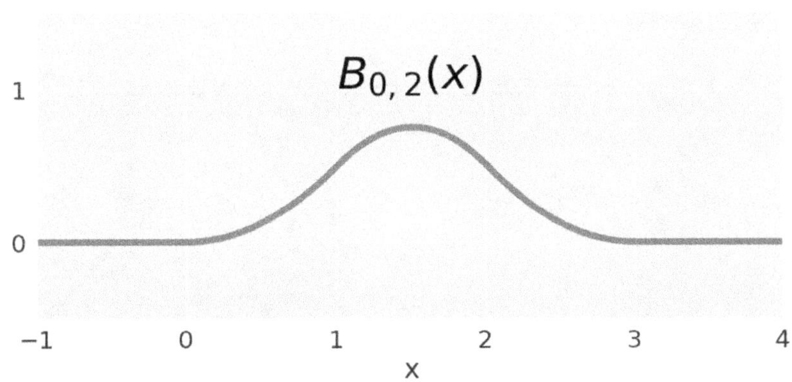

Figure 6.8: A second degree (quadratic) B-spline, having knots at $x = 0$, 1, 2 and 3.

We can then fit to a feature (x) using a linear combination of these basis functions

$$y = \sum_{i=1}^{n} \beta_i B_{i,j}(x) \tag{6.5}$$

where the β are the learnable scalar coefficients associated with each basis function, n is the number of basis splines to use, and j is the degree of the basis spline. Details regarding the determination of the positions of the knot points (the simplest approach being to use knots situated uniformly between the support end points) and fitting the values of the coefficients is beyond the scope of this chapter.

Sample code

Here is some sample code for fitting a quadratic B-spline (k=2) to a 1-dimensional dataset using `make_splrep`:

```
from scipy.interpolate import make_splrep

y_spline = make_splrep(X, y, k=2, s=0 )(X)
```

6.2 Smoothing

We have seen that interpolation is noise oblivious. For noisy data we can use smoothing; in the case of k-NN we can increase k, and in the case of the spline, increase s.

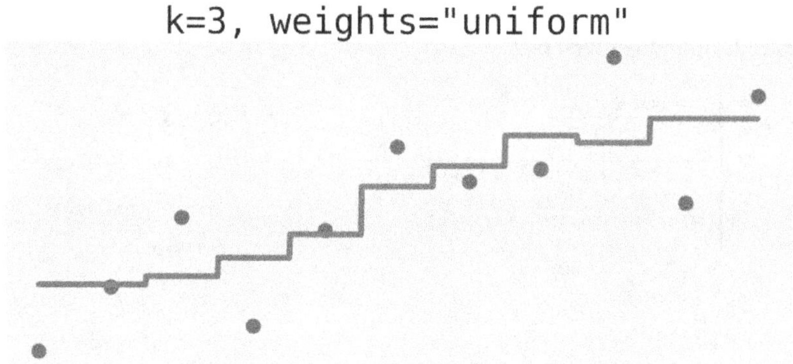

Figure 6.9: Anscombe 'A' with k-NN where $k = 3$.

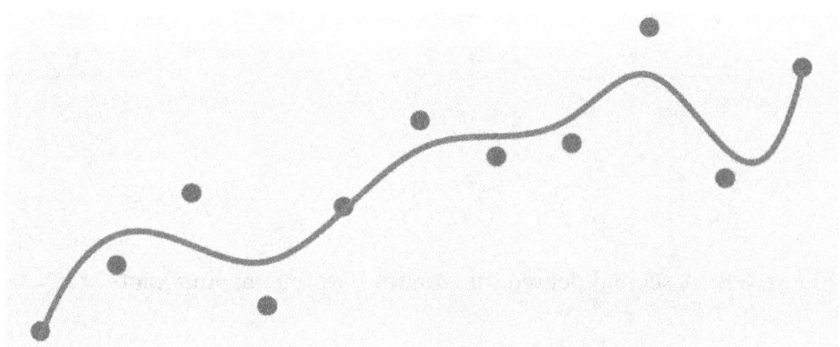

Figure 6.10: Anscombe 'A' with `splrep` where $k = 3$ and $s = 5$.

6.3 Summary

We have seen that interpolation is a *local* technique; for example in `lerp` the predicted values are based on solely on the values either side of the point we are predicting, and all other points are irrelevant. This is known as a *lazy learner* in that the dataset is effectively the model and one directly accesses the dataset at prediction time (that said there are may clever algorithms to speed up the process of finding the nearest neighbors, so in reality one does actually perform a fit). In the next chapter we shall look at regression, which is a *global*, technique that takes into account *all* of the training data point positions when fitting the model. We shall see that, for example with linear regression, we can compress the model down into a simple functional form along with just a handful of parameters (indeed machine learning can be seen from one viewpoint as being a form of lossy (non-invertible) compression).

Recommended reading

Papers

- Jerome H. Friedman *"Multivariate Adaptive Regression Splines"*, Annals of Statistics **19** pp. 1-67 (1991)
- Paul H. C. Eilers, Brian D. Marx *"Flexible smoothing with B-splines and penalties"*, Statistical Science **11** pp. 89-121 (1996)
- Paul H. C. Eilers, Brian D. Marx, Maria Durbán *"Twenty years of P-splines"*, SORT **39** pp. 1-38 (2015)

Books

- Tom Lyche and Knut Mørken "*Spline Methods*", University of Oslo (2018)
- Michael S. Floater "*An Introduction to Spline Theory*", University of Oslo (2025)

Other

- `statsmodels` LOWESS - locally weighted scatterplot smoother

Packages

- `py-earth` - a python implementation of the MARS algorithm, in the style of scikit-learn.

7. Regression

> You can do linear regression without thinking about whether the phenomenon you're modeling is actually close to linear. But you shouldn't.[1]
>
> *Jordan Ellenberg*

A regression problem in one in which the target values belong to the set of real numbers ($y \in \mathbb{R}$). From a machine learning standpoint our task is to produce point predictions (expectation values) and/or prediction intervals for previously unseen feature vectors. The term regression has its origins in the work of Galton[2] in 1886 when studying hereditary stature (the heights of children with respect to their parent's heights) and in the case of tall or short parents, empirically finding that their children's heights tend to gravitate (revert or regress) back towards that of the population mean. This can easily be understood if offspring heights are somewhat independent of their parent's heights; very tall or short parents represent extreme values, and is is much more likely that the next random sample seen will not be as extreme. It was in his quantification of the aforementioned 'somewhat' that a fit to the average of the two parent's heights versus the adult child height was performed in order to obtain the 'constant fraction' *i.e.* the regression coefficient, henceforth leading to the terminology regression for such an analysis.

In this chapter we shall look at the very simplest statistical (parametric) model, namely linear regression. We shall also look at the very simplest machine learning (non-parametric) model, namely the decision tree. We shall also see quantile regression (which includes median regression) and calculate prediction intervals using conformal prediction.

[1] George E. P. Box *"Science and Statistics"*, Journal of the American Statistical Association **71** pp. 791-799 (1974)

[2] Francis Galton *"Regression Towards Mediocrity in Hereditary Stature"*, The Journal of the Anthropological Institute of Great Britain and Ireland **15** pp. 246-263 (1886)

7.1 Regression baseline model

Our very first model should *always* be the baseline model. The baseline model is simply the expectation value. This is a model 'no-model' in that we make no use at all of the **X** values, only the target column, y.

Equation: Our regression baseline model, which we shall call $\hat{y}_0$, is

$$\hat{y}_0 = \mathbb{E}[f(x)] = \bar{y} \ \forall \ \hat{y} \tag{7.1}$$

It is worth mentioning that $\sum(y_i - \hat{y}_0) = 0$.

What does the baseline model look like?

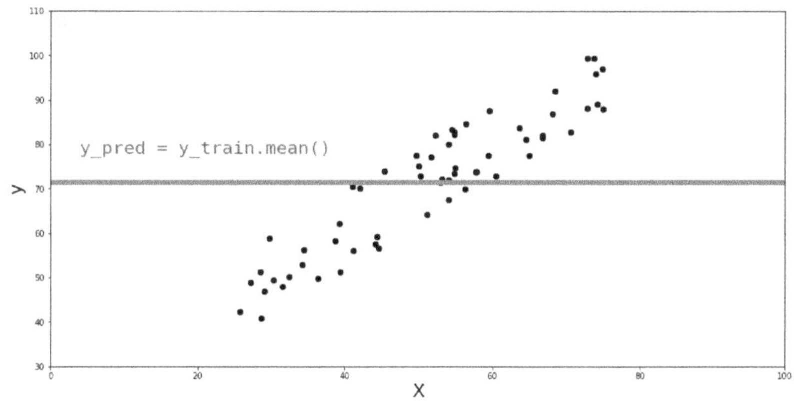

Figure 7.1: A regression baseline model.

This model embodies the notion that there is no learnable signal in any of the features in the data; it is all useless noise. There is no principled way to create a model that performs worse than this one. We then calculate our metric of choice for this model and use this to gauge our progress; if our more complex models fail to significantly outperform the baseline model it is entirely possible that our dataset is not amenable to machine learning.

7.2 Linear regression

Let us create a model that now has two degrees of freedom; positional and orientational. We can shift our straight line up or down by way of a parameter that we shall β_0, and we can rotate the line so as to have an inclination, β_1. Note that in general the β_1 and β_0 parameters are coupled; changing β_1 (*i.e.* rotating the regression line) would result in a change in β_0. They only become decoupled when the data is standardized so that $\bar{x} = 0$, hence will pivot about $x = 0$ thus leaving β_0 unchanged.

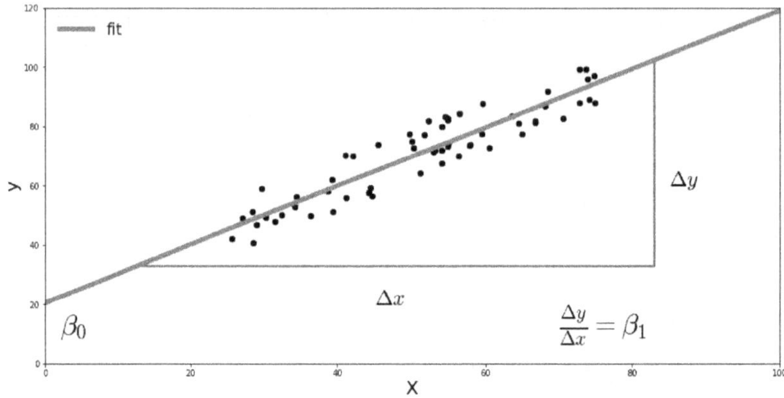

Figure 7.2: A straight line fit (green) to the datapoints (black).

Equation: Linear regression model

$$\hat{\mathbf{y}} = \mathbb{E}[y|\mathbf{x}] = \hat{\beta}_1 \mathbf{x}_1 + \hat{\beta}_0 \tag{7.2}$$

where β_1 is the *gradient* or *weight*, and β_0 is the *bias* term. $\mathbf{x}_1$ is a feature consisting of the coefficients $(x_0, x_1, ..., x_m)$.

For a dataset with multiple features the value of the bias (β_0) corresponds to the situation when $x = 0$ for every feature, and every feature, $\mathbf{x}_n$, will have its own corresponding β_n value.

Remark: Linear regression is known by statisticians as a *parametric* model: the functional form (here a straight line) is fixed, and we are only allowed to play with the parameters (β_1 and β_0). However, it is called a parametric model not because of β_1 and β_0 but because in the context of statistical modeling the assumption is made that the underlying population data that is being modeled is sampled from a parametric probability distribution, usually the Gaussian distribution having the parameters μ and σ, and that β_1 and β_0 reflect said parameters.

7.3 Calculating β_1 and β_0

7.3.1 Ordinary least squares

Equation: One can estimate β_1 and β_0 using ordinary least squares, for example:

$$\hat{\beta}_1 = \frac{\Sigma((x_i - \bar{x})(y_i - \bar{y}))}{\Sigma((x_i - \bar{x})^2)} \equiv \frac{cov(x,y)}{var(x)} \tag{7.3}$$

and then

$$\hat{\beta}_0 = \bar{y} - \hat{\beta}_1 \bar{x} \tag{7.4}$$

Sample code

```
import numpy as np

def OLS(x, y):
    beta_1 = (np.sum((x - np.mean(x))*(y - np.mean(y))))/ \
             (np.sum((x - np.mean(x))**2))
    beta_0 = np.mean(y) - (beta_1 * np.mean(x))
    return beta_1, beta_0

beta_1, beta_0 = OLS(x, y)
```

7.3.2 Normal equation

We can envisage our `DataFrame` as if it were a system of linear equations where β_n is associated with variable (*i.e.* feature) n, and the x_m in our dataframe represent the coefficients:

$$\begin{cases} x_0.\beta_1 & + & 1.\beta_0 & = & y_0 \\ x_1.\beta_1 & + & 1.\beta_0 & = & y_1 \\ \vdots & + & \vdots & = & \vdots \\ x_m.\beta_1 & + & 1.\beta_0 & = & y_m \end{cases} \tag{7.5}$$

Our task is to find the global parameter β_0 (note the insertion of a constant column of 1's to facilitate this, *i.e.* $\mathbf{x}_0 = \mathbf{1}$) and the β associated with each column.
In matrix notation:

$$\mathbf{X1} = \begin{bmatrix} x_0 & 1 \\ x_1 & 1 \\ \vdots & \vdots \\ x_m & 1 \end{bmatrix}, \quad \beta = \begin{bmatrix} \beta_1 \\ \beta_0 \end{bmatrix}, \quad \mathbf{y} = \begin{bmatrix} y_0 \\ y_1 \\ \vdots \\ y_m \end{bmatrix} \tag{7.6}$$

where **X1** is sometimes known as the design matrix.
For multiple (feature) linear regression with n features we have

$$\begin{aligned} y &= y_n + ... + y_1 + y_0 \\ &= \beta_n \mathbf{x}_n + ... + \beta_1 \mathbf{x}_1 + \beta_0 \mathbf{x}_0 \end{aligned} \tag{7.7}$$

which can be written as

$$\mathbf{X} = \begin{bmatrix} x_{0n} & \cdots & x_{01} & 1 \\ x_{1n} & \cdots & x_{11} & 1 \\ \vdots & \ddots & \vdots & \vdots \\ x_{mn} & \cdots & x_{m1} & 1 \end{bmatrix}, \quad \beta = \begin{bmatrix} \beta_n \\ \vdots \\ \beta_1 \\ \beta_0 \end{bmatrix}, \quad \mathbf{y} = \begin{bmatrix} y_0 \\ y_1 \\ \vdots \\ y_m \end{bmatrix} \tag{7.8}$$

where we have $m+1$ rows of data (note here the use of zero-based indexing) and n features which can be written much more compactly as

$$\mathbf{X}\beta = \mathbf{y} \tag{7.9}$$

With a view to solving this equation if we write this as

$$(\mathbf{X}^\mathsf{T}\mathbf{X})\beta = \mathbf{X}^\mathsf{T}\mathbf{y} \tag{7.10}$$

in linear algebra this is known as the *normal equation*. To find the values for the β's this can be re-written as

$$\beta = (\mathbf{X}^\mathsf{T}\mathbf{X})^{-1}\mathbf{X}^\mathsf{T}\mathbf{y} \equiv \mathbf{X}^{+}\mathbf{y} \tag{7.11}$$

where $\mathbf{X}^{+}$ is known as the pseudoinverse and $(\mathbf{X}^\mathsf{T}\mathbf{X})$ is known as the *Gram* or *normal* matrix. We see now why (perfect) multicollinearity is problematic for linear regression as this matrix would become singular (*i.e.* $\det(\mathbf{X}^\mathsf{T}\mathbf{X}) = 0$) and thus non-invertible, *i.e.* we want $\mathbf{X}$ to be full column rank.

Sample code

First we create the design matrix (**X1**) with the 1's column on the right hand side

```
import numpy as np
import statsmodels.api as sm

# create a design matrix with the 1 column on the RHS
# using statsmodels
X1 = sm.add_constant(X, prepend=False).to_numpy()
# using numpy
X1 = np.column_stack(( X, np.ones(len(X)) ))
```

calculate $\beta_n, \ldots, \beta_0$ where `@` is the `numpy.matmul` (matrix multiplication) operation

```
betas = np.linalg.inv(X1.T @ X1) @ X1.T @ y
print("beta_n,...,beta_0", betas)
```

7.3.3 Scikit-learn `LinearRegression`

Using the scikit-learn `LinearRegression` estimator

Sample code

```
from sklearn.linear_model import LinearRegression

regressor = LinearRegression( fit_intercept=True )
regressor.fit(X_train, y_train)
y_pred = regressor.predict(X_validation)
```

where the default `fit_intercept=True` option adds the column of 1's to facilitate the calculation of β_0. Scikit-learn can output the parameters via

```
beta_1 = regressor.coef_
beta_0 = regressor.intercept_
```

7.3.4 statsmodels OLS

From a statistical modeling perspective one can perform ordinary least squares by using the OLS routine from the statsmodels library

```
import statsmodels.api as sm

X = sm.add_constant(X)
model   = sm.OLS(y,X)
results = model.fit()
print(results.summary())
```

```
                            OLS Regression Results
==============================================================================
Dep. Variable:                      y   R-squared:                       0.998
Model:                            OLS   Adj. R-squared:                  0.998
Method:                 Least Squares   F-statistic:                 1.217e+05
Date:                Thu, 09 Jan 2025   Prob (F-statistic):          4.09e-278
Time:                        05:00:57   Log-Likelihood:                -314.20
No. Observations:                 200   AIC:                             632.4
Df Residuals:                     198   BIC:                             639.0
Df Model:                           1
Covariance Type:            nonrobust
==============================================================================
                 coef    std err          t      P>|t|      [0.025      0.975]
------------------------------------------------------------------------------
const          0.0288      0.165      0.175      0.861      -0.296       0.354
x1             0.9998      0.003    348.846      0.000       0.994       1.005
==============================================================================
Omnibus:                       18.962   Durbin-Watson:                   2.343
Prob(Omnibus):                  0.000   Jarque-Bera (JB):               69.062
Skew:                          -0.126   Prob(JB):                     1.01e-15
Kurtosis:                       5.868   Cond. No.                         115.
==============================================================================
```

Figure 7.3: statsmodels OLS output example

where x1 corresponds to $\hat{\beta}_1$ and const is $\hat{\beta}_0$.

Confidence intervals

One can now obtain the confidence interval of the β parameters via

```
print("beta_0", results.conf_int(alpha=0.05)[0])
print("beta_1", results.conf_int(alpha=0.05)[1])
```

where setting alpha=0.05 returns the 95% confidence intervals.

7.4 Assumptions of linear regression

No assumptions at all are required in order to fit a straight line, just as long as there is more than one datapoint. However, suffice to say the linear model is most effectively used when there is a linear relationship between the independent variable (x) and the dependent variable (y), the target column. To visually get an idea as to whether is is indeed the case or not, when performing EDA one can use the `seaborn.lmplot` which will overlay a linear fit to the data, along with the confidence interval (`ci`) associated with the parameters.

```
sns.lmplot(x=X, y=y, data=data, ci=95)
```

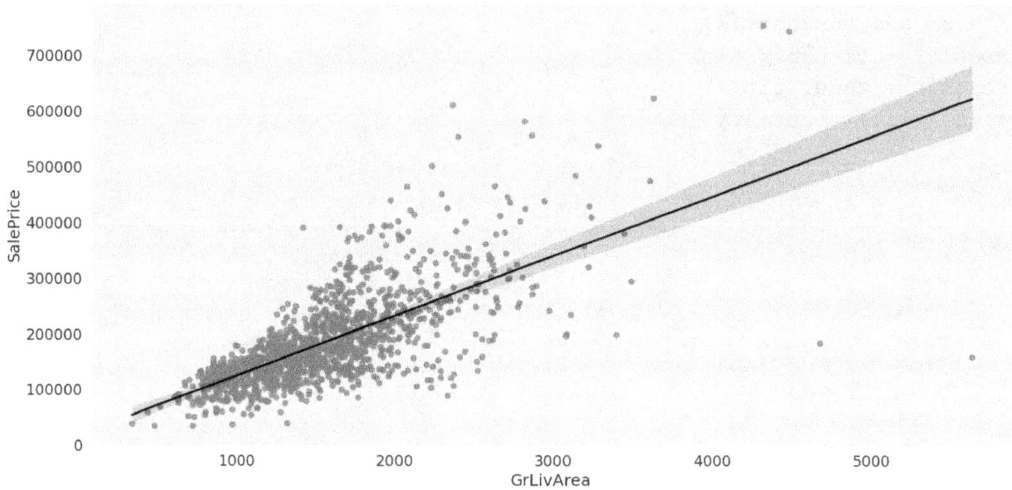

Figure 7.4: Example seaborn lmplot.

Furthermore, when it comes to inference for the regression coefficients and confidence intervals to be reliable and comparable the errors should be:

- **i.i.d.**: every error point is independent of the other errors, *i.e.* no autocorrelation (one can test this using the Durbin-Watson statistic)
- **have constant variance**: $\sigma^2 \neq f(x)$. This is known as homoskedasticity.
- **have a Gaussian distribution** *i.e.* $\forall\, i \in n, \varepsilon_i \sim \mathcal{N}(0, \sigma^2)$.
- $\mathbb{E}(\varepsilon) = 0$

That said, the importance of the errors being Gaussian is sometimes over-exaggerated[3].

> Remark: For small datasets that do not meet these conditions the `TheilSenRegressor` presents an interesting alternative.

7.4.1 Heteroscedasticity

In Fig 7.5 we plot the errors in our prediction (the difference between the true value and the predicted value) with respect to the predicted values. We can see that the dispersion (variance) in the errors is not uniform, and this non-uniformity is known as heteroscedasticity.

[3] Knief, Forstmeier "*Violating the normality assumption may be the lesser of two evils*", Behavior Research Methods **53** pp. 2576-2590 (2021)

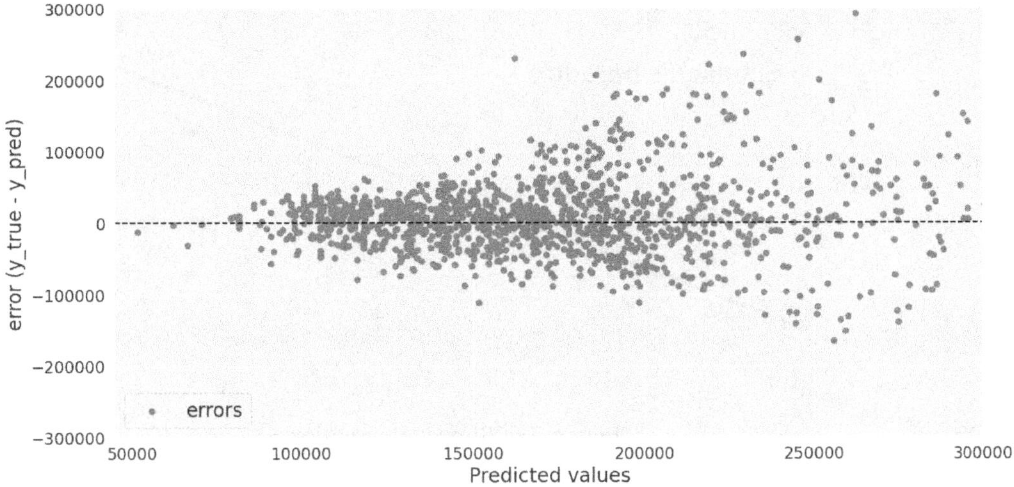

Figure 7.5: Error plot: An example of heteroscedasticity.

Sample code

One can create an error plot using

```
errors = y_validation - y_pred

fig = plt.figure(figsize=(16, 8))
plt.scatter(y_pred, errors, s=35, label = 'errors')
plt.axhline(y = 0, color = 'black', linestyle = 'dashed')
plt.legend(loc='lower left')
plt.xlabel('Predicted values')
plt.ylabel('error (y_true - y_pred)');
```

> Remark: An oft suggested solution for heteroscedasticity is to transform the dependent variable (y) by taking the logarithm or square root. However, it may not necessarily be a good idea to transform the target values if there is more than one feature, which in machine learning is basically always the case. For an in-depth discussion see the paper "The When and How of Target Variable Transformations".

7.4.2 Simpson's paradox

Simpson's paradox,[4] or aggregation bias, is the result of undertaking a univariate linear regression without taking into account a missing (confounding) categorical feature (here with the nominal values 'green' and 'orange'). Perhaps more than anything this highlights the importance of performing a through exploratory data analysis.

[4] E. H. Simpson *"The Interpretation of Interaction in Contingency Tables"*, Journal of the Royal Statistical Society, Series B (Statistical Methodology) **13** pp. 238-241 (1951)

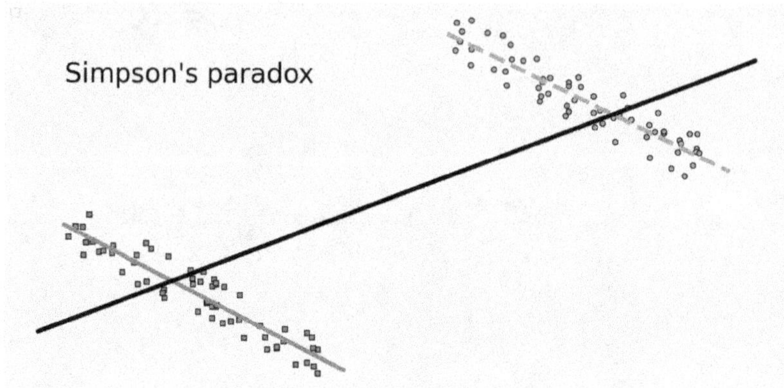

Figure 7.6: Simpson's paradox.

It is worth mentioning that with a multivariate dataset, during the process of feature selection the dropping of said categorical feature may possibly not be overly harmful to the performance of ones predictions. However, from an interpretability standpoint it would be a disaster. Indeed we can see form the somewhat extreme example depicted in Figure 7.6 that the β_1 regression coefficients for the points associated with both the 'green' and the 'orange' categories have the opposite sign of the β_1 associated with the global fit (black).

7.5 Polynomial regression

It is not at all unusual to have data to which a curve would be a much better fit than a straight line (remember dataset B of Anscombe's quartet).

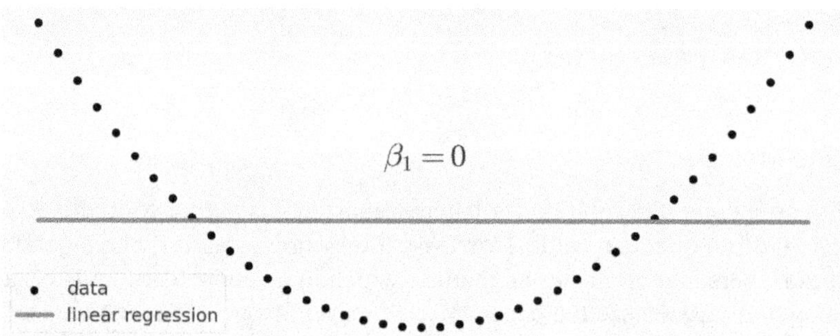

Figure 7.7: A straight line fit to data on a parabola.

We can incorporate curvature by way of adding more terms to the polynomial:

$$\hat{y}(\mathbf{X}) = \hat{\beta}_2 x^2 + \hat{\beta}_1 \mathbf{x} + \hat{\beta}_0 \tag{7.12}$$

for example in Pandas via
`df["x_squared"] = df["x"]**2`
this new feature has allowed us to incorporate curvature into our model.

Remark: This is still a linear function in terms of β; to the estimator the x^2 term is simply another feature column, *i.e.* a column of coefficients that remain unchanged throughout the learning process. It is the β that play the role of the variable.

One can use the scikit-learn `PolynomialFeatures` to automatically create the interaction features when one is performing multiple linear regression. For example if we have the features a, b, and c then for degree 2 this will also produce the new features a^2, b^2, and c^2 as well as the ab, ac, and bc interaction features.

Sample code

Here is an example of obtaining the parameters of a polynomial regression of degree 3 for the univariate feature x using numpy `polyfit`

```
beta_3, beta_2, beta_1, beta_0 = np.polyfit(X, y, deg=3)
```

7.6 Extrapolation

John von Neumann quipped *"...with four parameters I can fit an elephant, and with five I can make him wiggle his trunk."*. In Figure 7.8 we fit polynomials of increasing degree to a dataset. We can see that they all do rather well as long as there is data to fit to. However, as soon as there is no data their tails are pretty much free to do as they like (see also Runge's phenomenon). Such extrapolations make for extremely bad predictions so we wish to avoid extrapolation whenever we can (unless we are forecasting!)

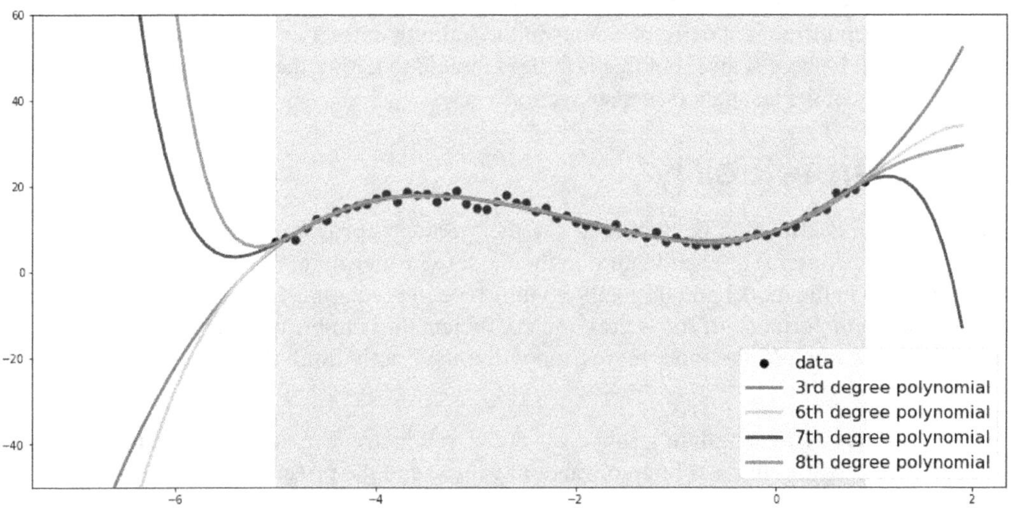

Figure 7.8: The danger of extrapolation

Remark: Broadly speaking interpolation is when we make predictions within the convex hull of our training data, and extrapolation occurs when we make predictions outside of the convex hull of our training data.

7.6.1 Convex hull

When it comes to making predictions one cannot filter out outliers; one does not simply say *'I am not going to produce a prediction for that particular point'*.

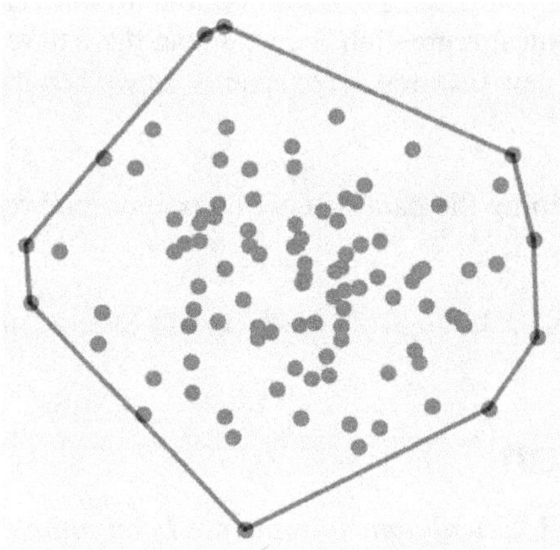

Figure 7.9: The 2D convex hull (black lines) for a set of points.

Thus in order to avoid having to extrapolate it is desirable that the convex hull of the training data at least spans the very same volume as the convex hull of the test data. For this reason it is convenient in machine learning to keep infrequent extreme values in the training dataset as they serve to expand the convex hull. This space will be very sparse, but this is still preferable to letting the estimator extrapolate if it encounters extreme values in the test data (see also Section 10.5).

7.7 Interpretability

The regression coefficients β_1, that is to say the gradients, provide very valuable information regarding the importance (weight) of each feature in the model. Furthermore, if a feature has $\beta_1 \approx 0$ this feature has very little role in the model and basically no influence in predicting $\hat{y}$. Note that for a correct interpretation of the relative importance of the regression coefficients it is important that each of the features have the same scale and in multiple linear regression will only strictly hold of none of the variables (features) are correlated.

> **Example** Say that a length of string costs 500€ per metre. We now create a dataset with the features length (cm), length (m), a column of random values, and the price of said piece of string

length (cm)	length (m)	random	price (€)
0.0	0.00	5.365885	0.0
1.0	0.01	1.309530	5.0
...	...	...	...
99.0	0.99	6.474448	495.0
100.0	1.00	2.622857	500.0

leading to a coefficient of 4.9995 for length (cm), a coefficient of 0.049995 for length (m), and a coefficient of 0 for the random column, *i.e.*

$$\mathbf{4.9995} \times \text{length(cm)} + \mathbf{0.049995} \times \text{length(m)} + \mathbf{0} \times \text{random} = \text{price}$$

We can now see the absolute importance of each of the features in predicting the price. Whilst correct, it gives the impression that the length (cm) feature is 100 times more important than the length (m) feature, which here we know is simply an artifact due to the unit of measurement. If we now normalize the dataset so that all of the features have the range $[0,1]$ we now obtain the relative importance's of 250 for length (cm), a coefficient of 250 for length (m), and a coefficient of 0 for the random column, leading to

$$\mathbf{250} \times \text{length(cm)}[0,1] + \mathbf{250} \times \text{length(m)}[0,1] + \mathbf{0} \times \text{random}[0,1] = \text{price}$$

indicating that length (cm) and length (m) have equally importance in predicting the price of a length of string. We may have noticed that these length features are perfectly correlated (collinear), thus we have redundancy and either one of these features can be (indeed should be) dropped with impunity. If we do this the remaining length feature now has a coefficient of 500, indicating that this feature alone completely describes the price.

We can view the regression coefficients (weights) for example using ELI5:

```
import eli5

feature_names = X_train.columns.tolist()
eli5.show_weights(regressor, top=None, feature_names= feature_names)
```

which gives us

Weight?	Feature
+390135.335	m2_edificados
+378177.833	<BIAS>
+355886.998	precio_zona
+63058.702	exterior
+16381.696	orientación_norte
+4314.874	planta
+3809.496	año_construción
+1.025	precio_aparcamiento
-595.693	necesita_reforma
-4027.583	orientación_sur
-4077.580	n_baños
-6322.717	n_habitaciones
-7899.945	m2_útiles
-14058.596	orientación_este
-14204.718	orientación_oeste
-24590.137	aparcamiento
-26983.654	nueva_construcción
-80908.585	ascensor
-118913.261	precio_alquiler

Figure 7.10: The weights (β_1) for each feature and the bias (β_0) for a multiple linear regression.

where BIAS corresponds to β_0. One can also calculate the confidence intervals (CI) associated with the coefficients with `statsmodels.regression.linear_model.OLS` using `conf_int`.

7.8 The loss function and cost functional

How does an estimator find the optimal parameters? We shall introduce the *loss* (L) and the *cost* (J):

- *loss* is a measure of distance[5] between the two points y, the true value, and $\hat{y}(\beta)$, our predicted value
- *cost* is the average over all of the individual losses: $\bar{L}$, *i.e.*

$$J[\beta] = \frac{1}{n}\sum^{n} L^p(y, \hat{y}(\beta))$$

where n is the number of samples. Our objective in machine learning is to identify the location of the minimum of $J[\beta]$.

Remark: Sometimes the loss function is known as the *error* function and the cost functional is known as the *risk* or *objective*. I would suggest the use of the letter J has its origins in variational calculus, notably in the Euler-Lagrange equation.

[5] See the p-norm and Lebesgue spaces.

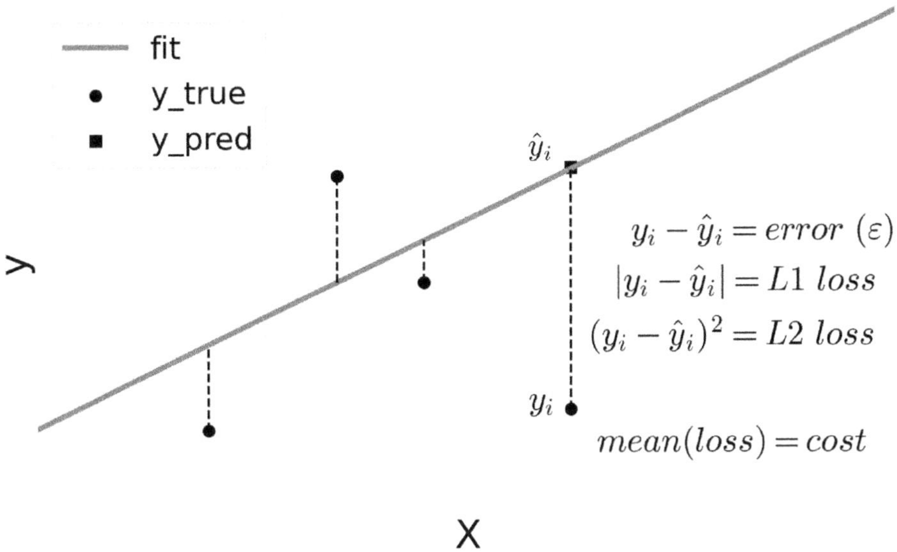

Figure 7.11: Fitting errors.

Remark: A valid loss function should have the following properties; it should be symmetric, *i.e.*

$$L(\hat{y}, y) = L(y, \hat{y})$$

it should be positive

$$L(\hat{y}, y) > 0, \qquad \hat{y} \neq y$$

and should satisfy the triangle inequality

$$L(\hat{y}, y) \leq L(\hat{y}, z) + L(z, y)$$

i.e. $L(\hat{y}, y)$ is the shortest distance between $\hat{y}$ and y.

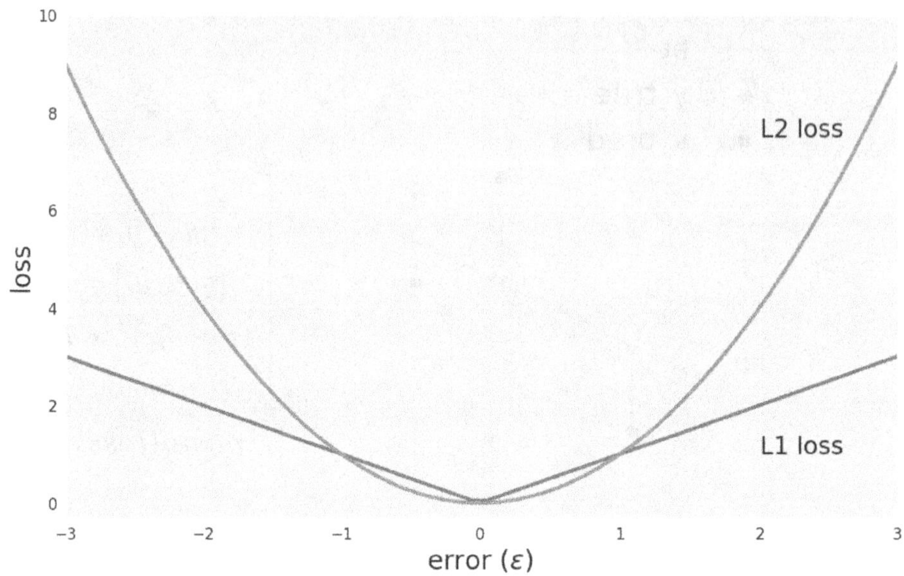

Figure 7.12: The $L1$ and $L2$ loss functions.

As code we have $y \to$ `y_true` and $\hat{y} \to$ `y_pred`.

Equation: ε (error) = `(y_true - y_pred)`

- $L1$ loss = AE (absolute error) = `abs(y_true - y_pred)`
- $L1$ cost = MAE (mean absolute error) $= \frac{1}{n}\sum_{i=1}^{n} |y_i - \hat{y}_i|$
- $L2$ loss = SE (squared error) = `(y_true - y_pred)**2`
- $L2$ cost = MSE (mean squared error) $= \frac{1}{n}\sum_{i=1}^{n} (y_i - \hat{y}_i)^2$

As mentioned, the optimal solution is found when the cost functional is at its minimum. For example, when performing linear regression using ordinary least squares, as the very name suggests, we use the $L2$ loss function, so we wish to minimize the $L2$ cost functional where:

$$
\begin{aligned}
J[\beta] &= MSE \\
&= \frac{1}{n}\sum_{i=1}^{n} (y_i - \hat{y}_i)^2 \\
J[\beta_1, \beta_0] &= \frac{1}{n}\sum_{i=1}^{n} \left(y_i - (\hat{\beta}_1 \mathbf{X}_i + \hat{\beta}_0 \mathbf{1})\right)^2
\end{aligned}
$$

The optimal values of β_1 and β_0 are those associated with $\text{argmin}(J)$.

Remark: If we use the $L1$ loss we are performing *median* regression (or least absolute deviations (LAD) regression), which is more robust than the standard mean regression (see also quantile regression).

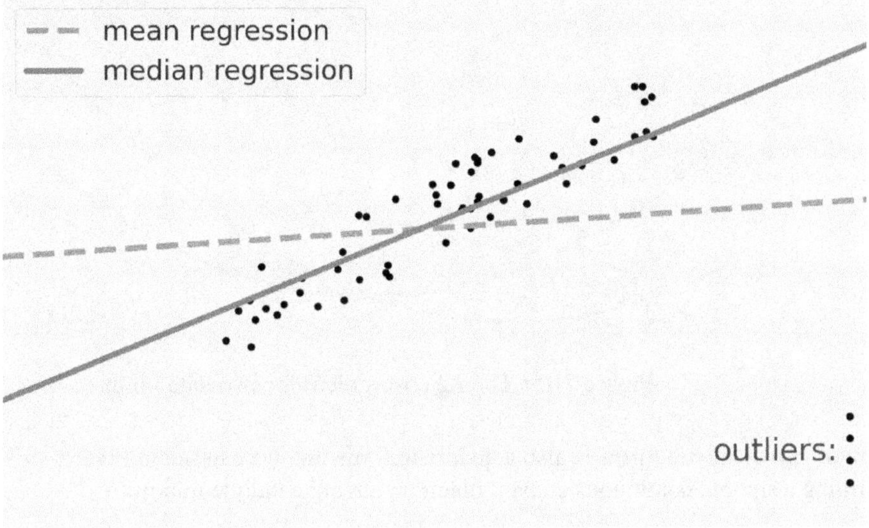

Figure 7.13: Median regression is robust to outliers.

Unlike linear regression, whose parameters can be obtained for example via OLS, LAD has no analytical solution and a solver such as those found in HiGHS is required. As a consequence this makes median regression computationally more expensive than linear (mean) regression.

What form does the $L1$ cost take for two points?

Figure 7.14: The $L1$ cost (green) for two data points.

In Figure 7.14 we can see the $L1$ cost functional (green) for two datapoints (blue and red). We can see that the resulting cost is piece-wise continuous, and may not have a unique minima, hence the optimal parameters are not unique. What form does the $L2$ cost take for two points?

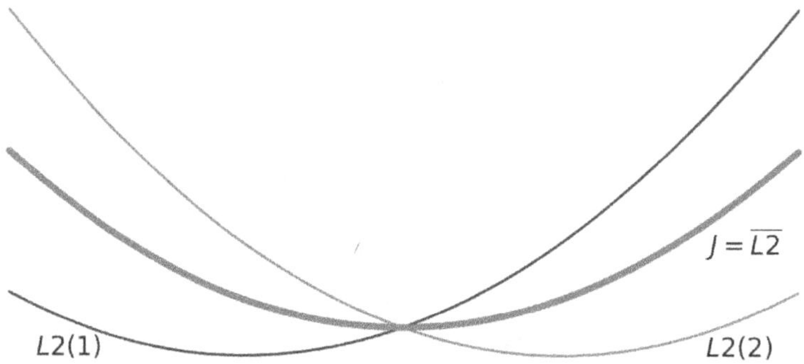

Figure 7.15: The $L2$ cost (green) for two data points.

The sum of two quadratic forms is also a quadratic form, and we can see in Figure 7.15 the $L2$ cost (green) also forming a smooth continuous convex function, having a unique minima.

Huber loss

A hybrid loss function, combining a quadratic loss for smaller errors within the range $\pm\delta$, and a linear loss for larger errors, is that of the Huber loss (L_H) given by

$$L_H = \begin{cases} \frac{1}{2}L2, & \text{if } |\varepsilon| \le \delta \\ \delta(L1 - \frac{1}{2}\delta), & \text{if } |\varepsilon| > \delta \end{cases} \tag{7.13}$$

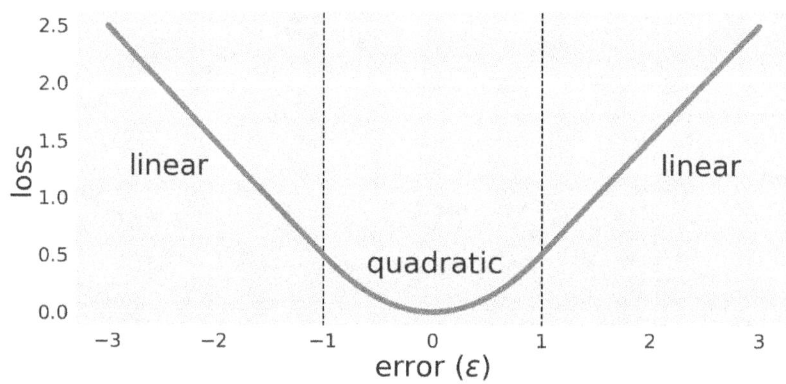

Figure 7.16: The Huber loss function (here for $\delta = 1$).

Indeed this loss function forms the core of the scikit-learn `HuberRegressor`.

7.9 Gradient descent

What does the cost functional for the $L2$ loss look like for two features? The cost functional is now two-dimensional. For linear regression with one feature the function was a parabola. In two dimensions we now have a surface, known as a paraboloid.

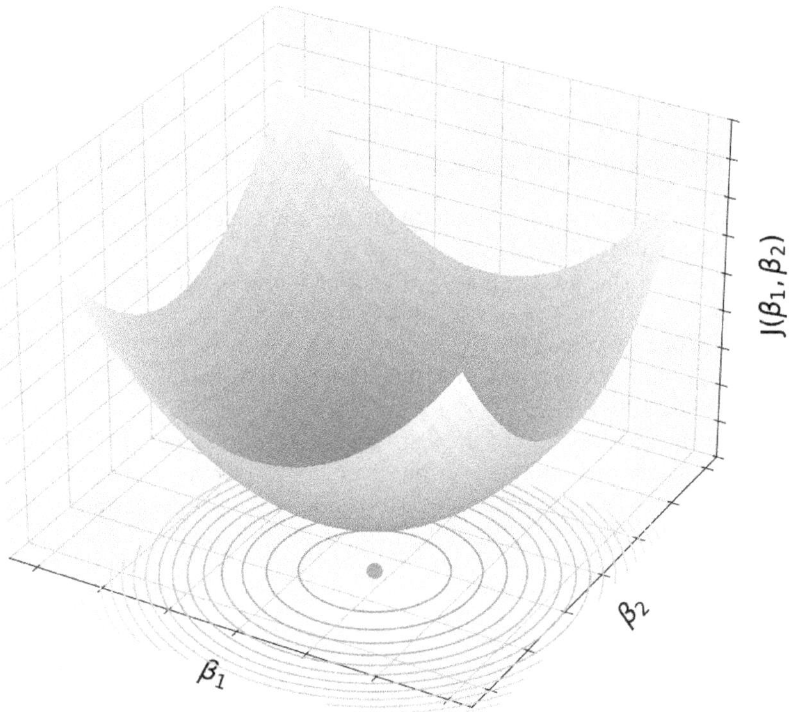

Figure 7.17: A 2-dimensional parabolic surface (paraboloid). The orange circle represents a projection of the location of the minima of the surface, and hence the optimal values for β_1 and β_2.

We shall now introduce a very powerful and general numerical technique for finding local minima called gradient descent[6] which goes back to Augustin Louis Cauchy in 1847 who used it to aid in the calculation of planetary orbits[7]. Here our objective is to find the position if the global minimum of the cost surface (although there is no guarantee of being able to do this for a complicated surface, and we may end up in what is known as a local minimum).

Remark: Any local minimum of a convex function is also a global minimum.

The gradient (G) of the cost surface (J) is given by

$$G = \frac{\partial J[\beta]}{\partial \beta} \tag{7.14}$$

where β are the parameters of our fit.

Equation: Gradient descent *update rule*

[6] Sebastian Ruder *"An overview of gradient descent optimization algorithms"*, arXiv:1609.04747 (2017)
[7] Claude Lemaréchal "*Cauchy and the gradient method*", Optimization Stories pp. 251-254 (2012)

$$\beta \leftarrow \beta - \eta \frac{\partial J[\beta]}{\partial \beta} \tag{7.15}$$

where η is the *learning rate* parameter.

Algorithm: First we choose a random point on the surface to start from, then:

1. calculate the gradient $(\partial J/\partial \beta)$
2. multiply by -1 to change the sign (*i.e.* the direction we shall step)
3. scale by η
4. this becomes our new value for β
5. repeat process until β converges to within a specified tolerance (for example $\Delta J < 0.001$).

In Figure 7.18 we can see the effect of the learning rate hyperparameter. If the value of η is small we take many small steps towards the minima. We can speed up the process by choosing a larger value of η, but if it is too large than we can end up 'bouncing' from side to side of the surface, each time overshooting the location of the minima.

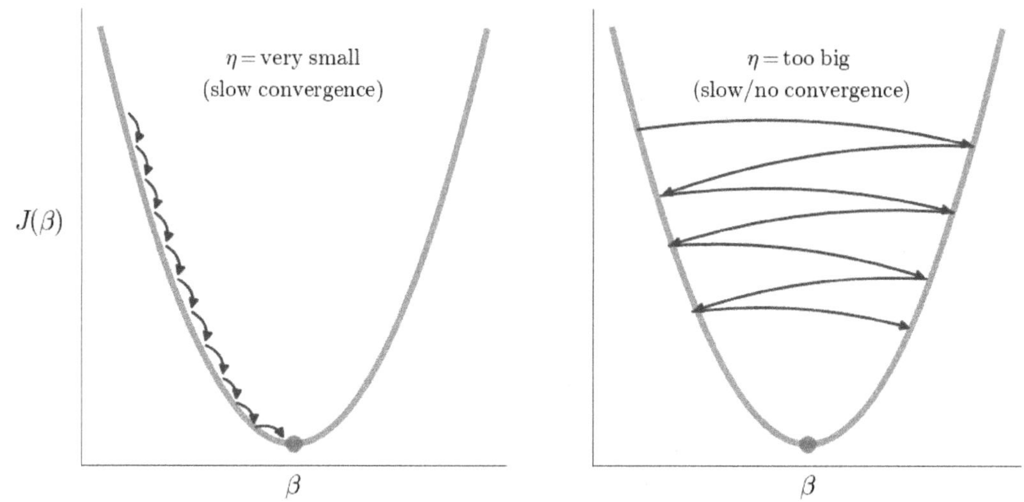

Figure 7.18: Effect of the learning rate hyperparameter (η).

We can assess our choice of η by plotting the learning rate (Figure 7.19), observing the reduction in the cost functional w.r.t. iteration. In the upper plot our choice of η was too small leading to slow convergence. In the lower figure we have a much better choice of η leading to faster convergence. Note however that if we become too enthusiastic and choose a very large learning rate the cost functional can diverge or 'explode'; we overshoot the other side of the function and start climbing up until the computer has a numerical overflow. Recent work[8] has indicated that faster convergence can be obtained by using non-constant step sizes whilst occasionally performing long steps.

[8] Benjamin Grimmer *"Provably Faster Gradient Descent via Long Steps"*, arXiv:2307.06324 (2023)

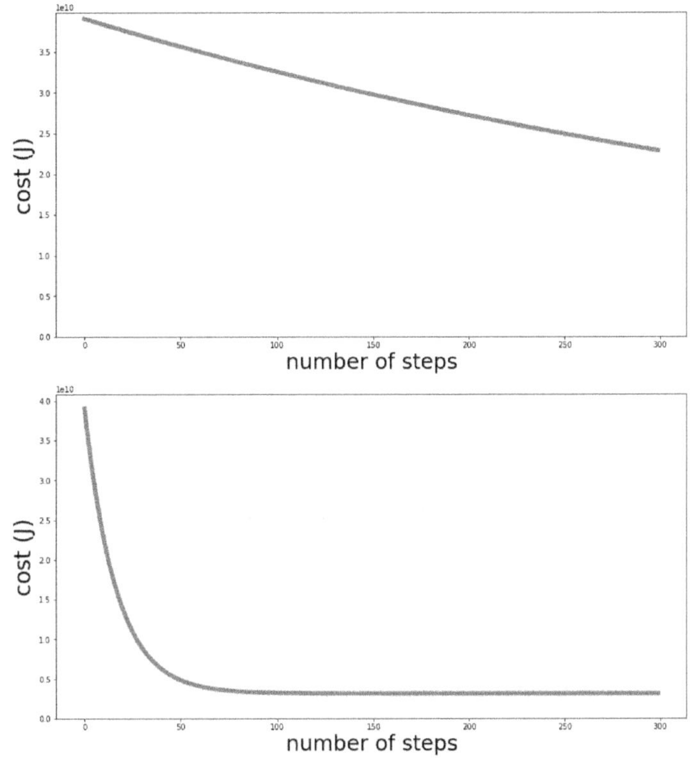

Figure 7.19: Different learning rates (η). In the upper figure the choice of learning rate is too conservative, in the lower figure we have a good learning rate.

We can use gradient descent for linear regression; the cost functional for the MSE is

$$
\begin{aligned}
J[\beta] = \text{MSE} = \frac{1}{n}\left(\varepsilon^{\mathsf{T}}\varepsilon\right) &= \frac{1}{n}\left(\hat{\mathbf{y}}-\mathbf{y}\right)^{\mathsf{T}}\left(\hat{\mathbf{y}}-\mathbf{y}\right) \qquad (7.16)\\
&= \frac{1}{n}\left(\mathbf{X}\beta-\mathbf{y}\right)^{\mathsf{T}}\left(\mathbf{X}\beta-\mathbf{y}\right)\\
&= \frac{1}{n}\left(\beta^{\mathsf{T}}\mathbf{X}^{\mathsf{T}}-\mathbf{y}^{\mathsf{T}}\right)\left(\mathbf{X}\beta-\mathbf{y}\right)\\
&= \frac{1}{n}\left(\beta^{\mathsf{T}}\mathbf{X}^{\mathsf{T}}\mathbf{X}\beta-\beta^{\mathsf{T}}\mathbf{X}^{\mathsf{T}}\mathbf{y}-\mathbf{y}^{\mathsf{T}}\mathbf{X}\beta-\mathbf{y}^{\mathsf{T}}\mathbf{y}\right)\\
&= \frac{1}{n}\left(\beta^{\mathsf{T}}\mathbf{X}^{\mathsf{T}}\mathbf{X}\beta-2\beta^{\mathsf{T}}\mathbf{X}^{\mathsf{T}}\mathbf{y}-\mathbf{y}^{\mathsf{T}}\mathbf{y}\right)\\
\frac{\partial J[\beta]}{\partial\beta} &= \frac{1}{n}\left(2\mathbf{X}^{\mathsf{T}}\mathbf{X}\beta-2\mathbf{X}^{\mathsf{T}}\mathbf{y}\right)\\
&= \frac{1}{n}2\mathbf{X}^{\mathsf{T}}\left(\mathbf{X}\beta-\mathbf{y}\right)\\
&= \frac{2}{n}\mathbf{X}^{\mathsf{T}}\left(\hat{\mathbf{y}}-\mathbf{y}\right) \qquad (7.17)
\end{aligned}
$$

giving

$$\beta \leftarrow \beta - \frac{\eta}{n}\mathbf{X}^{\mathsf{T}}\varepsilon \tag{7.18}$$

where the factor of 2 has been absorbed into the learning rate, η.

Sample code

Note that we first standardize our data before performing gradient descent (gist)

```
def gradient_descent(X, y_true, eta=0.1, n_iterations=5_000, tol=0.001):
    """
    X : a min-max scaled numpy matrix, shape (m_rows, n_feats)
    y_true : a numpy matrix, shape (m_rows, 1)
    returns : beta, shape (n_feats+1, 1)
    """
    # create design matrix from X having a column of 1s for beta_0
    X1 = np.column_stack( (X, np.ones(len(X)) ) )
    # select a random starting point
    rng = np.random.default_rng()
    beta = rng.uniform( size= X1.shape[1] ).reshape(-1,1)
    costs = [] # save the costs for plotting
    n_points = np.shape(y_true)[0]

    for i in range(n_iterations):
        y_pred = X1 @ beta # linear regression
        #y_pred = sigmoid(X1 @ beta) # logistic regression
        error = y_pred - y_true
        # cost == MSE
        cost = np.sum(error**2)/ n_points
        # early stopping
        if (cost) < tol: break
        costs.append(cost) # save for plotting
        gradient = X1.T @ error
        # update the betas
        beta = beta - (eta/ n_points) * gradient

    return beta, costs

from sklearn.preprocessing import MinMaxScaler
X = MinMaxScaler().fit_transform(X)
y = y.to_numpy().reshape(-1, 1)

beta, costs = gradient_descent(X, y)
```

In Figure 7.20 we have an example where the two features have very different scales. This makes life difficult for our gradient descent algorithm; a good value of η for the 'narrow' feature will will take a long time to explore the 'wide' feature. On the other hand a good η for the wide feature could be a disaster when exploring the narrow feature, leading to divergence. The solution to this is to scale the features (see the section Feature scaling: standardization and normalization in Chapter 4) beforehand.

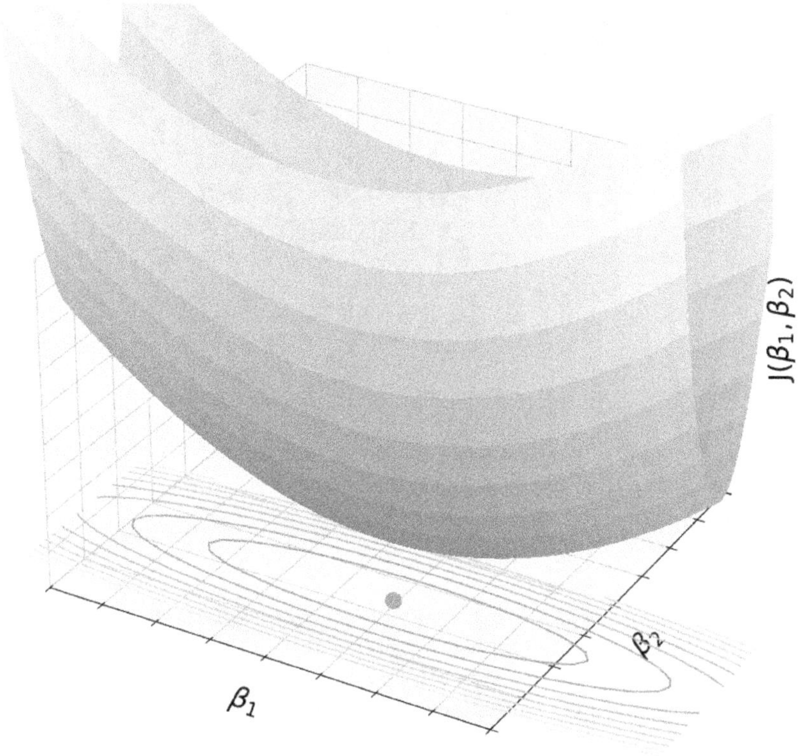

Figure 7.20: Two features with two very different scales. The orange circle represents a projection of the location of the minima of the surface, and hence the optimal values for β_1 and β_2.

Although there are indeed analytical solutions for a simple surface such as that of the linear regression cost functional, in Figure 7.21 we see an example loss surface of a neural network, where suffice to say no analytical solution exists and we have to use numerical methods.

Figure 7.21: Example of a cost surface of a neural network. (Image adapted from: Li, Xu, Taylor, Studer, Goldstein *"Visualizing the Loss Landscape of Neural Nets"*, arXiv:1712.09913 (2018), produced using their interactive 3D visualizer.)

> Remark: Ordinary least squares (OLS) has a time complexity of $\mathcal{O}(nm^2)$ where n is the number of rows of data, and m is the number of columns (features), whilst gradient descent (GD) has a time complexity of $\mathcal{O}(nmi)$ where i is the number of iterations. So if the number of iterations required to locate the minima is less than the number of features then GD will be faster than OLS.

7.9.1 Stochastic gradient descent regressor

With gradient descent the cost surface is constructed from all of the individual losses, *i.e.* the entire batch of training data. One could also construct the cost surface from a subset of the losses (known as a mini-batch), or even use a single loss, which is known as stochastic gradient descent. With scikit-learn one can perform linear regression using stochastic gradient descent via the `SGDRegressor`.

7.10 Metrics

How well did our model do? One way to visualize the performance of our model is to create a scatter plot of the predicted values against the true values. If our predictions were perfect all of the points would lie on the identity line. Points above the identity line represent cases where we overestimate, and points below the identity line represent underestimates.

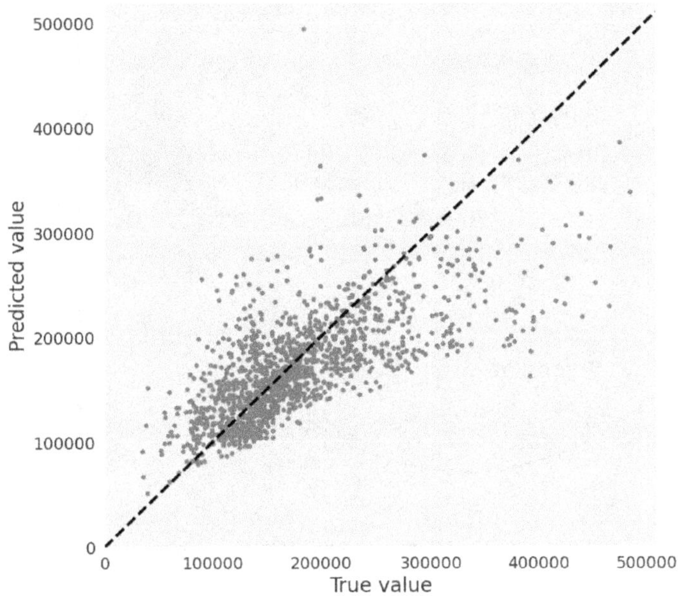

Figure 7.22: True value vs. predicted value plot.

For example, in Figure 7.22 we can see that for smaller predictions we have a similar dispersion of points either side of the $y = x$ line, which is to be expected. However, for larger values we see that in this example we always underestimate the true value, indicating that there is something missing in our model (and probably in our dataset) in this region.

Sample code

```
fig, ax = plt.subplots(figsize=(7, 7))
ax.axline([0, 0], [1, 1],
          color="red", linestyle='--', lw=3, zorder=3)
ax.scatter(x=y_validation, y=y_pred,
          color="blue", label="data")
minimum = min( y_pred.min(), y_validation.min() )
plt.xlim(minimum)
plt.ylim(minimum)
plt.xlabel('True')
plt.ylabel('Predicted')
plt.show();
```

Another interesting plot is a histogram of the prediction errors. Ideally the histogram should be symmetric, narrow and centred on our prediction (expectation value) and even better (from a statisticians perspective) have a Gaussian distribution. The broader the histogram the greater the errors, and if it is strongly skewed (biased) this could indicate underfitting.

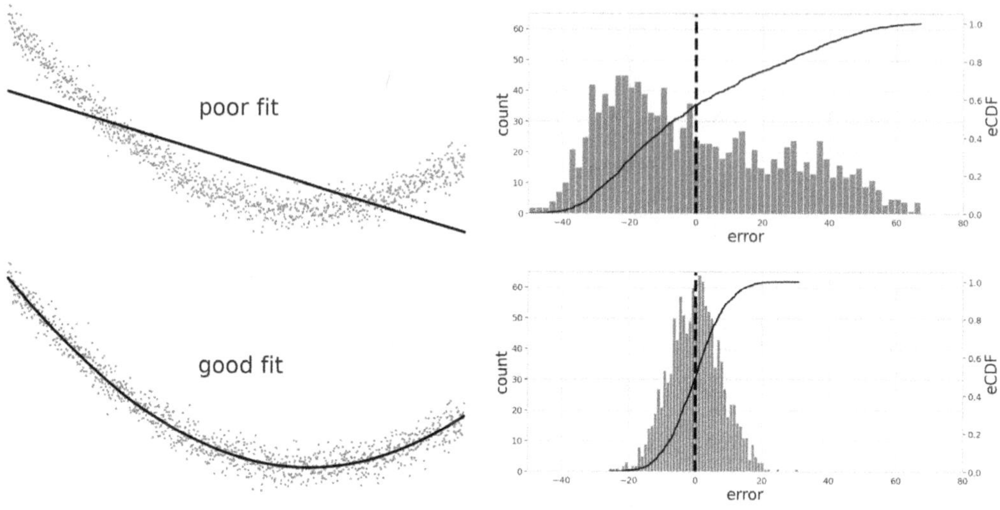

Figure 7.23: Histograms + eCDF of our prediction errors.

Sample code

```
residual_mean = (y_validation - y_pred).mean()

sns.displot( (y_validation - y_pred), height=6, aspect=2)
plt.xlabel('residual')
# add a mean value indicator
plt.axvline(residual_mean, color="red", lw=1);
```

That said, what we would really like is a single numerical value that indicates our overall performance.

> Remark: The performance of our fitted model on previously unseen data is called the *generalization error* (also known as the *test error*, the *out-of-sample error*, the *test risk*, or the *true risk*). The generalization error is calculated using a metric.

7.10.1 Root mean squared error (RMSE)

The most natural and logical metric to follow if we are using the *L2* loss function is the root mean squared error (RMSE).

Equation: Root mean squared error

$$\text{RMSE} := \sqrt{\varepsilon^2} = \sqrt{\frac{1}{n}\sum_{i=1}^{n}(y_i - \hat{y}_i)^2} \qquad \in [0, +\infty) \tag{7.19}$$

> Remark: A machine learning metric is not the same thing as a business key performance indicator (KPI) for example customer churn rate or growth in revenue, and optimizing the machine learning metric is

not the same thing as optimizing a KPI. Often it is not easy at all to connect the two. One can use the scikit `make_scorer` to craft a bespoke metric.

Sample code

As of scikit-learn version 1.4 there is now:

```
from sklearn.metrics import root_mean_squared_error

RMSE = root_mean_squared_error(y_true, y_pred)
```

and prior to version 1.4:

```
from sklearn.metrics import mean_squared_error

RMSE = mean_squared_error(y_true, y_pred, squared=False)
```

Here is some example code to calculate the RMSE of the baseline model ($\hat{y}_0$) for the out-of-sample validation set

```
from sklearn.metrics import root_mean_squared_error as metric

y_train_mean = np.full( len(y_validation), np.mean(y_train) )
metric(y_validation, y_train_mean)
```

(The in-sample baseline RMSE can be calculated via `np.std(y_train)`).

7.10.2 Mean absolute error (MAE)

If we are using the $L1$ loss function the natural metric is the mean absolute error (MAE).

Equation: The mean absolute error (MAE) is given by:

$$\text{MAE} := \frac{1}{n}\sum|\varepsilon| = \frac{1}{n}\sum_{i=1}^{n}|y_i - \hat{y}_i| \qquad \in [0, +\infty) \tag{7.20}$$

Sample code

```
from sklearn.metrics import mean_absolute_error

MAE = mean_absolute_error(y_true, y_pred)
```

7.10.3 MAE $\leq$ RMSE

In the incredibly improbable situation that all of the errors (ε) are of the same magnitude we have, here using two observations, $\varepsilon_1 = \varepsilon_2 = \varepsilon$

$$\text{MAE} = \left(\frac{|\varepsilon| + |\varepsilon|}{2}\right) = \left(\frac{2|\varepsilon|}{2}\right) = |\varepsilon|$$

and

$$\text{RMSE} = \sqrt{\left(\frac{\varepsilon^2 + \varepsilon^2}{2}\right)} = \sqrt{\left(\frac{2\varepsilon^2}{2}\right)} = \sqrt{\varepsilon^2} = |\varepsilon|$$

hence in this special case

$$\text{MAE} = \text{RMSE}$$

In general, again using two observations, we have

$$\text{MAE}^2 = \left(\frac{|\varepsilon_1| + |\varepsilon_2|}{2}\right)^2 = \frac{(\varepsilon_1^2 + \varepsilon_2^2) + 2|\varepsilon_1||\varepsilon_2|}{4}$$

and

$$\text{RMSE}^2 = \left(\frac{\varepsilon_1^2 + \varepsilon_2^2}{2}\right) = \frac{2(\varepsilon_1^2 + \varepsilon_2^2)}{4} = \frac{(\varepsilon_1^2 + \varepsilon_2^2) + (\varepsilon_1^2 + \varepsilon_2^2)}{4}$$

We can show that

$$2|\varepsilon_1||\varepsilon_2| \leq (\varepsilon_1^2 + \varepsilon_2^2)$$

since

$$0 \leq (\varepsilon_1 - \varepsilon_2)^2 = (\varepsilon_1^2 + \varepsilon_2^2) - 2|\varepsilon_1||\varepsilon_2|$$

hence in general

$$\text{MAE} \leq \text{RMSE}$$

7.10.4 Coefficient of determination (R^2)

A popular regression metric, especially amongst statisticians for comparing the goodness of fit of explanatory models, is the R^2 score, also known as the coefficient of determination.

Equation: The R^2 score is given by:

$$R^2 := 1 - \frac{\sum_{i=1}^{n} (y_i - \hat{y}_i)^2}{\sum_{i=1}^{n} (y_i - \bar{y}_i)^2} \equiv 1 - \frac{MSE}{Var(y)} \qquad \in (-\infty, 1] \tag{7.21}$$

The mean baseline model has an R^2 score of zero since $\hat{y} = \bar{y}$, and the perfect fit (perfect overfitting) has an R^2 score of 1 since the $MSE = 0$. However, the normalized range provided by R^2 tends to obfuscate the interpretability afforded by directly reporting the cost functional. For example, if one has an MAE of 500 in units of € when predicting house prices we know that, on average, each of our predictions has an error of 500€ .

> *"At this point, you might be wondering just what R^2 is good for — what job it does that isn't better done by other tools. The only honest answer I can give you is that I have never found a situation where it helped at all. If I could design the regression curriculum from scratch, I would never mention it. Unfortunately, it lives on as a historical relic"*
> The Truth about Linear Regression by Cosma Rohilla Shalizi (§10.3.2)

Sample code

```
def R_squared(y_true, y_pred):
    SS_res = np.sum((y_true - y_pred)**2)
    SS_tot = np.sum((y_true - np.mean(y_true))**2)
    return 1 - (SS_res/SS_tot)
```

7.11 Linear regression learning curve

How much data do we need to learn from in order to produce a good fit using univariate linear regression? In Figure 7.25 we look at the learning curve where we examine the expectation value of the MSE, obtained from a multitude of fits to random samples taken from a large dataset here having a straight line signal plus Gaussian noise.

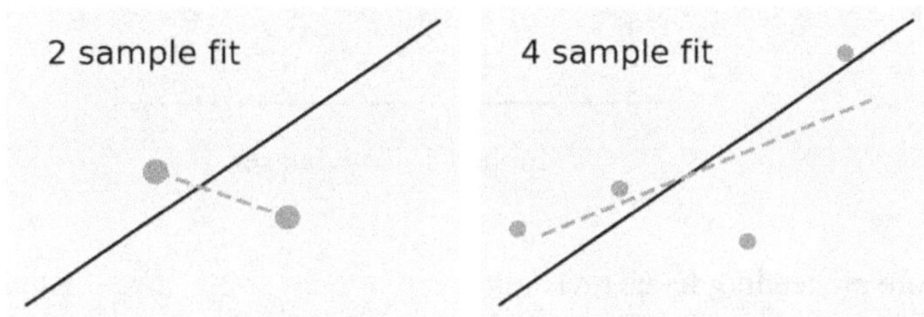

Figure 7.24: On the LHS we see a fit to two randomly selected training samples. Such a 2-sample fit has no in-sample error, but has very poor out-of-sample performance. On the RHS we can see that a 4-sample fit now has an in-sample error, but will lead to better out-of-sample performance. (The solid black line represents the ground truth function.)

We see that for just two samples the in-sample error is zero; this is because a straight line can fit two data points perfectly having no error. However, fitting to just two of data points leads to the worst out-of-sample error (well above the range of the plot below). On the other hand we can see that beyond having used around 15 training samples to produce our fit the out-of-sample error has now almost converged upon the the best possible error which, for the MSE metric, is the variance of the noise component in the dataset, $\mathbb{E}[\varepsilon^2] = \sigma^2$ given that in this example the signal component is completely learnable with our model.

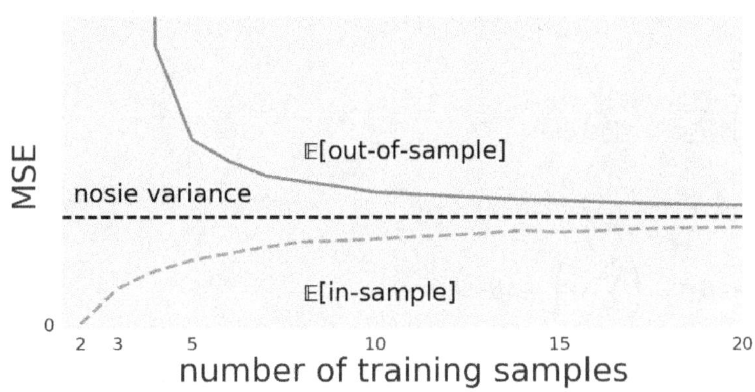

Figure 7.25: Learning curve for univariate linear regression. Suffice to say the more samples we have the better we can learn the signal.

Remark: To facilitate the calculation of a learning curve for any given estimator and dataset scikit-learn provides the `sklearn.model_selection.learning_curve` routine.

7.12 Decision tree regressor

The linear regression model has the virtue of being very easy to interpret by way of the β parameters associated with each feature. However, it only works well if the relationship between each feature (x) and y is linear, which is frequently not the case. Let us take for example the following toy dataset in Table 7.1:

X	y_true
1	1
2	1
4	2
5	2

Table 7.1: Toy dataset.

Remark: Before proceeding let us revisit the regression baseline model which was simply the mean of the target $\bar{y}$. Let us this time find the optimal constant value, β_0, that corresponds to the minimum of the $L2$ cost functional

$$
\begin{aligned}
J[\beta_0] &= MSE \\
&= \frac{1}{n}\sum_{i=1}^{n}(y_i - \beta_0)^2
\end{aligned}
$$

we wish to find the minima of $J[\beta_0]$

$$
\begin{aligned}
\frac{\mathrm{d}J[\beta_0]}{\mathrm{d}\beta_0} &= 0 \\
&= \frac{1}{n}\sum_{i=1}^{n} 2\,(y_i - \beta_0)\cdot(-1)
\end{aligned}
$$

we now solve

$$
\left(\frac{-2}{n}\right)\cdot\sum_{i=1}^{n}(y_i - \beta_0) = 0
$$

Given that $(-2/n)$ cannot be zero we have

$$
\sum_{i=1}^{n}(y_i - \beta_0) = \left(\sum_{i=1}^{n} y_i\right) - n\beta_0 = 0
$$

leading to

$$\beta_0 = \frac{1}{n}\sum_{i=1}^{n} y_i = \bar{y} \tag{7.22}$$

so we see now that our mean baseline model was actually the **optimal constant model**.

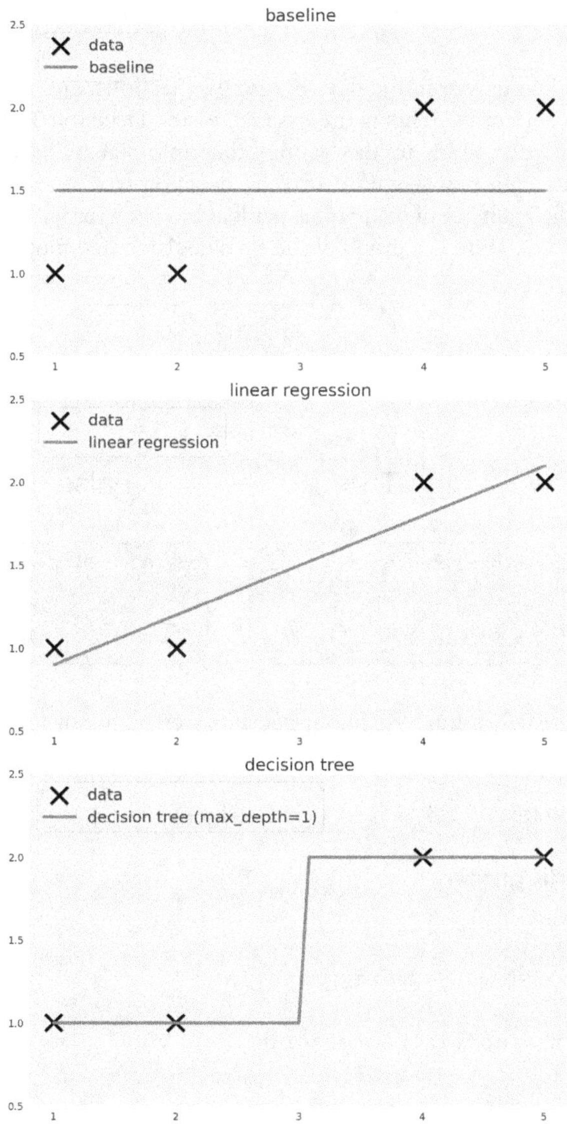

Figure 7.26: Baseline, linear regression, and decision tree predictions for our toy dataset.

In Figure 7.26 the uppermost plot represents the mean baseline model. In the middle plot we can easily see that it is not possible for a straight line to pass through all four points simultaneously; thus such a fit will have a non-zero error.

model	RMSE
Baseline	0.5
Linear regression	0.158
Decision tree	0

Table 7.2: Toy dataset RMSE results.

However, if we judiciously split the dataset into two sections, and fit a mean baseline model to either side, we can obtain a perfect fit. This is the essence of the Decision Tree regressor. Decision Trees use recursive binary splitting to divide up the training data into plateau known as *leaves*. The value of each leaf is the mean of the data points within it. The decision tree stops splitting when a specified depth (`max_depth`) or specified number of data points per leaf has been (or will be) reached (`min_samples_leaf` or `min_samples_split`). Here is a graph of the final decision tree model for the aforementioned dataset:

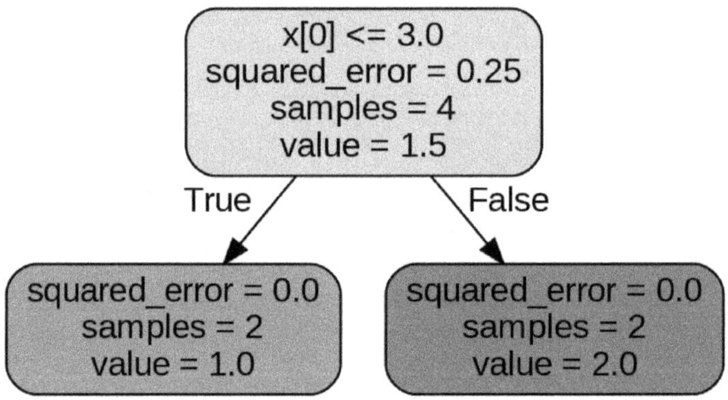

Figure 7.27: graphviz of our decision tree regressor for the toy dataset.

> **Remark:** A decision tree of `max_depth=1` is also known as a 'decision stump'.

Sample code for the graph

```
import graphviz
from sklearn.tree import export_graphviz

dot_data = export_graphviz(regressor,
                           filled=True,
                           rounded=True,
                           proportion=False)
graphviz.Source(dot_data)
```

where we can see that the initial squared error (*i.e.* the $L2$ loss) is 0.25, containing 4 data points, with a mean value of 1.5. Upon splitting at $X \leq 3$ two leaves are produced, both having zero error, containing two data points, the left hand leaf having a mean of 1, and the right hand leaf a mean value of 2. Indeed we can even describe our model in two sentences:

- if x is less than 3 then $\hat{y}$ is 1
- if x is greater than 3 then $\hat{y}$ is 2

The position (cut-point) of the binary split is chosen to be the one that most minimizes the cost, *i.e.* the total of the squared error ($L2$ loss).

> Example For our toy dataset making the split between the first and second datapoints (*i.e.* at $X = 1.5$) would lead to the LHS split having a squared error of 0 and for the RHS we first create the mean baseline $(1+2+2)/3 = 1.66$, then calculate the total error for the points w.r.t. this baseline $(1-1.66)^2+(2-1.66)^2+(2-1.66)^2 = 0.66$. If we now split between the second and third datapoint (*i.e.* at $X = 3$) both sides have a squared error of zero, and finally If we split between the second and third datapoint (*i.e.* at $X = 4.5$) we have a LHS baseline of $(1+1+2)/3 = 1.33$ and squared error of 0.66. Thus we find the optimal split, having the smallest error, is located at $X = 3$.

Say we have a two feature dataset. In this case first we split on feature 1 and calculate the sum of the squared errors (ΣSE) where ΣSE = SE(LHS) + SE(RHS), then we split on feature 2 and also calculate the corresponding ΣSE. Whichever feature has the lowest ΣSE is the is the split that is kept in the tree.

In general the improvement (I) afforded by performing a given split is provided by

$$I = \left(\sum_{i=1}^{N} (y_i - \bar{y})^2 \right) - \left(\sum_{i=1}^{N_{LHS}} (y_i - \bar{y})^2 + \sum_{i=N_{LHS}+1}^{N} (y_i - \bar{y})^2 \right) \tag{7.23}$$

$$\equiv Var(y_{\text{before split}}) - \left(\frac{N_{LHS}}{N} Var(y_{LHS}) + \frac{N_{RHS}}{N} Var(y_{RHS}) \right) \tag{7.24}$$

and the cut-point is that at the position associated with argmin(I), where N is the total number of points. In other words, we are looking for the split that most reduces the variance.

> Remark: The scikit-learn decision tree has a `random_state` parameter. This is used as a tiebreaker when multiple features afford the very same cost reduction.

Feature scaling

From this example it is clear that for this non-parametric estimator the solver (binary splitting) does not require that the features be scaled.

Hyperparameters

Unlike the linear regressor we now have what are known as hyperparameters. Linear regression has no hyper-parameters:

```
regressor = LinearRegression()
```

but now our decision tree model has two very important hyperparameters

```
regressor = DecisionTreeRegressor(max_depth=5, min_samples_leaf=1)
```

7.12.1 Hyperparameter: `max_depth`

By far the most influential hyperparameter for a decision tree is its depth – although height would perhaps be a more apt name for a tree. In Figure 7.28 we see fits of a decision tree of `max_depth=1` and `max_depth=2` to the same dataset

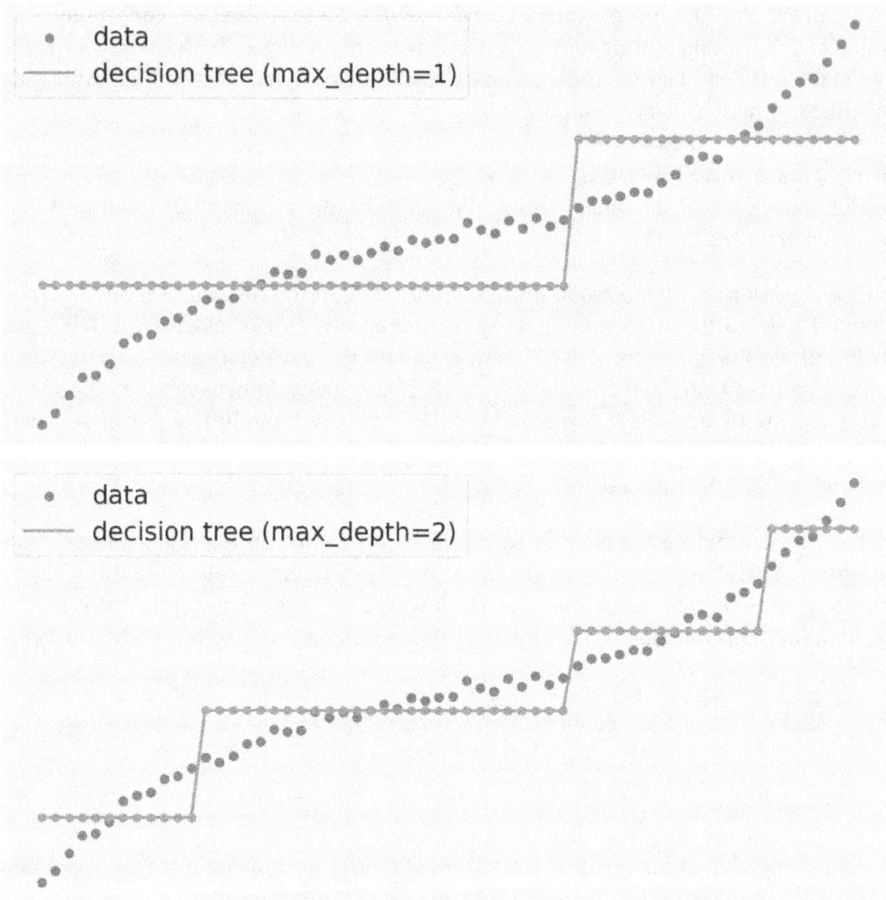

Figure 7.28: Decision trees (green) for `max_depth=1` (upper) and `max_depth=2` (lower).

Here we can see the tree in action; at depth 1 the tree splits the data into two plateaux then, for depth 2 the the position of the initial split is maintained and the tree then independently splits the left hand side plateau again into two, and the right hand side plateau into two, creating a total of four plateaux which correspond to the four leaves of the tree.

> Remark: Although the depth=1 split may be optimal, there may be a more optimal split for depth=2 by not maintaining the position of the first split. The decision tree is an example of a greedy algorithm.

As we increase the depth the number of leaves has the potential to grow exponentially. Eventually we will have the capacity to assign a leaf to each and every data-point, thus fitting any dataset perfectly with zero error:

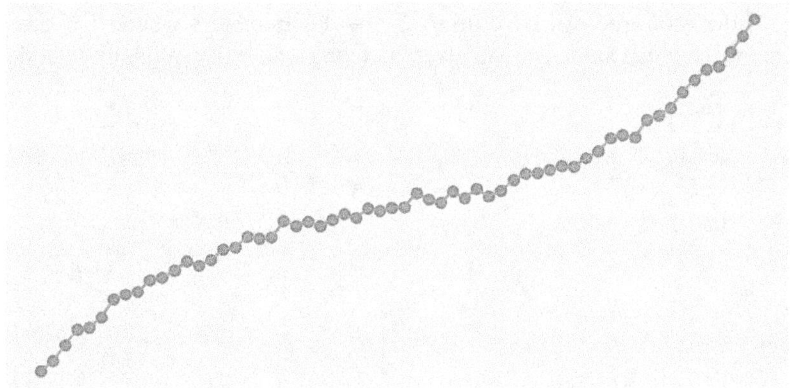

Figure 7.29: With sufficient max_depth we will eventually get a perfect fit to the training data.

This seems fantastic, but is actually a complete disaster! Let us plot the RMSE metric with respect to the tree depth for our fit to the training data, and also for an out-of-sample test dataset having the same underlying signal, but having different random noise.

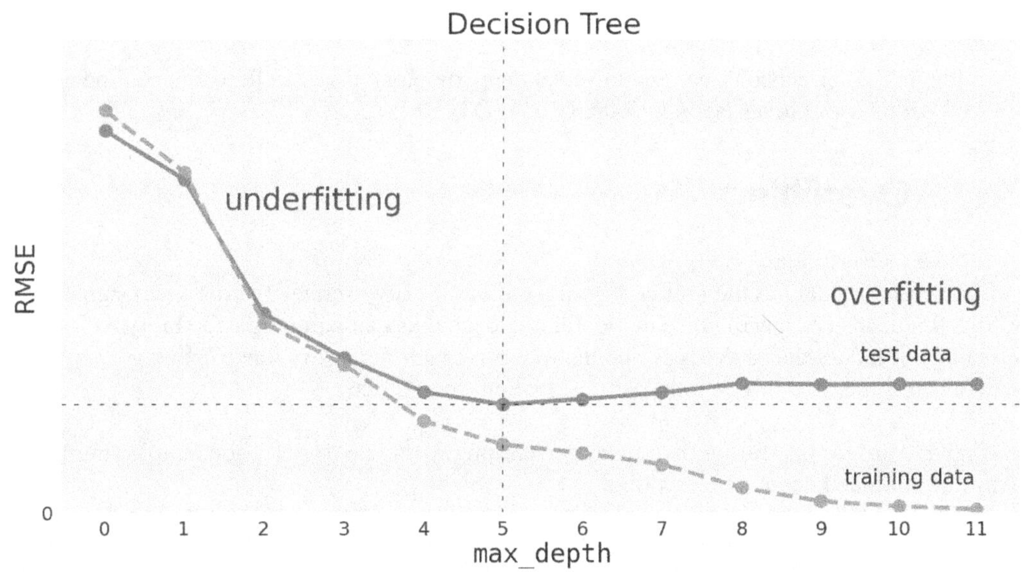

Figure 7.30: An Occam curve showing performance as a function of model complexity (here max_depth).

The important things in Figure 7.30 are that, with sufficient depth, a decision tree can perfectly fit any training dataset (it is a universal approximator); eventually every single datapoint will have its very own leaf with each leaf having zero error. However, on the unseen test data (in green) we see that, in the above example, the best performance (lowest out-of-sample RMSE) was achieved at `max_depth=5`, and indeed the results even become very slightly worse for deeper trees as the models fitted to more and more of the noise. The greater the variance of the noise component, the worse the fit will become. In this example beyond `max_depth=5` we start what is known as overfitting.

Remark: A decision tree can have up to $2^{d+1}-1$ parameters where $d =$ `max_depth`. 2^d of those parameters are the mean values of each leaf, and the rest are the splits of the nodes.

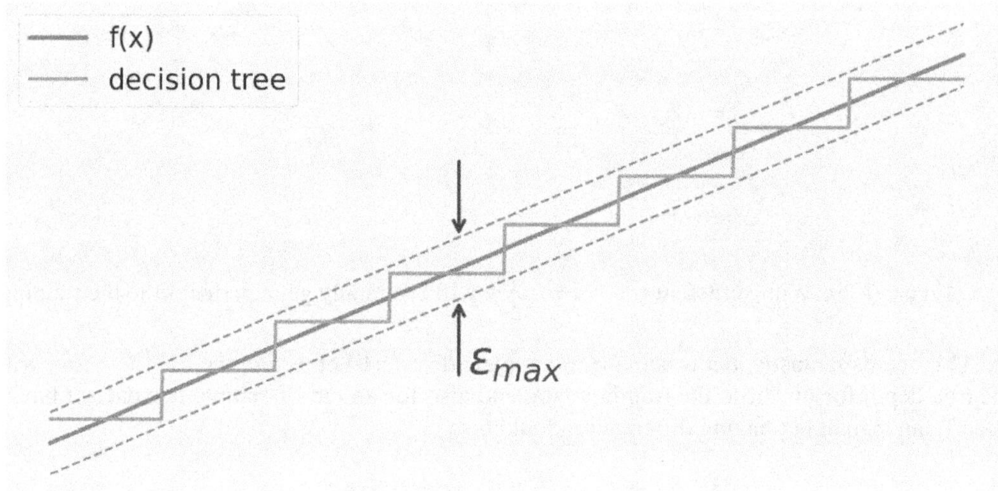

Figure 7.31: Decision trees are universal approximators; they can fit to any continuous function to within an arbitrary error, *i.e.* $\sup_x |f(x) - \mathrm{DT}(x)| < \varepsilon_{max}$

7.13 Overfitting

Remark: Overfitting:
Effect: Our model has the ability to fit not only to the low frequency (variance) signal but also to the high frequency (variance) noise in the training data, thus damaging transferability.
Cause: A model that overfits is one that has too much flexibility due to having too many adjustable parameters (degrees of freedom) per observation (row) of data.

If it were not for overfitting then machine learning would be trivial; for example simply fit a decision tree of unlimited depth to everything!

Overfitting can be understood as when we have fitted to all of the signal, and we now start fitting to the stochastic noise (aleatoric uncertainty) component. If our train and test datasets are i.i.d., which is a basic requirement for machine learning to actually work, then we fully expect the signal that we learn from the training data to be present in the previously unseen test data, thus making a model that learns the training signal to then be transferable to the signal in the test data. However, on the other hand the specific noise values seen in the training dataset, due to its random nature, are not the same as the noise values present in the test data, so we would do well to not let our model learn anything at all about the noise component in the training data. Such overfitting will occur when our model has more complexity or flexibility than the absolute minimum required required to learn the signal component[9], *i.e.* our model should be parsimonious; it should be as simple as possible (but no simpler).

[9] Douglas M. Hawkins *"The Problem of Overfitting"*, Journal of Chemical Information and Computer Sciences **44** pp. 1-12 (2004)

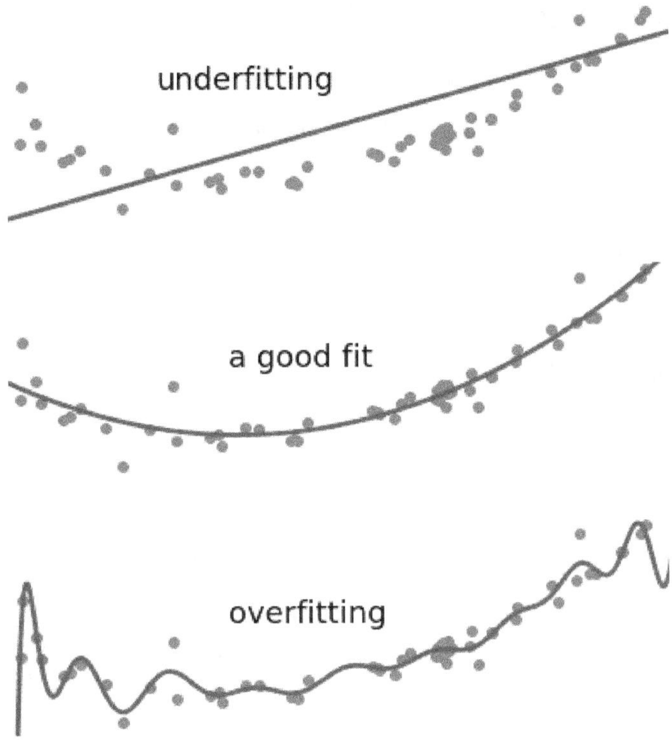

Figure 7.32: Underfitting vs. good fit vs. overfitting. In underfitting we capture some of the signal. In a good fit we capture all of the signal, and in overfitting we capture the signal and some of the random noise.

It should be mentioned that, due to the epistemic uncertainty (*i.e.* gaps in the data) even if we were fortunate enough to have a dataset with absolutely no noise component whatsoever, a model can still overfit if we have very little data to work with, and the sparse regions should be filled with the simplest possible model; otherwise an overly complex model will fill said regions with a very poor approximation, leading to very bad out-of-sample predictions.

7.13.1 Parametric models: regularization

Remark: **Warning**: One should normalize the features before using regularization.

How do we reduce overfitting in parametric models? *shrinkage* via regularization. We have seen that linear regression using a single parameter (*i.e.* β_1) tends to underfit our target if said target is non-linear, but if we have a great many features where each additional feature introduces a new adjustable parameter, we can eventually overfit the target (see kitchen sink regression). To reduce, or even remove, the influence of parameters associated with features that are of little importance (basically noise) we can use regularization (remember, if a given feature has a $\beta = 0$ this feature forms no part of the model).

Equation: Regularization = cost functional (J) + penalty term

The $L1$ penalty (also known as LASSO) is $|\beta|$

$$J \leftarrow J + \lambda \sum |\beta| \tag{7.25}$$

which can be written as $\|\beta\|_1$, known as the Manhattan norm.
The $L2$ penalty (Ridge) is β^2

$$J \leftarrow J + \lambda \sum \beta^2 \tag{7.26}$$

which can be written as $\|\beta\|_2^2$, the Euclidean norm. For ridge regression the coefficients can be found by solving

$$\beta = (\mathbf{X}^\mathsf{T}\mathbf{X} + \lambda \mathbf{I})^{-1}\mathbf{X}^\mathsf{T}\mathbf{y} \tag{7.27}$$

where $\mathbf{I}$ is the identity matrix.

λ is the regularization hyperparameter; the larger the value of λ the stronger the penalty.

In scikit-learn these penalties available via the following estimators:

- LASSO regression – Linear least squares with $L1$ regularization
- Ridge regression – Linear least squares with $L2$ regularization
- ElasticNet regression – Linear least squares with both $L1$ and $L2$ regularization

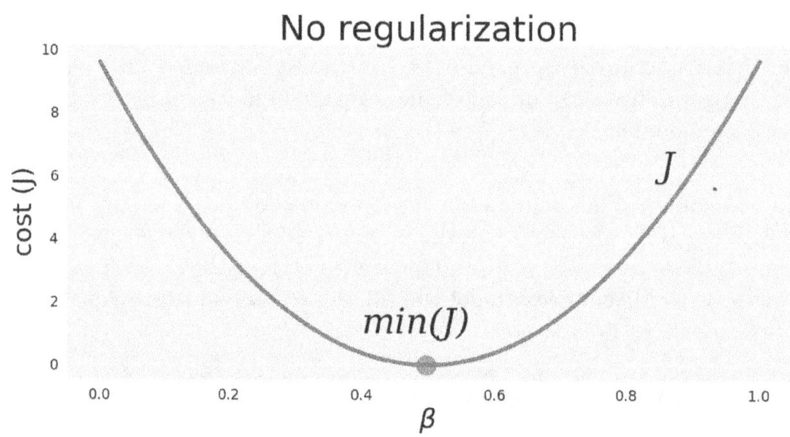

Figure 7.33: No regularization. Orange circle indicates the optimal value of β.

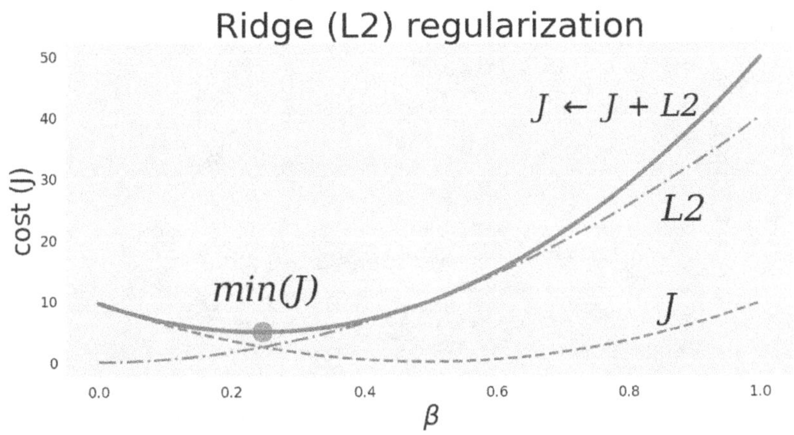

Figure 7.34: The effect of adding L2 (ridge) regularization. We see that the optimal value of β has shifted to a lower value.

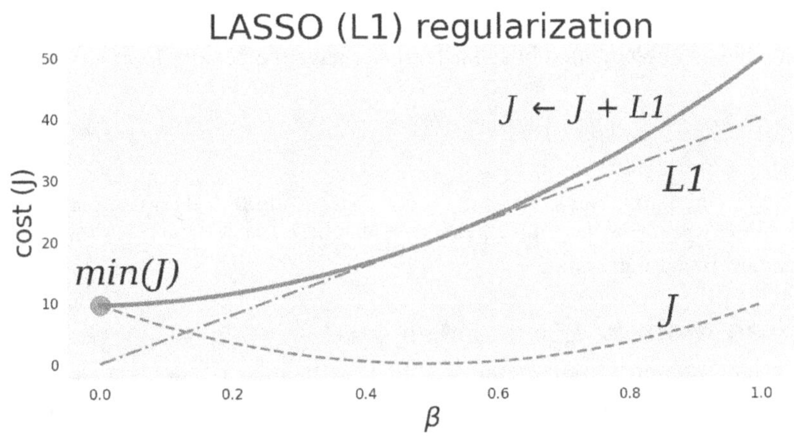

Figure 7.35: The effect of adding L1 (LASSO) regularization. Here β has become zero.

In Figure 7.33 we have no regularization, corresponding to standard linear regression. The optimal value of β is found at the minima of the cost functional (solid line), and has been marked with an orange dot. In Figure 7.34 we apply the $L2$ penalty (dot-dashed line), which is quadratic. When we add the $L2$ penalty to the original cost functional (dashed line) we find that the minima of our new cost functional (orange dot) has been shifted to a lower value. In Figure 7.35 this time we apply the $L1$ penalty which is linear. We can now see that it is possible to shrink the value of β all the way down to zero. Remember that when a feature has a β of zero, this feature no longer forms part of the model.

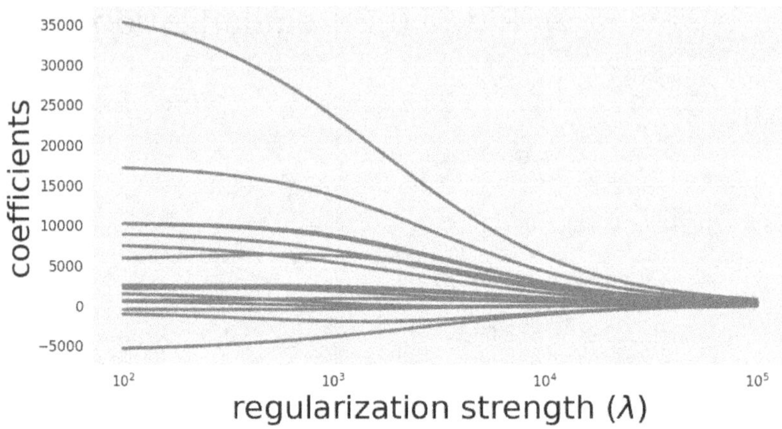

Figure 7.36: Ridge regressor coefficients as λ is increased. We can see the shrinkage in the coefficient paths.

In the situation where the number of features is much greater than the number of samples, such as in the area of DNA microarray analysis, the elastic net[10] has been shown to outperform both LASSO and Ridge. For the elastic net as implemented in scikit-learn we have the penalty term

$$\lambda \left(\rho \|\beta\|_1 + \frac{(1-\rho)}{2} \|\beta\|_2^2 \right) \tag{7.28}$$

where ρ is the mixing parameter (`l1_ratio`) such that setting $\rho = 0$ corresponds to just the $L2$ penalty, and setting $\rho = 1$ corresponds to just the $L1$ penalty. When λ (`alpha`) $= 0$ we turn off all regularization and revert to standard linear regression.

7.13.2 Tree models: `min_samples_leaf`

How do we reduce overfitting in decision tree models? by doing some gardening! In Figure 7.29 we saw a tree that was over-fitted so as to have one single datapoint in each leaf. This is where the `min_samples_leaf` hyperparameter comes into play. We stop the splitting when reaching the specified number of samples per leaf. We can also make shallower trees by limiting the `max_depth` hyperparameter.

[10] Zou, Hastie *"Regularization and Variable Selection Via the Elastic Net"*, Journal of the Royal Statistical Society Series B: Statistical Methodology **67** pp. 301-320 (2005)

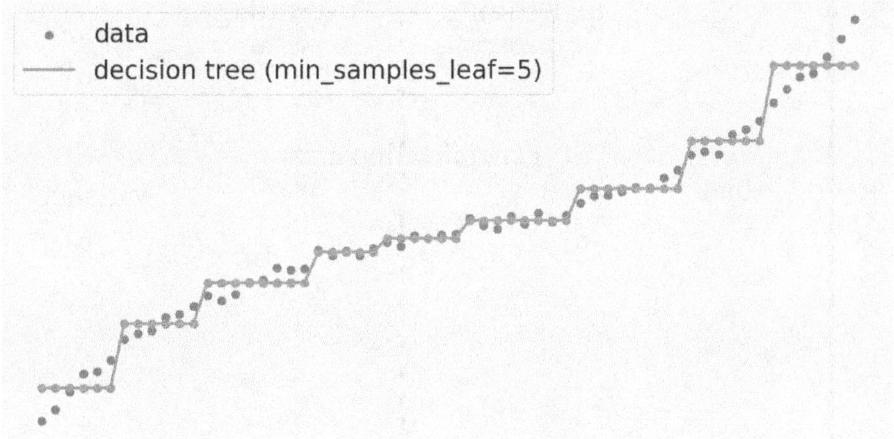

Figure 7.37: A decision tree with unlimited depth and `min_samples_leaf`=5.

(We can also perform 'pruning' using the `ccp_alpha` hyperparameter).

> Remark: **Warning**: The default scikit-learn `DecisionTreeRegressor()` has no `max_depth` and `min_samples_leaf` is 1 so it creates "fully grown unpruned trees", which is basically an elegant way of saying it is **guaranteed to overfit**.

7.14 Bias-variance tradeoff and decomposition

As mentioned in the chapter on cross-validation, bias is when we consistently either overestimate or underestimate a statistic. The linear regression is a high bias model; for all but the simplest of datasets it will always result in a sub-optimal generalization error. On the other hand, a fully grown decision tree is a high variance model; it can perfectly fit to all of the points in the training dataset, but at the cost of generalizability, again resulting in a sub-optimal generalization error. The larger the bias, the more the model is said to underfit; *i.e.* not capture all of the signal in the data. The larger the variance the more the model is said to overfit; *i.e.* capture the signal as well as all of the noise in the data. Between these two extremes there is a sweet spot.

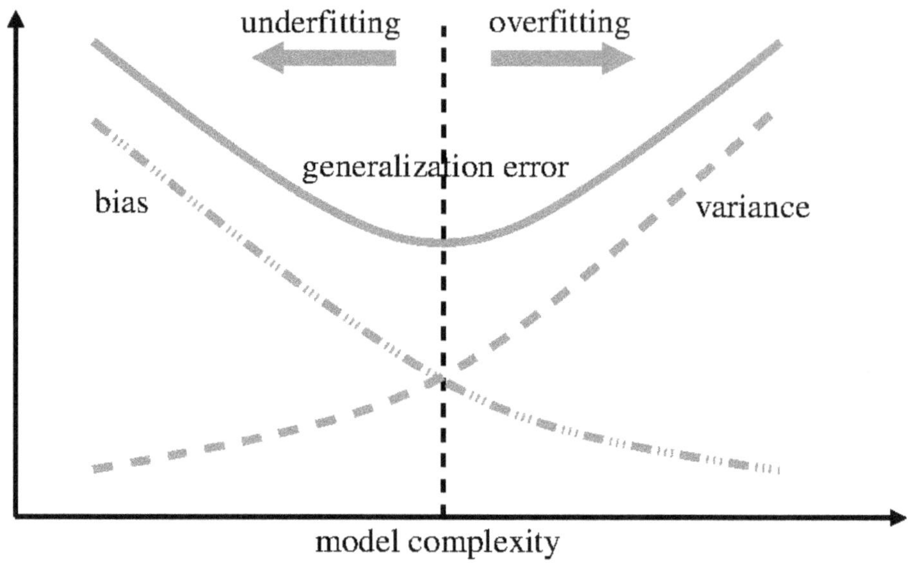

Figure 7.38: A schematic Occam curve showing the bias/variance tradeoff. Image adapted from Brown, Ali "*Bias/Variance is not the same as Approximation/Estimation*", Transactions on Machine Learning Research (02/2024).

When it comes to evaluating the generalization error in terms of the mean squared error (MSE) we can see that it looks similar to the formula for the variance. However, with the MSE we are measuring distances of our predictions w.r.t. the true value (`y_true`) whereas the variance measures distances w.r.t. the mean of the values themselves, $\overline{y_i}$. For the mean squared error we can perform a bias-variance decomposition[11] which, for a 'deterministic' dataset (*i.e.* that has no stochastic noise component), is given by

Equation: The bias-variance decomposition for the mean squared error

$$\underbrace{\frac{1}{n}\sum_{i=1}^{n}(y_i-\hat{y}_i)^2}_{\text{MSE}} = \frac{1}{n}\sum_{i=1}^{n}\underbrace{\left(y_i-\overline{\hat{y}_i}\right)}_{\text{bias}(\hat{y})}{}^2 + \underbrace{\frac{1}{n}\sum_{i=1}^{n}\left(\overline{\hat{y}_i}-\hat{y}_i\right)^2}_{\text{Var}(\hat{y})} \tag{7.29}$$

In words this simply states that the average distance of our model is from the true values is given by how far the model is from the average model plus how far the average model is from the true value.

The bias-variance decomposition looks great on paper, but actually calculating the bias and variance of a model is not a trivial task, specifically calculating the expectation value of the model, $\mathbb{E}(\hat{y})$, which in practical terms involves calculating the mean of the predictions produced by a large number of fits, $\overline{\hat{y}}$, for example via bootstrap sampling of the training data.

7.15 Monotonic constraints

Monotonic constraints are an excellent way to embed domain knowledge into a fit, or to simply impose common sense on either real or ordinally encoded features. For example, it is our intuition that the larger a

[11] Geman, Bienenstock, Doursat "*Neural Networks and the Bias/Variance Dilemma*", Neural Computation **4** pp. 1-58 (1992)

house, the greater the sale price. Now in reality this may not always hold true and there will be exceptions; for example a big house that happens to be in extremely poor condition, or is unappealingly situated next to a very busy road may have a less than expected value. However, on the whole we may well find that imposing this constraint can lead to more stable, and interpretable, results. A linear regression will naturally be monotonic in nature. However, for tree based estimators this is not the case.

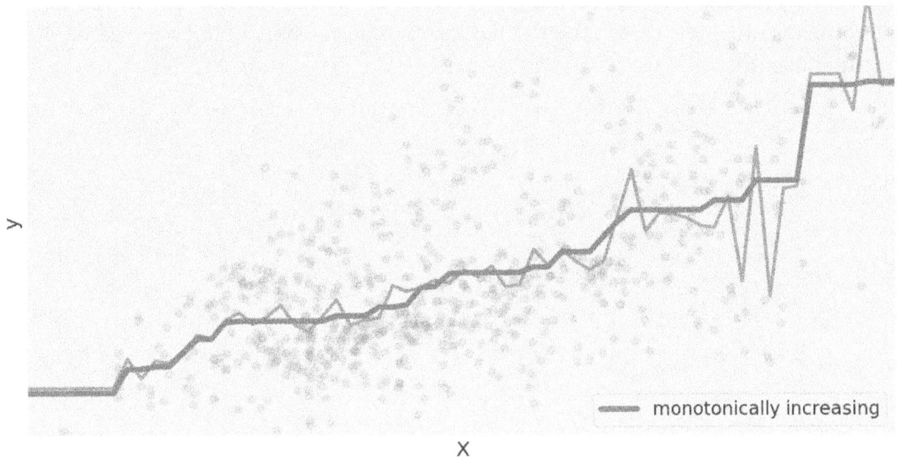

Figure 7.39: A standard fit (orange) and a monotonically increasing fit (green).

Monotonic constraints are available in both XGBoost and CatBoost using the parameter `monotone_constraints`. LightGBM and the scikit-learn `DecisionTree`, `RandomForest`, and `HistGradientBoosting` regression and classification routines use the `monotonic_cst` parameter. One simply specifies the name of the feature(s) to be constrained, and whether it is monotonically increasing (`1`) or decreasing (`-1`). For example

```
HistGradientBoostingRegressor( monotonic_cst={"feature_0":  1,
                                              "feature_7": -1} )
```

7.16 Quantile regression and prediction intervals

Thus far we have produced what are known as point predictions, *i.e.* for a new feature vector we use our model to tell us $\hat{y}$. However, it is arguably much more useful, especially when it comes to decision making, to calculate prediction intervals. For example, say our model for house prices gave us a point prediction of 121,516€ for a given property. If we saw a house with the very same characteristics on sale for 120,000€ ¿Is that a bargain? If we put an asking price of 125,000€ on the house ¿Will it sell, or is it overpriced? This is where prediction intervals can really help us to make a decision. A good technique for producing prediction intervals is quantile regression[12, 13]. We can specify a coverage (say 80%) and then produce a model. That model could return a lower price of say 110,000€ and an upper price of 130,000€ for said house. With this data we are now confident that if we see a house with the same characteristics on sale for 100,000€ then this property is below market value, and could be a very good investment opportunity. Or on the other hand we could confidently try to sell the property at 130,000€ without leaving money on the table.

[12] Bassett, Koenker "*Regression Quantiles*", Econometrica **vol 46** pp. 33-50 (1978)

[13] Koenker, Hallock "*Quantile Regression*", Journal of Economic Perspectives **vol 15** pp. 143-156 (2001)

7.16.1 Pinball loss function

For quantile regression one uses the quantile or 'pinball' loss, which is given by

$$L_p = \begin{cases} \tau\,|y_i - \hat{y}_i|\,, & \text{if } \varepsilon \geq 0 \\ (1-\tau)\,|y_i - \hat{y}_i|\,, & \text{if } \varepsilon < 0 \end{cases} \tag{7.30}$$

where τ is the quantile, $\tau \in [0,1]$. The pinball loss can be considered to be the generalization of the $L1$ loss to a specified quantile.

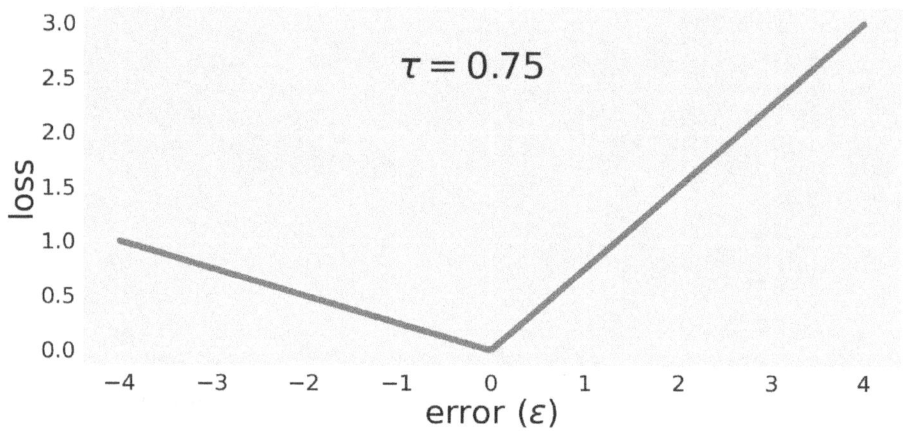

Figure 7.40: The pinball loss function for $\tau = 0.75$.

> Remark: If $\tau = 0.5$ the pinball loss reduces to the half the $L1$ loss and we perform median (Q2) regression.

Some estimators that can be used to perform quantile regression in python:

- `sklearn.linear_model.QuantileRegressor`
- `sklearn.ensemble.GradientBoostingRegressor`
- `sklearn.ensemble.HistGradientBoostingRegressor`
- `XGBoost` / `LightGBM` / `CatBoost`

There is also the `quantile-forest` package that implements quantile regression forests. What does quantile regression look like? For a linear model:

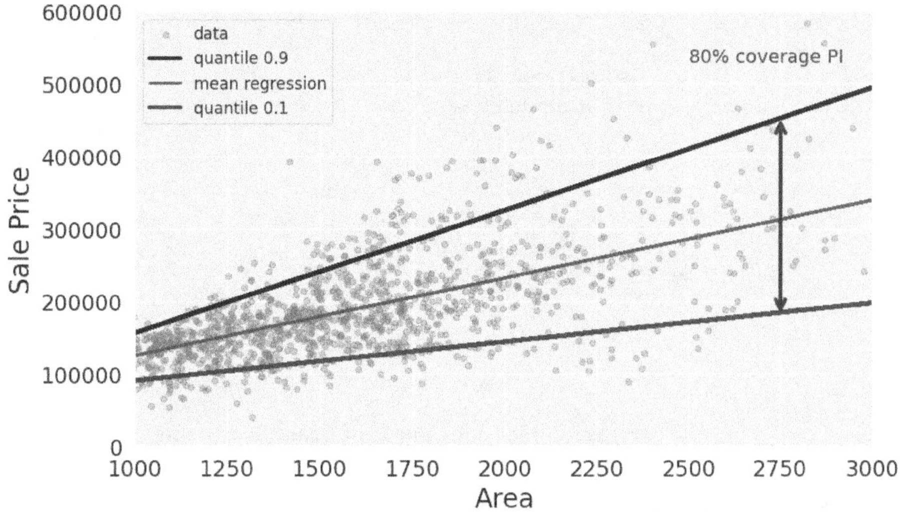

Figure 7.41: 80% prediction interval from a linear model

and for a non-parametric tree model

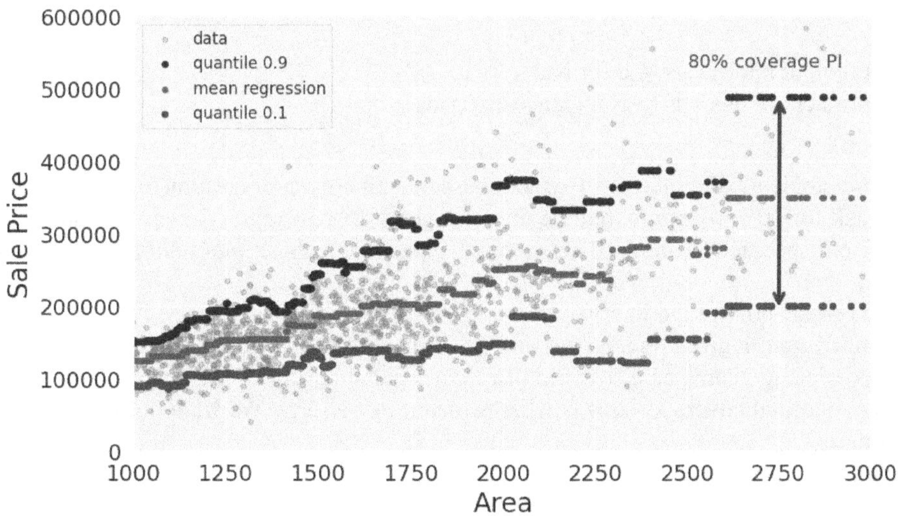

Figure 7.42: 80% prediction interval from a tree model

N Jupyter Notebook: PI competition I: Quantile regression

Quantile crossing

There exists the potential, particularly with linear quantile regression performed on heteroscedastic data, for what is known as quantile crossing, leading to nonsensical negative prediction intervals.

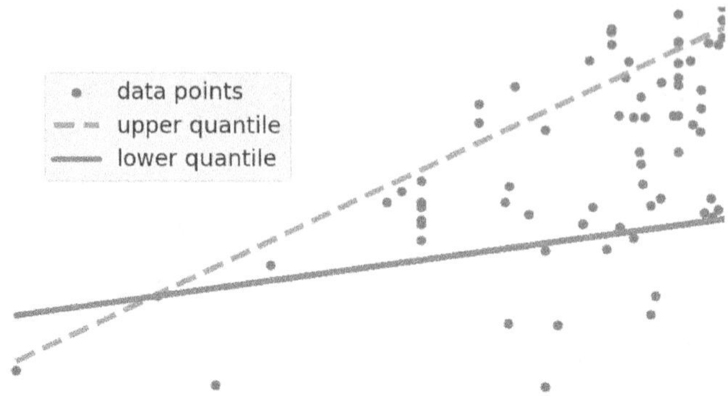

Figure 7.43: An example of quantile crossing.

7.17 Conformal prediction intervals

Conformal prediction is a framework designed to provide valid uncertainty quantification and for an excellent introduction to this technique see the book "Practical Guide to Applied Conformal Prediction in Python" by Valeriy Manokhin.

> **Remark:**
>
> - prediction intervals $\not\equiv$ error bars
> - prediction intervals $\not\equiv$ confidence intervals

What is the problem? The intervals from our base quantile regression estimator may be wrong. For example, we may ask for 80% coverage, but we may not get 80% coverage. However, conformal prediction will guarantee our specified coverage. There are two types of coverage: *marginal* and *conditional*. For, say 80% coverage:

- **marginal**: 80% of the intervals will contain `y_true`
- **conditional**: a given interval has an 80% chance of containing `y_true`

It is not possible to guarantee distribution-free conditional coverage[14]. However, conformal prediction does guarantee marginal coverage - this is what is meant by validity. We want our prediction intervals to have three things:

- **validity**: guaranteed marginal coverage
- **efficiency**: intervals to be as narrow as possible
- **adaptability**: in cases of heteroscedasticity have variable lengths

conformal prediction provides the validity, the base estimator provides the efficiency (validity can also help the efficiency; overcoverage is inefficient), and the quantile regression provides the adaptability[15]. Conformal prediction comes in two 'flavours':

- **transductive** (*full* or *online*): no calibration set needed, but computationally expensive: multiple fits
- **inductive** (*split* or `prefit`): needs hold-out data for a calibration set, but is computationally efficient: just one fit

[14] Barber, Candès, Ramdas, Tibshirani *"The limits of distribution-free conditional predictive inference"*, arXiv:1903.04684 (2020)

[15] Zecchin, Park, Simeone, Hellström *"Generalization and Informativeness of Conformal Prediction"*, arXiv: 2401.11810 (2024)

Requirements: for machine learning to work correctly our splits should be i.i.d. samples. For conformal prediction to work we only need *exchangeability*[16] ¿What is exchangeability? It is when one can `shuffle` or `sort` the rows of a dataset and it will make no difference to the predictions. Exchangeability is a weaker condition than i.i.d., so if we are i.i.d. we are good to go.

> Remark: Exchangeability becomes problematic for time series data, where the order of the rows is indeed important.

One can think of the conformal prediction process as a calibration of ones prediction intervals.

7.17.1 Conformalized quantile regression (CQR)

We shall describe the conformalized quantile regression (CQR) technique by Emmanuel Candès and co-workers[17, 18] which adds conformal prediction to standard quantile regression. Conformalized quantile regression is essentially a six step process:
1) train your two quantile regressors, Q_{lower} and Q_{upper}, on `X_train`, `y_train`
2) predict the two quantiles for the `X_calibrate` data

```
# calculate lower and upper quantile values of the calibration set
y_pred_lower_upper = qrf.predict(X_calib,
                                 quantiles=[alpha/2, 1-alpha/2])
```

3) for each `y_true` in `y_calibrate` calculate a conformity score E_i

$$E_i := \max(Q_{lower} - \texttt{y\_true}, \texttt{y\_true} - Q_{upper})$$

```
calibration_df = pd.DataFrame(y_calib.values, columns = ['y_true'])
calibration_df["lower"] = y_pred_lower_upper[:,0]
calibration_df["upper"] = y_pred_lower_upper[:,1]
a  = (calibration_df["lower"]-calibration_df["y_true"]).values
b  = (calibration_df["y_true"]-calibration_df["upper"]).values
calibration_df["Ei"] = (np.vstack((a, b)).T).max(axis=1)
```

4) calculate `s` being the value of the $(1-\alpha)(1+1/n_{calib})$ quantile of this set of conformity scores $\{E\}$ where $\alpha :=$ (100-coverage%)/100, and n_{calib} is the number of calibration rows

```
s = calibration_df["Ei"].quantile((1-alpha)*(1+(1/(len(calibration_df)))))
```

5) predict the two quantiles for `X_test`
6) obtain validity by subtracting `s` from Q_{lower} and adding `s` to Q_{upper}

```
predictions["conformal_lower"] = predictions["lower"] - s
predictions["conformal_upper"] = predictions["upper"] + s
```

---

[16] Kuchibhotla "*Exchangeability, Conformal Prediction, and Rank Tests*", arXiv:2005.06095 (2021)
[17] Romano, Patterson, Candès "*Conformalized Quantile Regression*", NeurIPS **vol 32** (2019)
[18] Sesia, Candès "*A comparison of some conformal quantile regression methods*", Stat **vol 9** e261 (2020)

> **Remark:** For the CQR calibration dataset (`X_calibrate`, `y_calibrate`) I would suggest using between 1000 and 2000 rows of data. For more details on calibration sample sizes see Table 1 in *"Universal distribution of the empirical coverage in split conformal prediction"*.

Jupyter Notebook: For a worked example see: Prediction intervals: Quantile Regression Forests

7.17.2 Locally-weighted conformal regression

In locally-weighted conformal regression[19] we use two estimators, one fitted to the training data ($\hat{\mu}$), and the other estimator ($\hat{\rho}$) is fitted to the errors, *i.e.* the difference between the predictions output by the model fitted to the training data (`y_pred_train`), and the `y_true` (Y) values. We denote our estimator as $\hat{\mu}$ as generally most machine learning regressors return a mean expectation value since the default loss function is usually $L2$, *i.e.* the squared error.

$$\mu(x) = \mathbb{E}(Y|X=x) \tag{7.31}$$

The locally-weighted residuals R_i are given by

$$R_i = \frac{|Y_i - \hat{\mu}(X_i)|}{\hat{\rho}(X_i)} \tag{7.32}$$

```
model_means  = regressor_mean.fit(X_train, y_train)
y_pred_train = model_means.predict(X_train)

# calculate the absolute deviations
AD = np.abs(y_pred_train - y_train)
# fit a model to these deviations
model_residuals = regressor_residual_mean.fit(X_train, AD)
```

now we apply these two models to the calibration data and calculate the conformity of each row (i)

```
y_pred_calib = model_means.predict(X_calib)
MAD_calib    = model_residuals.predict(X_calib)

R_i = np.abs(y_calib - y_pred_calib) / MAD_calib
```

and calculate the final conformity score (d), here for 90% coverage (*i.e.* $\alpha = 0.1$) (note the small finite sample correction)

$$d = \text{quantile}((1-\alpha)(1+1/n_{calib})) \tag{7.33}$$

where n_{calib} is the number of rows in the calibration set.

```
alpha = 0.1 # i.e. 90% coverage
n = len(X_calib)
d = R_i.quantile( (1-alpha)*(1+(1/n)) )
```

[19] Jing Lei, Max G'Sell, Alessandro Rinaldo, Ryan J. Tibshirani, and Larry Wasserman *"Distribution-Free Predictive Inference for Regression"*, Journal of the American Statistical Association, **113** pp. 1094-1111 (2018)

now for the test data

```
y_pred   = model_means.predict(X_test)
MAD_pred = model_residuals.predict(X_test)
```

our lower and upper conformal prediction intervals are calculated as

$$[\hat{\mu}(X_i) - \hat{\rho}(X_i)d,\ \hat{\mu}(X_i) + \hat{\rho}(X_i)d] \tag{7.34}$$

```
predictions = y_test.to_frame()
predictions.columns = ['y_true']
predictions["point prediction"] = y_pred

# create our conformal predictions
predictions["lower"] = y_pred - (MAD_pred * d)
predictions["upper"] = y_pred + (MAD_pred * d)
```

N Jupyter Notebook: Example notebook of performing locally-weighted conformal regression.

Here we plot the true value vs. predicted value of our point predictions along with their corresponding prediction intervals

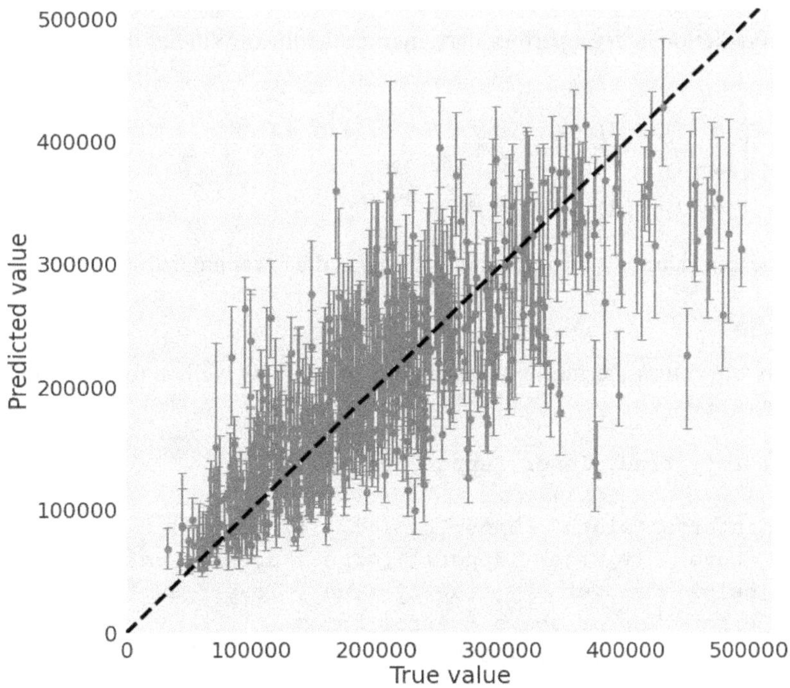

Figure 7.44: True value vs. predicted value plot with prediction intervals.

Sample code

Sample code to produce the true vs. predicted value plot with prediction intervals

```
fig, ax = plt.subplots(figsize=(7, 7))

plt.errorbar(predictions["y_true"], predictions["point prediction"],
        yerr=(predictions["point prediction"]-predictions["lower"],
              predictions["upper"]-predictions["point prediction"]),
              ecolor='grey', linestyle='', marker="o", capsize=5)

ax.axline([0, 0], [1, 1], color="black", linestyle='--',
                     lw=3, zorder=3 )
plt.xlim(0)
plt.ylim(0)
plt.xlabel('True value')
plt.ylabel('Predicted value')
plt.show();
```

7.17.3 Prediction interval metric: Winkler interval score

We can evaluate the performance of our prediction interval estimates using the Winkler interval score[20, 21]:

Equation: Prediction interval performance metric: the mean Winkler interval score

$$W_\alpha = \begin{cases} (u-l)+\frac{2}{\alpha}(l-y), & \text{if } y<l \\ (u-l), & \text{if } l \le y \le u \\ (u-l)+\frac{2}{\alpha}(y-u), & \text{if } y>u \end{cases} \tag{7.35}$$

where y is the true value, u is the upper prediction, l is the lower prediction, and α is (100-coverage%)/100.

Sample code

This function will return the mean Winkler interval score as well as the marginal coverage (written by AmbrosM) (gist)

```
def MWI_score(y_true, lower, upper, alpha):

    total_interval_width = upper.sum() - lower.sum()
    error_above = (y_true - upper)[y_true > upper].sum()
    error_below = (lower - y_true)[y_true < lower].sum()
    total_error = error_above + error_below
    MWIS = (total_interval_width+total_error*2/alpha)/len(y_true)
```

[20] Winkler *"A Decision-Theoretic Approach to Interval Estimation"*, Journal of the American Statistical Association **vol 67**, pp. 187-191 (1972)

[21] Brehmer, Gneiting *"Scoring interval forecasts: Equal-tailed, shortest, and modal interval"*, Bernoulli **vol 27**, pp. 1993-2010 (2021)

```
# marginal coverage
coverage = ((lower <= y_true) & (y_true <= upper)).mean()
return MWIS, coverage
```

7.18 Expectile regression

In quantile regression we have seen the pinball loss, which is a generalization of the $L1$ loss to any quantile. Expectile regression[22] uses a generalization of the $L2$ loss, given by

$$L_e = \begin{cases} \tau (y_i - \hat{y}_i)^2, & \text{if } \varepsilon \geq 0 \\ (1-\tau)(y_i - \hat{y}_i)^2, & \text{if } \varepsilon < 0 \end{cases} \tag{7.36}$$

where τ is the expectile, $\tau \in [0, 1]$.

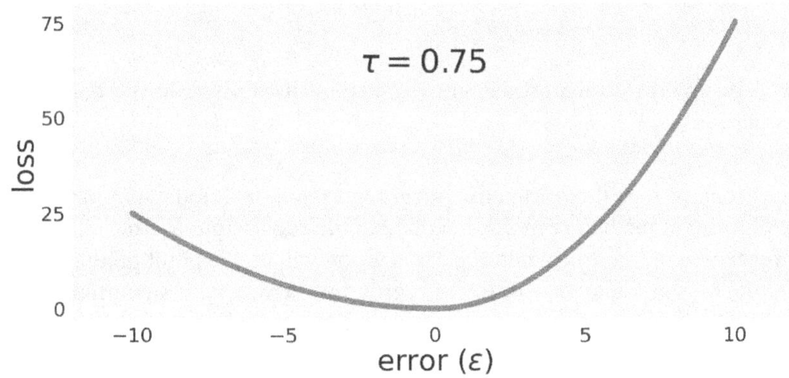

Figure 7.45: The expectile loss function for $\tau = 0.75$.

For $\tau = 0.5$ the expectile loss becomes half of the $L2$ loss and we effectively perform standard mean regression.

[22]James L. Powell, Whitney K. Newey *"Asymmetric Least Squares Estimation and Testing"*, Econometrica **55** pp. 819-847 (1987)

7.19 Summary

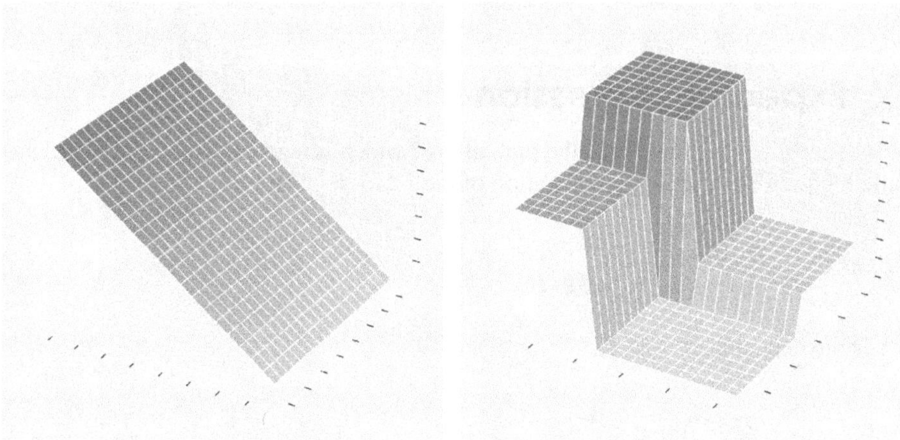

Figure 7.46: With two features linear regression fits a plane to the data, and a decision tree creates plateaux.

In this chapter we have seen the parametric linear regression model, the non-parametric decision tree model, and have also looked at median regression with quantile regression. We have looked at prediction intervals as a more informative option to calculating expectation values *i.e.* point predictions. In Figure 7.46 we can see the inductive bias associated with linear regression, which learns continuous function, and inductive bias of decision trees, which learns a piece-wise continuous surface.

Recommended reading

Papers

- Cawley, Talbot "*On Over-fitting in Model Selection and Subsequent Selection Bias in Performance Evaluation*", The Journal of Machine Learning Research **11** pp. 2079-2107 (2010)
- Mikhail Belkin, Daniel Hsu, Siyuan Ma, Soumik Mandal *"Reconciling modern machine-learning practice and the classical bias–variance trade-off"*, PNAS **116** pp. 15849-15854 (2019)
- Sebastian Raschka "*Model Evaluation, Model Selection, and Algorithm Selection in Machine Learning*", arXiv:1811.12808 (2020)
- Angelopoulos, Bates "*A Gentle Introduction to Conformal Prediction and Distribution-Free Uncertainty Quantification*", arXiv:2107.07511 (2022) (§2.2)

Books

- Cosma Rohilla Shalizi "*The Truth about Linear Regression*", (2024)
- Wessel N. van Wieringen *"Lecture notes on ridge regression"*, arXiv:1509.09169 (2023)
- Peng Ding *"Linear Model and Extensions"*, arXiv:2401.00649 (2024)
- Andrew Gelman, Jennifer Hill, Aki Vehtari *"Regression and Other Stories"*, Cambridge University Press (2023)
- Valery Manokhin "*Practical Guide to Applied Conformal Prediction in Python*", Packt Publishing Limited (2023) (Chapter 7)

Packages

- quantile-forest by Reid Johnson
- MAPIE - Model Agnostic Prediction Interval Estimator
- Puncc
- crepes by Henrik Boström

8. Classification

> The only useful function of a statistician is to make predictions, and thus to provide a basis for action.
>
> *W. Edwards Deming*

A classification problem in one in which the target values (often called *labels*) belong to a set of classes. Quintessential classification problems are identifying penguin species or iris flowers, and who manages to get off a sinking ship. From a machine learning standpoint our task is to estimate the probability of examples of new feature vectors belonging to each of these classes. The most frequent problem is known as binary classification, where the training labels are set to either `0` or `1`, *i.e.* $y \in \{0, 1\}$, chosen so as to facilitate the computation of the log loss function.

> **Remark:** Class 1 is often called the *positive* class and correspondingly is not unusual to see the class 0 to logically be called the *negative* class.

In regression our challenge was to find a line that was as close as possible to all of the datapoints at the same time

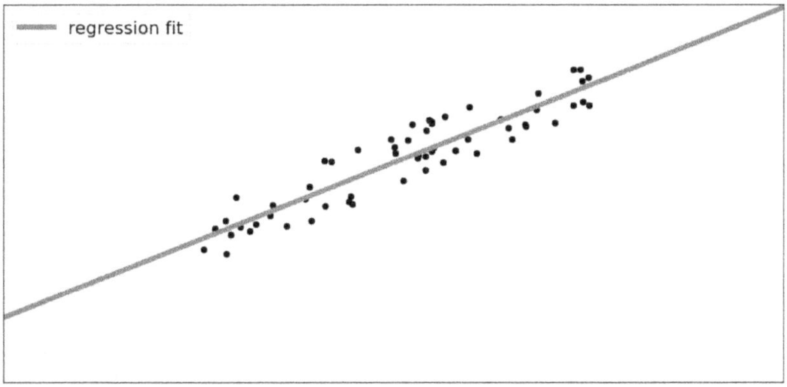

Figure 8.1: Linear regression

However, now in classification we would like to find the line that best divides the two classes, called the *decision boundary*.

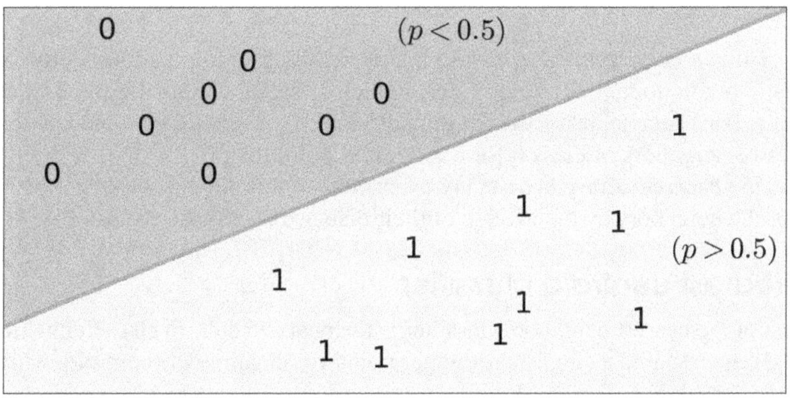

Figure 8.2: Classification with the (linear) decision boundary in orange for the $p = 0.5$ decision threshold.

8.1 Nearest neighbors classifier (k-NN)

Perhaps the simplest, and most venerable classifier, going back to 1951, is the k-nearest neighbors classifier. Remember that our data ($\mathbf{X}$) consists of rows each of which are feature vectors; each feature is the component of said vector $(x_1, x_2, ..., x_n)$ in an n-dimensional space, and the target (or label in this case) y is a the value at the head (endpoint) of the vector. When asked to predict a class for a new feature vector it inspects the k nearest Euclidean (*i.e.* Minkowski distance $p = 2$) neighbors to the endpoint of the vector and assigns a class to a point based on a majority vote if $k > 1$, or simply mimics the class of its single nearest neighbour if $k = 1$. The nearest neighbors classifier stands out as the model is the training data itself, it has no loss function to be minimized, and no fit is made. Just like interpolation it is local; neighbours beyond k have no influence whatsoever on the prediction.

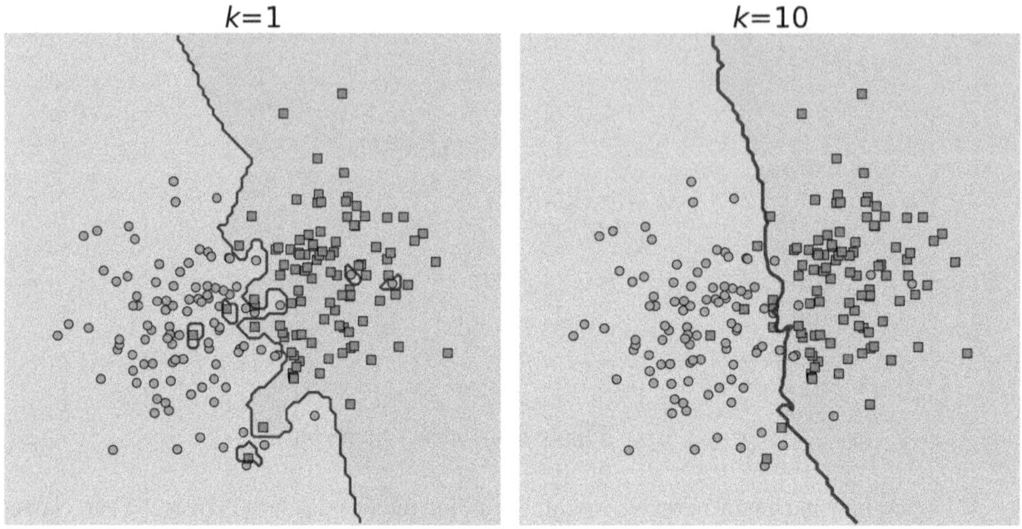

Figure 8.3: Example of the k-NN classifier in 2D

For $k = 1$ it is a *consistent classifier* in that it fits the training data perfectly. Scikit-learn can return a probabilistic prediction (`predict_proba`), which is calculated as the fraction of the classes for the k nearest points. For example, if we use the default value `n_neighbors=5` and encounter three neighbors of class 1 and two neighbors of class 0 for a requested point then $P(\hat{y} = 1) = 3/5 = 0.6$. Suffice to say that over the last 75 years there have been many extensions of this simple classifier, the most obvious being the weighting of the neighbors by the inverse of their distance (`weights='distance'`).

8.1.1 Nearest centroid classifier

An extension of the nearest neighbors classifier is the nearest centroid classifier, which aggregates all of the points of a given class into a single 'prototype' point, for example the centroid, which is calculated via

$$\mathbf{C}_0 = \frac{1}{n_0} \sum_{x \in 0} \mathbf{x}, \quad \mathbf{C}_1 = \frac{1}{n_1} \sum_{x \in 1} \mathbf{x}$$

where $\mathbf{x}$ are the n feature vectors belonging to said class. The class of a new point is then assigned by its proximity to either of the (in binary classification, two) centroids. This classifier is implemented in `sklearn.neighbors.NearestCentroid`. An underlying assumption is that the datapoints for each class form convex clusters.

8.2 Bernoulli regression

Without going far wrong, one can treat binary (probabilistic) classification as simply being a special case of regression, only here the target values are either 0 or 1, rather than being any number along $\mathbb{R}^1$. Upon calibration our predictions become probabilities, and upon dichotomization our probabilities become classes.

8.2.1 Linear regression

Given our univariate set of data-points depicted in Figure 8.4 the first thing we could try doing is to fit a linear regression to the data:

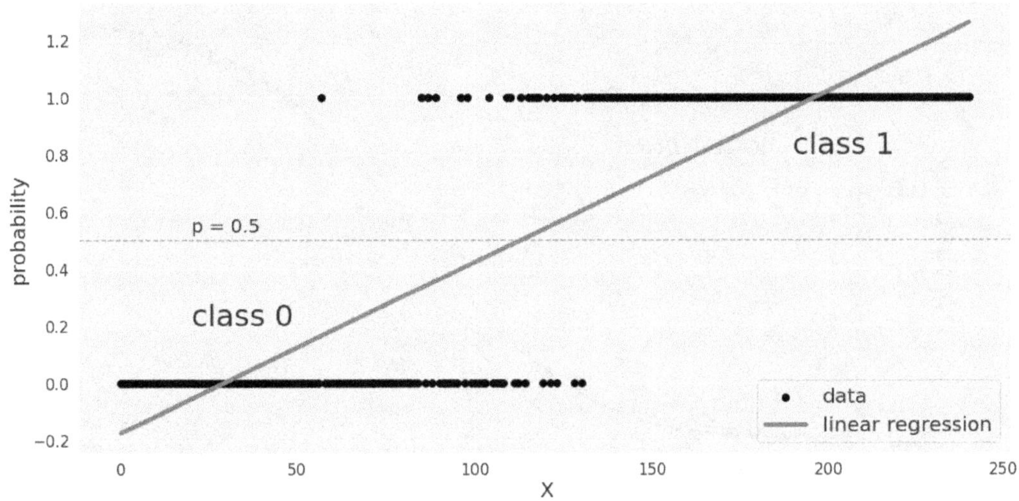

Figure 8.4: Linear regression fit (green line) to binary data (black points).

and indeed this is known as the linear probability model. However, there are some clear drawbacks to this model: for example unless the straight line we have fitted is horizontal ($\beta_1 = 0$) which due to the nature of the data cannot be the case, then there is no upper nor lower bound to our fit. If our fit is to represent a probability, clearly probabilities greater than one, and less than zero are meaningless. We could rectify this by Winsorizing the predictions by clipping our data on $[0,1]$ with something like
`df["y_pred"] = df["y_pred"].clip(lower=0,upper=1)`
but closer inspection reveals other problems. Here we are using our fit to represent the probability that for a given value of X our `y_pred` represents a probability of seeing the class 1. For example in Figure 8.4 at $X = 150$ our line indicated a probability of roughly 0.8 of seeing class 1. However we can see from the datapoints that there are no such events. Our straight line fit is evidently overly pessimistic.

8.2.2 Probit regression

The probit (a portmanteau of 'probability unit') function, $\Phi(x)$, is that of the Gaussian cumulative distribution function, which is given by

$$\Phi(x) = \text{CDF}(\mathcal{N}) = \frac{1}{\sqrt{2\pi}} \int_{-\infty}^{x} e^{-t^2/2}\, dt \tag{8.1}$$

hence the probit model is given by

$$\hat{y}(x) = p(y=1) = \frac{1}{\sqrt{2\pi}} \int_{-\infty}^{(\hat{\kappa}_1 x + \hat{\kappa}_0)} e^{-t^2/2}\, dt \tag{8.2}$$

Probit regression was for a time favoured due to its association with the Gaussian distribution, but whose calculation required the use of statistical Z tables. On the other hand the logit was deemed somewhat easier to compute, and gained ground over the probit from the 1970's onwards.[1]

[1] J. S. Cramer *"The Origins of Logistic Regression"*, Tinbergen Institute Working Paper No. 2002-119/4 (2003)

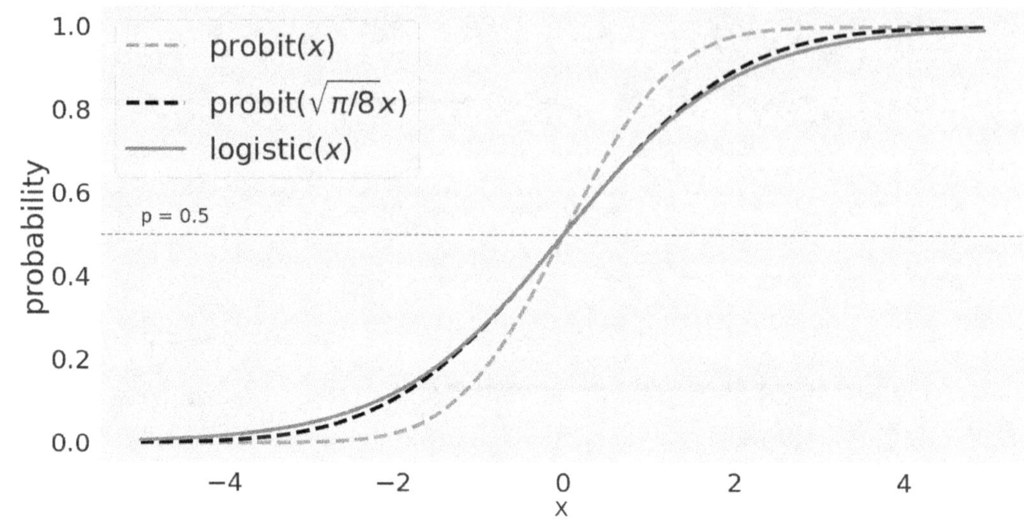

Figure 8.5: Comparison of the probit (dashed orange curve) and logistic (solid green curve) functions.

Of note is the approximation

$$\text{logistic}(x) \approx \Phi\left(\sqrt{\frac{\pi}{8}}x\right) \tag{8.3}$$

where the scaling factor is obtained by setting the derivative of the probit to be equal to that of the logistic curve at $x = 0$. Though ostensibly similar in form, there is no simple connection between the probit and sigmoidal logistic function.

8.2.3 Logistic regression

The straight-line fit to binary data can clearly be improved upon. A much better model was discovered long ago when fitting curves to data that saturates. A classic example can be found from chemistry in the form of an autocatalytic reaction in which the concentration of the product slows until all of the reactant is used up.

Equation: The logistic function, which can be used to map $\mathbb{R} \to (0,1)$

$$\text{logistic}(x) := \frac{1}{1+e^{-(\kappa_1 x+\kappa_0)}} \tag{8.4}$$

Observe that the term within the exp() function is the same as our linear regression model. Essentially we are simply squashing a linear regression to now fit between 0 and 1.

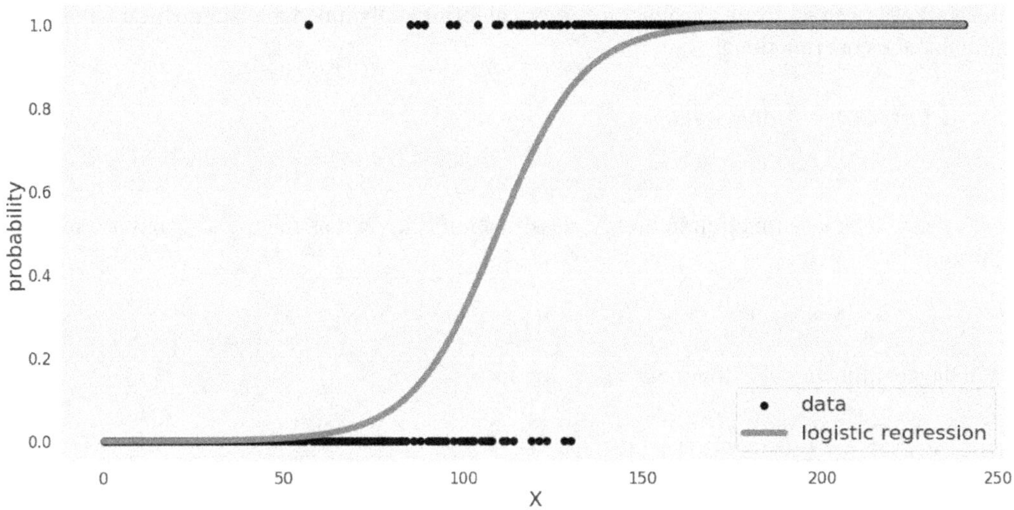

Figure 8.6: Fitting the data with a logistic function

Thus, in linear regression our task is to find the parameters $\hat{\beta}_1$ and $\hat{\beta}_0$ of the straight line that best fits our data.

$$\hat{y}(x) = \hat{\beta}_1 x + \hat{\beta}_0$$

In logistic regression similarly our task is to find the parameters $\hat{\kappa}_1$ and $\hat{\kappa}_0$ of the logistic function that best fits our data

$$\ln\left(\frac{\hat{y}}{1-\hat{y}}\right) = \hat{\kappa}_1 x + \hat{\kappa}_0 \tag{8.5}$$

The LHS of this equation is known as the *log-odds* or the logit link function (g).

Interpretability

Logistic regression, just like its homologue linear regression, has the virtue that its predictions are relatively easy to interpret.

N Jupyter Notebook: Titanic explainability: Why me? asks Miss Doyle

8.3 Log loss function

It is often computationally convenient to use log probability; it is worth reminding ourselves that the probability (of independent events) is multiplicative

$$p(A \cap B) = p(A) \cdot p(B)$$

and we have the logarithmic identity

$$\ln(p(A) \cdot p(B)) = \ln(p(A)) + \ln(p(B))$$

which allows us to go from a product to a more algoritmically amenable summation when we are trying to minimize the cost functional

$$\prod_{i=1}^{n} p(y_i|\mathbf{x}_i) = \sum_{i=1}^{n} \ln(p(y_i|\mathbf{x}_i))$$

Equation: The loss function in binary classification is known as the log loss and is a particular case of the cross entropy loss

$$L_{log} = -y\ln(p(\hat{y})) - (1-y)\ln(1-p(\hat{y})) \tag{8.6}$$

and the cost functional is the mean of the log losses

$$J_{log} = -\frac{1}{n}\sum (y\ln(p(\hat{y})) + (1-y)\ln(1-p(\hat{y}))) \tag{8.7}$$

where $p(\hat{y})$ is the probability of belonging to class 1, and thus $(1-p(\hat{y}))$ is the probability of belonging to class 0. Note that logarithms in the domain (0,1) have a negative range, hence the introduction of a negative sign so as to lead to positive contributions to the cost functional.

Remark: Just as in linear regression here the log loss cost functional is also convex (since the logarithm function is strictly concave), so we can always find the global minimum.

What does this loss function L_{log} look like? If the class of y is 0 then Equation 8.6 reduces to $L_{log} = -\ln(1-p(\hat{y}))$

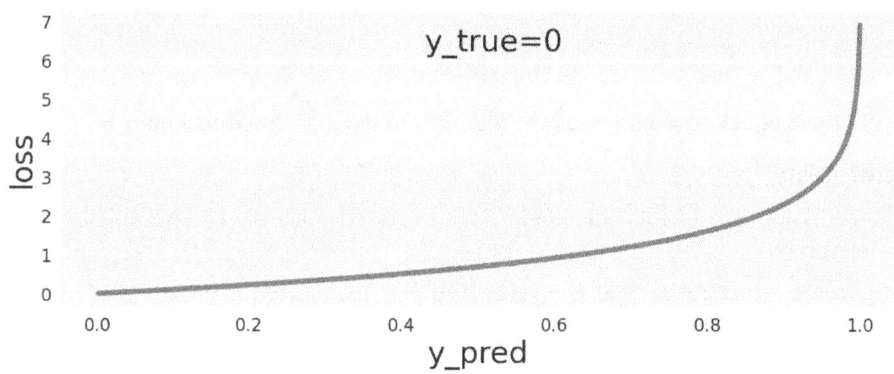

Figure 8.7: The loss for a given predicted probability when the true class is 0.

and if the class y is 1 then we have $L_{log} = -\ln(p(\hat{y}))$

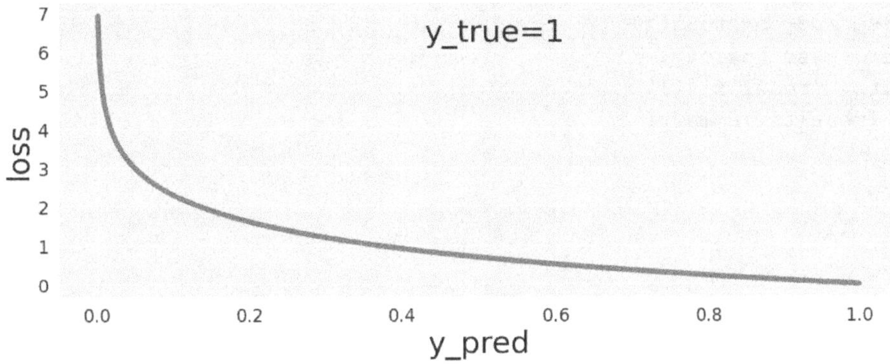

Figure 8.8: The loss for a given predicted probability when the true class is 1.

Note that both Figures 8.7 and 8.8 the loss has been clipped since the log loss for predicting a probability of 1 for an example whose true class is 0 tends to infinity (and vice versa).

8.4 Calculating κ_1 and κ_0

Unlike with β_1 and β_0 for linear regression there is no analytical closed-form solution for obtaining the logistic regression κ_1 and κ_0 coefficients, and iterative quasi-Newton methods such as the Broyden-Fletcher-Goldfarb-Shanno (BFGS) algorithm are used.

8.4.1 Scikit-learn `LogisticRegression`

Sample code

```
from sklearn.linear_model import LogisticRegression

classifier = LogisticRegression(C=np.inf, solver='lbfgs')
classifier.fit(X.reshape(-1, 1), y)
y_pred  = classifier.predict_proba(X.reshape(-1, 1))[:,1]

kappa_1 = classifier.coef_[0]
kappa_0 = classifier.intercept_
```

> Remark: By default the `sklearn LogisticRegression` routine is actually logistic regression + $L2$ (Ridge) regularization. Before scikit-learn version 1.8 in order to use standard logistic regression one must set `penalty=None`, and after version 1.8 one should set `C=np.inf`.

8.4.2 statsmodels `Logit`

Using `statsmodels`

```
import statsmodels.api as sm
```

```
X1 = sm.add_constant(X)
model   = sm.Logit(y, X1)
results = model.fit()
print(results.summary())
```

```
Optimization terminated successfully.
         Current function value: 0.266611
         Iterations 8
                           Logit Regression Results
==============================================================================
Dep. Variable:                      y   No. Observations:                  241
Model:                          Logit   Df Residuals:                      239
Method:                           MLE   Df Model:                            1
Date:                Thu, 25 Sep 2025   Pseudo R-squ.:                  0.6087
Time:                        08:59:48   Log-Likelihood:                -64.253
converged:                       True   LL-Null:                       -164.20
Covariance Type:            nonrobust   LLR p-value:                 2.210e-45
==============================================================================
                 coef    std err          z      P>|z|      [0.025      0.975]
------------------------------------------------------------------------------
const         -5.1132      0.703     -7.271      0.000      -6.491      -3.735
X              0.0504      0.007      7.719      0.000       0.038       0.063
==============================================================================
```

Figure 8.9: statsmodels Logit output example

8.4.3 Gradient descent

One can also find κ_1 and κ_0 via gradient descent. Using the log loss in conjunction with the logistic function we have the cost functional

$$J[\kappa] = \overline{\text{log loss}} = -\frac{1}{n}\sum\left(y\ln(p(\hat{y})) + (1-y)\ln(1-p(\hat{y}))\right) \tag{8.8}$$

where

$$p(\hat{y}) = \sigma(\hat{y}) := \frac{1}{1+e^{-\hat{y}}} = \frac{e^{\hat{y}}}{1+e^{\hat{y}}} \tag{8.9}$$

and where

$$\hat{y} = \kappa_1\mathbf{X} + \kappa_0\mathbf{1} = \mathbf{X}\kappa \tag{8.10}$$

We have

$$\frac{\partial J[\hat{y}]}{\partial \hat{y}} = -\frac{1}{n}\sum\left(\frac{ye^{\hat{y}} + y - e^{\hat{y}}}{1+e^{\hat{y}}}\right) \tag{8.11}$$

which after multiplying by $\frac{e^{-\hat{y}}}{e^{-\hat{y}}}$ gives

$$
\begin{aligned}
\frac{\partial J[\hat{y}]}{\partial \hat{y}} &= -\frac{1}{n}\sum\left(\frac{y+ye^{-\hat{y}}-1}{1+e^{-\hat{y}}}\right) \\
&= -\frac{1}{n}\sum\left(\frac{y(1+e^{-\hat{y}})}{1+e^{-\hat{y}}}-\frac{1}{1+e^{-\hat{y}}}\right) \\
&= -\frac{1}{n}\sum(y-p(\hat{y})) \\
&= \frac{1}{n}\sum(p(\hat{y})-y)
\end{aligned} \tag{8.12}
$$

When expressed in the form of matrices we have

$$
\frac{\partial J[\kappa]}{\partial \kappa} = \frac{1}{n}\mathbf{X}^{\mathsf{T}}\left(\sigma(\mathbf{X}\kappa)-y\right) \tag{8.13}
$$

arriving at the very same expression as that for linear regression

$$
\kappa \leftarrow \kappa - \frac{\eta}{n}\,\mathbf{X}^{\mathsf{T}}\varepsilon \tag{8.14}
$$

where ε is the error associated with each prediction. The python source code is the same as that for linear regression (gist), but where we also make use of

```
def sigmoid(x):
    return 1/(1 + np.exp(-x))
```

8.5 Probabilistic classification baseline model

Equation: Our probabilistic classification baseline model, which we shall call $\hat{y}_0$, is given by the probability of seeing the minority class ($y = 1$):

$$
\hat{y}_0 := \frac{n_{rows}|y=1}{n_{rows}} \equiv \bar{y} \tag{8.15}
$$

We can also take this opportunity to introduce the log of the odds (O) of seeing class 1, or logit, and its inverse

$$
\text{logit} = \ln\left(\frac{n_{rows}|y=1}{n_{rows}|y=0}\right) \tag{8.16}
$$

we can convert this log odds into a probability via the inverse transform, known as the logistic

$$
\hat{y}_0 = \frac{\exp(\text{logit})}{1+\exp(\text{logit})} \quad \forall\, \hat{y} \tag{8.17}
$$

For example, for a balanced dataset where there are equal numbers of examples of each class our baseline model will be $\ln(1) = 0$ thus $\exp(0)/(1+\exp(0)) = 0.5$. For an imbalanced dataset where 10% of the classes are 1 and 90% are class 0 we have $\ln(1/9) \approx -2.2$ thus $\exp(-2.2)/(1+\exp(-2.2)) = 0.1$.

For example, to calculate the baseline log loss

```
from sklearn.metrics import log_loss as metric

y_train_mean = np.full( len(y_validation), np.mean(y_train) )
metric(y_validation, y_train_mean)
```

8.6 Dichotomization

Dichotomization is a post-processing step applied to our probabilistic calculations; transforming an analogue input (real probabilities) to a digital output (binary classes). This is achieved by via the decision threshold, often set to a default value of $p = 0.5$. Predicted probabilities below the threshold now become class 0, and predicted probabilities above the threshold become class 1.

8.6.1 Linear classification: the perceptron

We can take our linear probability model seen in section 8.2.1 and encapsulate it within a Heaviside step function (H)

$$\hat{y}(x) = H(p(x) - d) \tag{8.18}$$

where

$$H(x) := \begin{cases} 1, & x \geq 0 \\ 0, & x < 0 \end{cases}$$

and where p is given by

$$p(x) = \hat{\beta}_1 x + \hat{\beta}_0 \tag{8.19}$$

where d is the value of our decision threshold. This is known as the perceptron classifier, introduced in 1958 by Frank Rosenblatt[2].

```
def perceptron(X, beta, d = 0.5):
    X1 = np.column_stack((X, np.ones(len(X))))
    p = X1 @ beta # p is our probability
    y = np.heaviside( p-d, 0)
    return y
```

8.6.2 Logistic classification

It is important to emphasize that with logistic regression, as the very name suggests, we are still performing regression, this time in probability space, *i.e.* the predictions lie on the surface of a probability simplex, having a dimension of $n - 1$ where n is the number of classes, rather than in real space as per linear regression. This only becomes classification upon the application of a decision threshold to assign class labels to our predicted probabilities.

[2] Rosenblatt *"The perceptron: A probabilistic model for information storage and organization in the brain."*, Psychological Review **65** pp. 386-408 (1958)

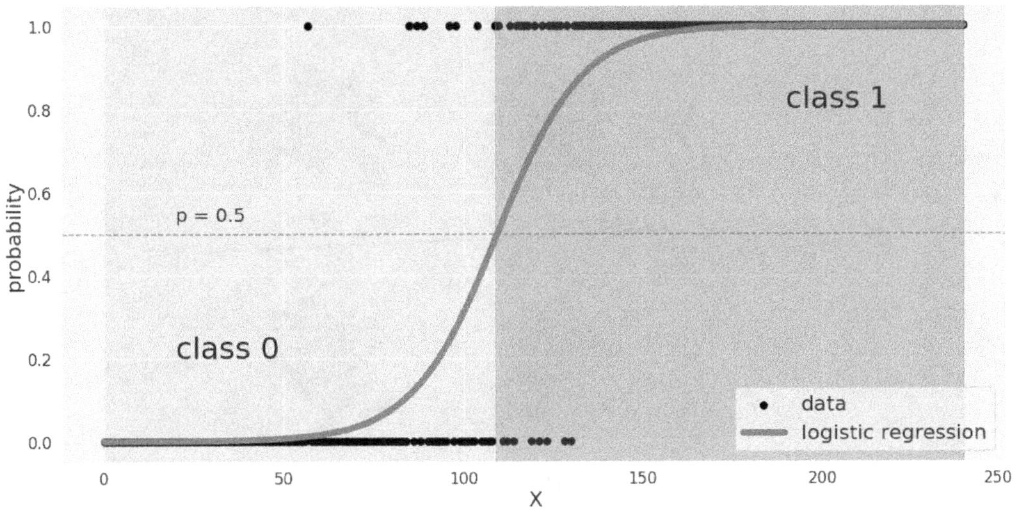

Figure 8.10: Dichotomized logistic fit

> Remark: It is worth mentioning that, for small tabular datasets, logistic regression has been found to hold its own against heavyweight AutoML routines, and should be the first port of call.[a]
>
> [a]Ricardo Knauer, Erik Rodner "*Squeezing Lemons with Hammers: An Evaluation of AutoML and Tabular Deep Learning for Data-Scarce Classification Applications*", arXiv:2405.07662 (2024)

8.7 Logistic regression and the XOR problem

In Fig 8.11 we fit a logistic regression to a non-linearly separable XOR-like dataset. In this dataset each of the four clusters, two clusters representing class 0 and the other two clusters representing class 1, have exactly the same number of points, thus simply by looking at the $p = 0.5$ decision boundary we can see that we have an accuracy score of 0.5 (*i.e.* half of the points are mis-classified). Indeed, for this particular fit our probabilities only ranged between $p_{min} = 0.48$ and $p_{max} = 0.52$. indicating just how little confidence there is in said fit.

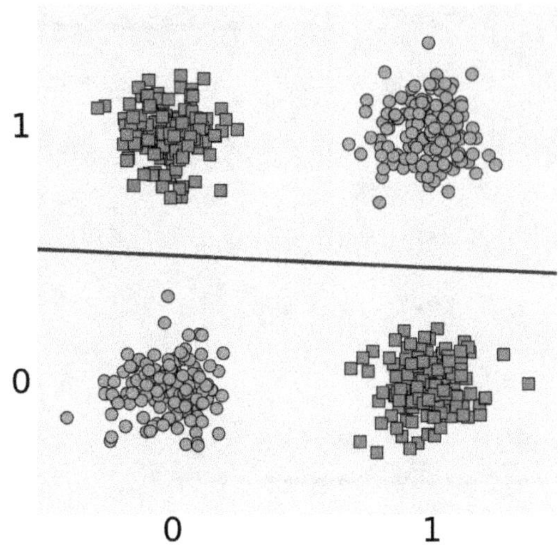

Figure 8.11: An example $p = 0.5$ decision boundary resulting from a logistic regression fit to the XOR dataset.

To solve this particular problem we can use feature engineering to go from 2-dimensions (*i.e.* the features x_1 and x_2) to 3-dimensions by creating the additional new feature $x_1 \times x_2$, for which the classes can now be perfectly separated with a plane.

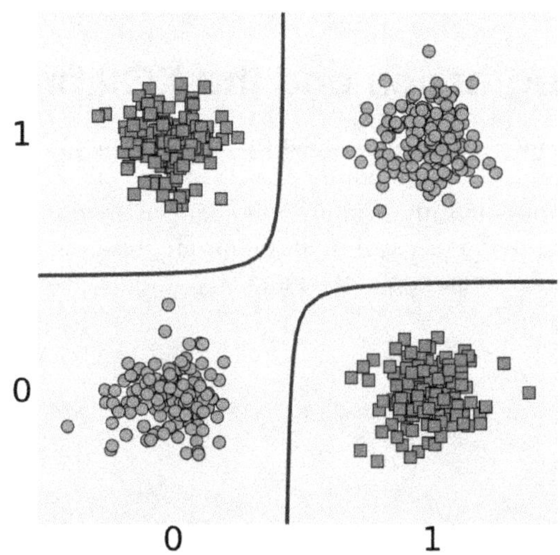

Figure 8.12: A logistic regression fit to the the 3-dimensional transformed XOR dataset. We see that when projected back into 2-dimensions the $p = 0.5$ decision boundary is now non-linear.

Indeed feature engineering is one of the most valuable tools in machine learning.

8.8 Decision tree classifier

Just as with regression, we can also perform classification using decision trees. Again we shall use a toy dataset

X	y_true
1	0
2	0
4	1
5	1

Table 8.1: Toy classification dataset.

and here is our decision tree fit to the data

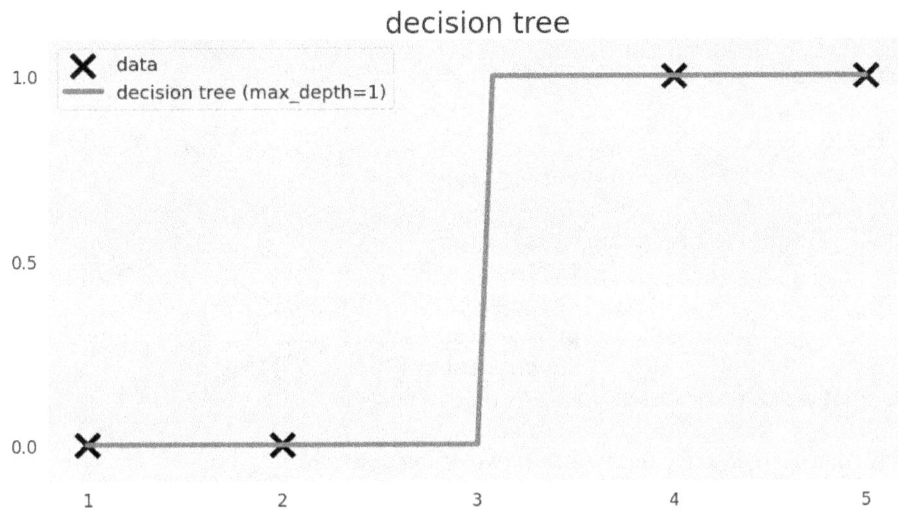

Figure 8.13: Decision tree classifier results for the toy dataset

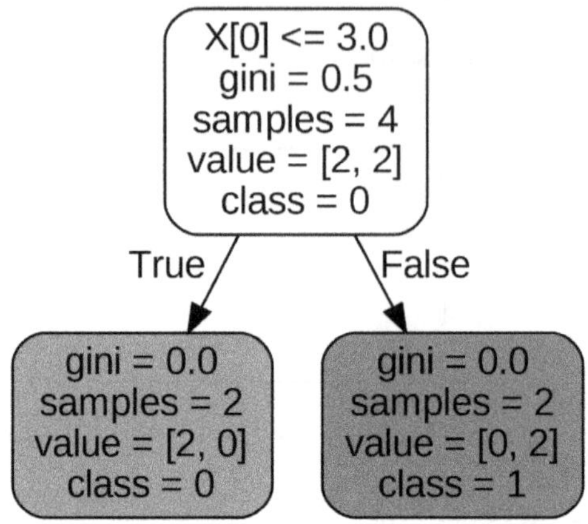

Figure 8.14: `graphviz` of our decision tree classifier for the toy dataset.

Sample code

```
import graphviz
from sklearn.tree import export_graphviz

dot_data = export_graphviz(classifier,
                           filled=True,
                           rounded=True,
                           proportion=False,
                           class_names=['0', '1'])
graphviz.Source(dot_data)
```

Indeed we can even describe our model in two sentences:

- if x is less than 3, $\hat{y}$ is 0
- if x is greater than 3, $\hat{y}$ is 1

This time instead of the squared error loss function used in regression we now use the *Gini diversity* (I_G) as the splitting function.

8.8.0.1 Splitting criteria: Gini diversity and Shannon entropy

Equation: The Gini index of diversity (I_G), named after Corrado Gini, is given by

$$I_G(p) := 1 - \sum_{i=1}^{J} p_i^2 \qquad \in [0, 0.5] \tag{8.20}$$

where p_i is the fraction of samples in class i. For binary classification this becomes

$$I_G = 1 - p(\text{zero})^2 - p(\text{one})^2 \tag{8.21}$$

The less diverse the configuration, the smaller the Gini index

mixture	Gini index
0 0 0 1 1 1	$I_G = 1 - \left(\frac{3}{6}\right)^2 - \left(\frac{3}{6}\right)^2 = 0.5$
0 0 0 1 1	$I_G = 1 - \left(\frac{3}{5}\right)^2 - \left(\frac{2}{5}\right)^2 = 0.48$
0 0 0 1	$I_G = 1 - \left(\frac{3}{4}\right)^2 - \left(\frac{1}{4}\right)^2 = 0.375$
0 0 0	$I_G = 1 - \left(\frac{3}{3}\right)^2 - \left(\frac{0}{3}\right)^2 = 0$
1 1 1	$I_G = 1 - \left(\frac{0}{3}\right)^2 - \left(\frac{3}{3}\right)^2 = 0$

Table 8.2: Example Gini index calculations

An alternative to using the CART based Gini diversity criterion is the Shannon information entropy (I_E) as used in the Iterative Dichotomiser 3 (ID3) and C4.5 classifiers originally developed by John Ross Quinlan.

Equation: The Shannon information entropy (I_E), named after Claude Shannon because of his 1948 paper *"A mathematical theory of communication"*, is given by

$$I_E(p) := -\sum_{i=1}^{J} p_i \log_2(p_i) \qquad \in [0,1] \tag{8.22}$$

As with regression trees (see Eq. 7.24) the improvement afforded by performing a particular split (ΔI) here is given by

$$\Delta I = I_{(\text{before split})} - \left(\frac{N_{LHS}}{N} I_{(LHS)} + \frac{N_{RHS}}{N} I_{(RHS)} \right) \tag{8.23}$$

where N is the number of samples before splitting. One then selects the split that offers the largest improvement. In Figure 8.15 we compare the Gini and Shannon functions.

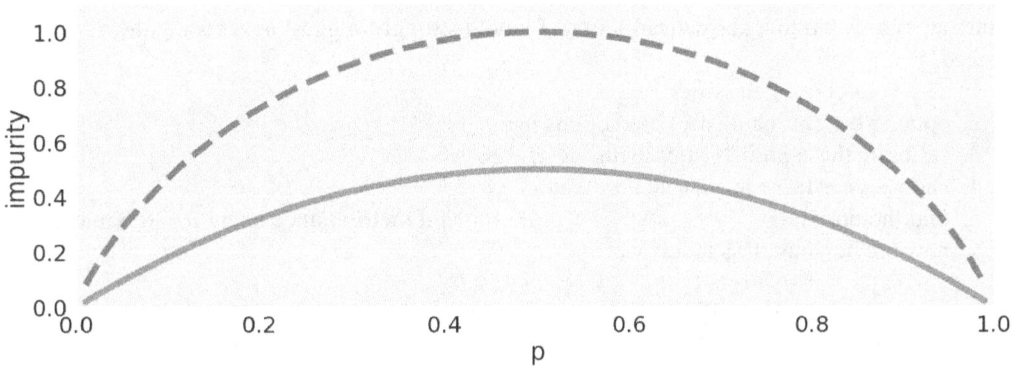

Figure 8.15: Plot of the Gini (orange) and Shannon (dashed green) functions.

However, it has been found that empirically there is little to choose between these two criteria in terms of classifier performance.[3]. Indeed in the book Classification and Regression Trees it was observed that *"...the*

[3] Laura Elena Raileanu, Kilian Stoffel *"Theoretical Comparison between the Gini Index and Information Gain Criteria"*, Ann. Math. Art. Int. **41** pp. 77-93 (2004)

tentative conclusion we have reached is that within a wide range of splitting criteria the properties of the final tree selected are surprisingly insensitive to the choice of splitting rule.".

N Jupyter Notebook: Titanic: some sex, a bit of class, and a tree...

> Remark: The Shannon information entropy splitting criterion corresponds to minimizing the log loss function, and the Gini diversity splitting criterion corresponds to minimizing the squared error loss[a].
>
> [a]Painsky, Wornell *"On the Universality of the Logistic Loss Function"*, arXiv:1805.03804 (2018)

8.8.0.2 Cross entropy and the Kullback-Leibler (KL) divergence

The cross entropy, $H(p,q)$, performs a comparison between two distributions (configurations), p and q, and is given by

$$H(p,q) = -\sum_{i=1}^{J} p_i \log_2(q_i) \tag{8.24}$$

and the Kullback-Leibler (KL) divergence is defined as

$$D_{KL}(p,q) := -\sum_{i=1}^{J} p_i \log_2\left(\frac{q_i}{p_i}\right) \equiv H(p,q) - I_E(p) \tag{8.25}$$

i.e. the difference between the cross entropy and the Shannon entropy. Via the log-sum inequality it can be shown that the KL divergence is at a global minima when $q_i = p_i \; \forall i$. Note that the KL divergence is asymmetric, *i.e.* $D_{KL}(p,q) \neq D_{KL}(q,p)$, hence is unsuitable as a supervised learning metric.

8.9 Classifier output: `predict` vs `predict_proba`

Most scikit-learn classifiers come with two prediction methods; the `predict` method will directly return class predictions, and `predict_proba` will return probabilities (note: these are not strictly $p(y|\mathbf{X})$ but rather are more akin to a normalized score). I would strongly suggest never using the `predict` method and instead:

1. `fit` your chosen classifier
2. obtain your (probabilistic) predictions using `.predict_proba()`
3. calibrate these probabilities using Venn-ABERS
4. choose your favorite classification metric
5. find the optimal dicotomization threshold for said metric (since using $p = 0.5$ may not be optimal)
6. now create your class labels via:

```
y_class = (y_prob[:,1] > threshold)*1
```

However, as data scientists the question arises as to whether we should actually create class labels at all (see the paper *"The Cost of Dichotomization"* by Jacob Cohen). For example, if our model is to be used as part of an automated process, such as the classic `SPAM/NOT SPAM` filter then fine. But when it comes to more serious issues such as medical conditions we should limit ourselves to providing the calibrated probabilities, and leave the decision taking process (for example whether to perform further tests, or even suggest treatment) to healthcare professionals (see the wonderful article *"Classification vs. Prediction"* by Frank E. Harrell Jr.).

8.10 Probabilistic metrics

8.10.1 Strictly proper scoring rules

A proper scoring rule is one for which the better our predictions (`y_pred`) with respect to the ground truth values (`y_true`) the better (*i.e.* smaller) our score

$$\text{score}(\texttt{y\_true}, \texttt{y\_true}) \leq \text{score}(\texttt{y\_pred}, \texttt{y\_true}) \quad \forall\, \texttt{y\_pred}, \texttt{y\_true} \tag{8.26}$$

A strictly proper scoring rule is one for which the very best possible score is obtained iff `y_pred` = `y_true`. In other words, there should be no way to construct a bad set of predictions that will return a better score than a good set of predictions would. Just as in regression, the most reasonable metrics are those that are aligned with the loss function and this leads to a set of strictly proper scoring rules[4]. Out of those those of particular note are the logarithmic score and the Brier score. The Brier score (B) is given by

$$B = \frac{1}{n}\sum_{i=1}^{n}(y_i - \hat{p}_i)^2 \qquad \in [0,1] \tag{8.27}$$

where y_i is the true class label ($y \in \{0,1\}$) and p_i is the predicted probability of $y_i = 1$.

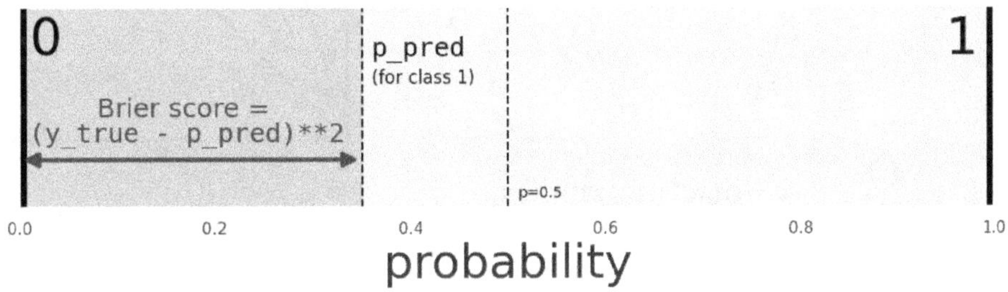

Figure 8.16: The Brier score (here shown for an individual prediction) is essentially the mean squared error (MSE).

Indeed the Brier score is analogous to the mean squared error (MSE) metric seen in regression. The perfect prediction will result in a Brier score of 0, and the worst possible score is a Brier score of 1.

> Remark: For binary classification with the Brier score one would obtain ones probabilities by performing regression using the squared error ($L2$) loss function.

It is safe to assume that ones classifier results are initially uncalibrated, and post hoc calibration will lead to an improvement in these metrics, indeed calibration is an absolutely essential step to perform in the classification process.

8.10.2 Calibration-refinement decomposition

Proper losses can be decomposed into[5]

$$\mathbb{E}(L) = \underbrace{\mathbb{E}(D_L)}_{\text{calibration error}} + \underbrace{\mathbb{E}(H_L)}_{\text{refinement error}} \tag{8.28}$$

[4]Gneiting, Raftery *"Strictly Proper Scoring Rules, Prediction, and Estimation"*, Journal of the American Statistical Association **102** pp. 359-378 (2007)

[5]Jochen Bröcker *"Reliability, Sufficiency, and the Decomposition of Proper Scores"*, arXiv:0806.0813 (2008)

where D_L is the divergence where $D_L(p,q) := L(p,q) - L(q,q)$ and H_L is the entropy $H(q) := L(q,q)$.

8.10.3 AUC ROC score

The AUC ROC is shorthand for the area under the receiver operating characteristic curve, a plot of the rate of true positives against false positives, and has it origins in assessing the ability to discriminate between a signal and random interference.[6] The better the classifier the more it is able to discriminate the two classes; the distance between the means of the distributions in units of σ is called the discriminability (or sensitivity) index (d') and a distance of 0 indicates that the classifier cannot distinguish between the two classes, whereas larger discriminability index values indicates better separation. This is shown on the LHS of Figure 8.17. On the RHS is the corresponding plot of the true positive rate against the false positive rate and it is the area under this curve that becomes the AUC ROC score[7].

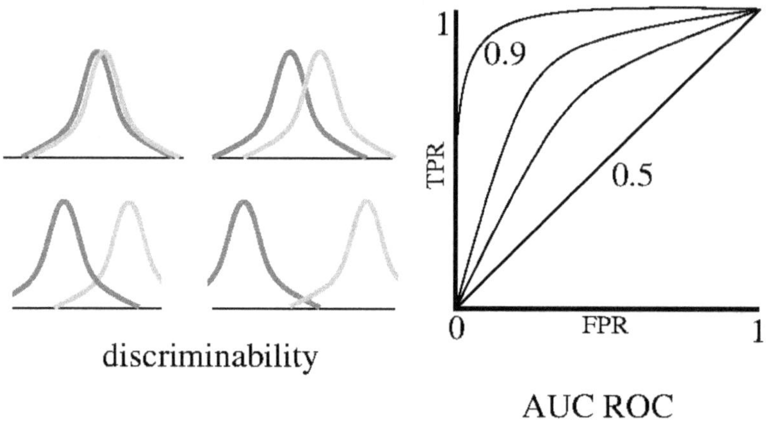

Figure 8.17: Discriminability index and the ROC curve.

An AUC ROC score of 0.5 is no better than random guessing, whilst a value of 1 represents perfect classification (`from sklearn.metrics import roc_auc_score`).

Equation:

$$\text{gini} = 2 \times \text{AUC} - 1 \tag{8.29}$$

Remark: It is worth stressing that the AUC ROC is a 'ranking' score measuring the discriminability between classes, and is in no way assessing the actual quality of the predicted probabilities; it is entirely possible for a poorly calibrated model to return a good AUC ROC score and *vice versa*[a]. In view of this, despite its popularity, the use of the AUC ROC score should be discouraged.

[a]Lobo, Jiménez-Valverde, Real *"AUC: a misleading measure of the performance of predictive distribution models"*, *Global Ecology and Biogeography* **17** *(2007)*

[6]Peterson, Birdsall *"The Theory Of Signal Detectability. Part 1. The General Theory"*, Technical Report No. 13, Electronic Defence Group, University of Michigan (1953)

[7]Tom Fawcett *"An introduction to ROC analysis"*, Pattern Recognition Letters **27** pp. 861-874 (2006)

8.11 Classifier calibration

As mentioned, for many classifiers `predict_proba` returns a relative score[8] Indeed one would do well to assume *a priori* that ones initial calculation, regardless of the technique used, is poorly calibrated. However, for cost-sensitive decision making it is imperative to work with good probabilities. For example, which fraud case is most worth investigating first?
uncalibrated:

- 500K€ fraud with $p = 0.61 \rightarrow$ expected cost = 305K
- 1M€ fraud with $p = 0.27 \rightarrow$ expected cost = 270K

calibrated:

- 500K€ fraud with $p = 0.59 \rightarrow$ expected cost = 295K
- 1M€ fraud with $p = 0.34 \rightarrow$ expected cost = 340K

We can see that incorrect probabilities will lead to incorrect decisions. Classifier probabilities are calibrated if they are unbiased conditional on their own predictions $\mathbb{E}[Y|p] = p$. One would do well to assume that all classifiers will benefit from calibration[9]. Predicted probabilities can be calibrated via a correction function fitted to empirical data so as to reflect the true probabilities[10].

8.11.1 Reliability diagrams

Visually one can inspect calibration via a reliability diagram as shown in Figure 8.18

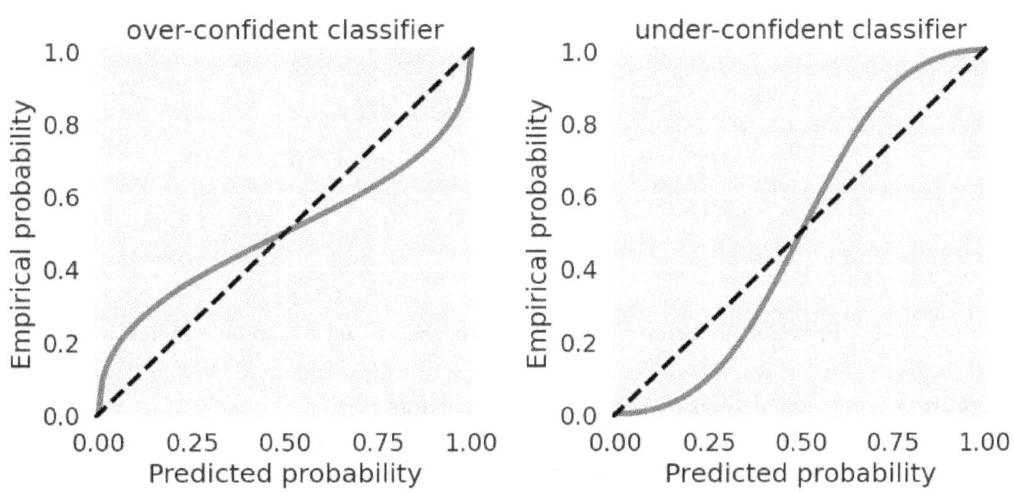

Figure 8.18: Miscalibration: over- and under-confident classifiers.

Some of the many post-hoc probability calibration techniques are:

- **Platt scaling** - this is a two-parameter (A and B) sigmoid correction, originally designed for the (underconfident) SVM classifier.

$$p_{calib} = \frac{1}{1 + \exp(Ap + B)} \tag{8.30}$$

[8]Sweidan, Johansson *"Probabilistic Prediction in scikit-learn"*, diva2:1603345 (2021)
[9]Cohen, Goldszmidt *"Properties and Benefits of Calibrated Classifiers"*, PKDD 2004, LNAI 3202, pp. 125-136 (2004)
[10]Niculescu-Mizil, Caruana *"Predicting good probabilities with supervised learning"*, ICML '05, pp. 625-632 (2005)

However, Platt scaling has the undesirable inclination to actually uncalibrate a well-calibrated classifier, and beta calibration is the superior alternative when working with small datasets. The beta calibration map has three adjustable parameters that need to be fitted, A, B and C where $A, B \geq 0$ and is given by

$$p_{calib} = \frac{1}{1+1/\left(\exp(C)\frac{p^A}{(1-p)^B}\right)} \tag{8.31}$$

- **Isotonic scaling** - non-parametric step-wise monotonic regression fitted to class 1 for $P(1)$ values
- **Venn-ABERS** method - double isotonic; fitted to both class 1 and class 0, then merge the two via

$$p = \frac{\text{fit}_{(1)}}{(1-\text{fit}_{(0)})+\text{fit}_{(1)}} \tag{8.32}$$

8.11.2 Venn-ABERS calibration

For the Venn-ABERS method [11, 12, 13] what do the two fits $p1$ and $p0$ look like?

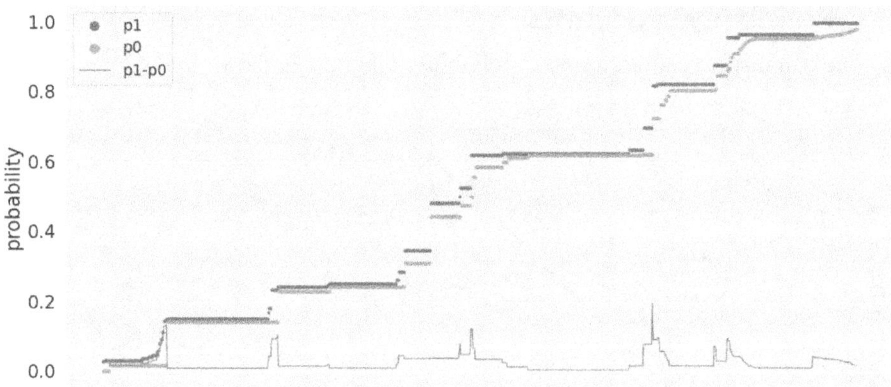

Figure 8.19: Venn-ABERS: plots for the $p0$ and $p1$ isotonic regressions.

There are two implementations of Venn-ABERS predictors

- **IVAP**: inductive (`"prefit"`) which requires a hold-out calibration set
- **CVAP**: cross-conformal: fit and calibrate k times via `StratifiedKFold`

First we install the `venn-abers` routine, written by Ivan Petej

```
!pip install -q venn-abers
from venn_abers import VennAbersCalibrator
```

IVAP example: split/`"prefit"` Venn-ABERS

```
p_cal  = classifier.predict_proba(X_calib)
p_test = classifier.predict_proba(X_test)
```

[11] Vovk, Shafer, Nouretdinov "*Self-calibrating Probability Forecasting*", NIPS'03 pp. 1133-1140 (2003)
[12] Vovk, Petej "*Venn-Abers Predictors*", arXiv:1211.0025 (2014)
[13] Vovk, Petej, Fedorova "*Large-scale probabilistic prediction with and without validity guarantees*", arXiv:1511.00213 (2015)

```
VAC = VennAbersCalibrator()
predictions = VAC.predict_proba(p_cal = p_cal,
                                y_cal = y_calib.values,
                                p_test = p_test)[:,1]
```

> Remark: For the IVAP calibration dataset (`X_calib`, `y_calib`) I would suggest for good results setting aside between 1000 and 2000 rows of data from the training data. For more details on calibration sample sizes see Table 1 in *"Universal distribution of the empirical coverage in split conformal prediction"*.

CVAP example: cross-conformal Venn-ABERS (no hold-out calibration set required)

```
VAC = VennAbersCalibrator(estimator=classifier,
                          inductive=False,
                          n_splits=5)

VAC.fit(X_train, y_train)
predictions = VAC.predict_proba(X_test)[:,1]
```

In Figure 8.20 we have the reliability diagram for an XGBoost calculation. We can see that it is clearly over-confident in its predictions (metric results: log loss 0.799, Brier score 0.190).

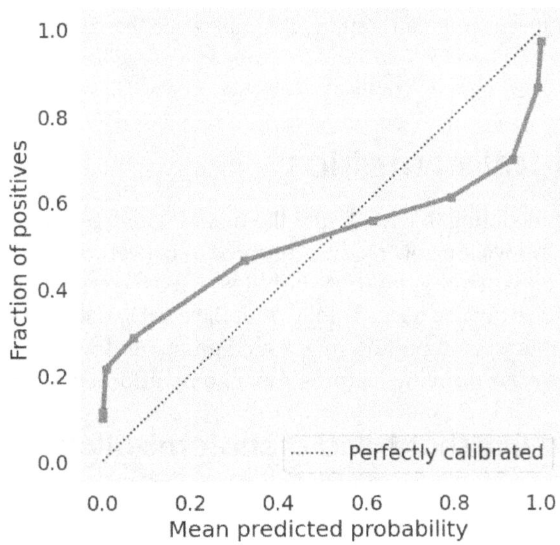

Figure 8.20: The reliability diagram for an XGBoost fit without calibration.

We now perform calibrated cross-conformal Venn-ABERS with the same estimator and the results show a marked improvement; log loss 0.496 and Brier score 0.163, as well as can be seen visually in Figure 8.21.

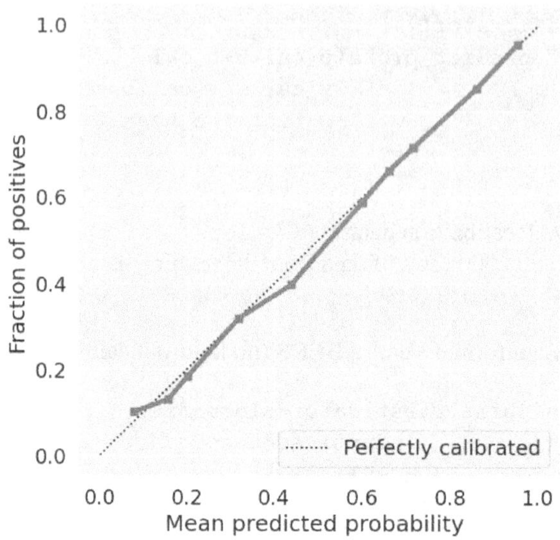

Figure 8.21: XGBoost fit with cross Venn-ABERS calibration.

N Jupyter Notebook: Classifier calibration using Venn-ABERS

For a head-to-head comparison of calibration techniques see the paper Valery Manokhin, Daniel Grønhaug "*Classifier Calibration at Scale: An Empirical Study of Model-Agnostic Post-Hoc Methods*", arXiv:2601.19944 (2026).

8.12 Classification metrics

Once we have finished modeling, having found the model with the lowest cost (for example in terms of the log loss or the Brier score) we are now ready to proceed to convert our probabilities into classes by assigning labels. The following classification metrics should be used for reporting purposes (and not as ersatz cost functionals), and should always be quoted along with the corresponding baseline performance. For example, a model having an accuracy score of 94% may sound great, until we learn that the baseline score was 91%, and at the end of the day our machine learning model only afforded a modest 3% improvement.

8.12.1 Decision threshold and dichotomization

Classification metrics work with class labels rather than the underlying probabilities. By default the decision threshold for converting probabilities into class labels is usually set at $p = 0.5$. However, optimizing the location of this threshold can lead to improvements in the aforementioned metrics. In Figure 8.22 we schematically envisage a histogram of our probabilistic predictions (for example from the scikit `predict_proba` method) along with a vertical dashed line representing the decision threshold. Predictions below the decision threshold are classed as `0` and predictions above the decision threshold are classed as `1`. We can see that negative class examples that lie above the decision threshold become false positives, and positive class examples that lie below the decision threshold become false negatives.

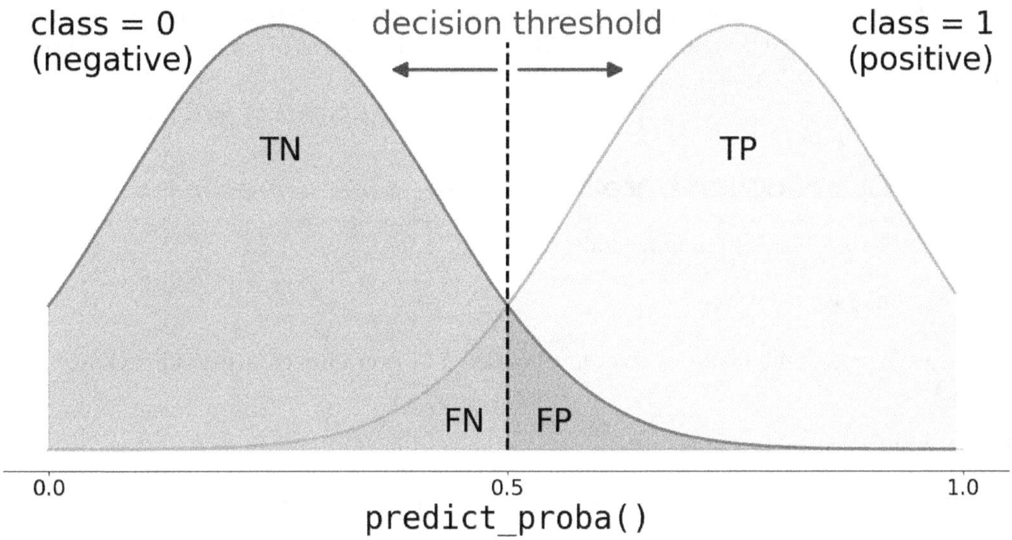

Figure 8.22: The decision threshold allows us to assign a class label to our predicted probability.

Sample code

If one is using a hold-out validation dataset then one can find the optimal threshold via the following code, which is nothing more fancy than a simple brute-force scan over a range of thresholds (gist):

```
def get_optimal_threshold(y_true, y_pred_proba, metric):
    score = 0.
    optimal_score = 0.
    thresholds = np.linspace(0, 1, 201)
    for threshold in range(len(thresholds)):
        new_score = metric(y_true, y_pred_proba >= thresholds[threshold])
        if new_score > score:
            score = new_score
            optimal_threshold = thresholds[threshold]
            optimal_score = new_score
    return optimal_threshold, optimal_score

# classification metric of choice
from sklearn.metrics import accuracy_score as metric

optimal_threshold, optimal_score = get_optimal_threshold(y_true,
                                          y_pred_proba, metric)

print("optimal decision threshold:", optimal_threshold)
print("optimal metric score:", optimal_score)
```

Note that the optimal threshold is metric specific; the ideal threshold for the accuracy score may well be very different from the ideal threshold for the F_1 score *etc.* Interestingly it has been observed that for the F_1 score *"...if the classifier outputs are well-calibrated conditional probabilities, then the optimal threshold is half the* *optimal F_1 score."*[14] with the implication being that the default setting of 0.5 is never the best threshold.

If one wishes to find the optimal threshold via cross-validation as of version 1.5 scikit-learn now includes the `TunedThresholdClassifierCV`.

N Jupyter Notebook: False positives, false negatives and the discrimination threshold.

8.12.2 Classification baseline model

Equation: Classification baseline model

$$\hat{y} = 0 \ \forall \ \hat{y} \tag{8.33}$$

We always predict the majority class label (often 0 by convention). This is also known as the ZeroR model.

For example, to calculate the baseline accuracy score

```
from sklearn.metrics import accuracy_score as metric

y_baseline = np.zeros( len(y_validation) )
metric(y_validation, y_baseline)
```

8.12.3 Confusion matrix

For binary labels there are four possible classifications

false positive (FP)	$y = 0$ and $\hat{y} = 1$
false negative (FN)	$y = 1$ and $\hat{y} = 0$
true positive (TP)	$y = 1$ and $\hat{y} = 1$
true negative (TN)	$y = 0$ and $\hat{y} = 0$

Table 8.3: The four possible binary classification assignments.

which are often presented in what is known as a contingency table or *confusion matrix* (see Fig. 8.23).

[14] Chase Lipton, Elkan, Narayanaswamy *"Thresholding Classifiers to Maximize F1 Score"*, arXiv:1402.1892 (2014)

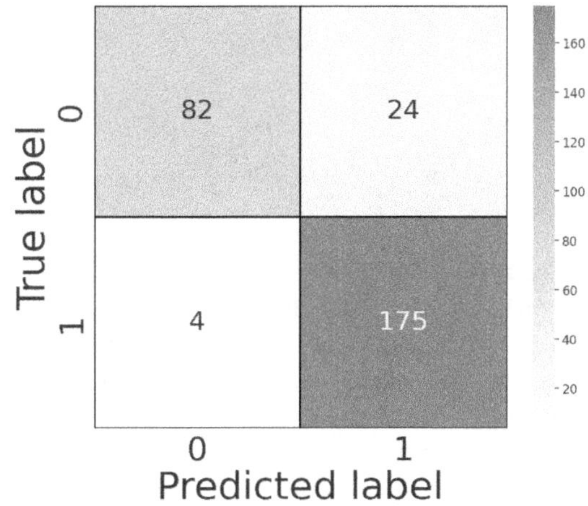

Figure 8.23: A example of a confusion matrix.

The true values are along the main diagonal, here TN=82, TP=175, and the off-diagonal has the false values; FN=4 and FP=24. If the classification were perfect the off-diagonal elements would all be zeros.

N Jupyter Notebook: "Titanic: In all the confusion..."

Sample code

```
from sklearn.metrics import confusion_matrix, ConfusionMatrixDisplay

cm = confusion_matrix(y_true, y_pred, labels=classifier.classes_)
disp = ConfusionMatrixDisplay(confusion_matrix=cm,
                              display_labels=classifier.classes_)
disp.plot();
```

8.12.4 Accuracy score

The accuracy score is the most popular, although somewhat blunt, classification metric; it is simply the fraction of correctly classified examples, *i.e.*

$$\text{accuracy} := \frac{TN+TP}{TN+FP+FN+TP} \quad \in [0,1] \tag{8.34}$$

The baseline accuracy score for a classification problem corresponds to the fraction of the majority class in the dataset.

We can see that the accuracy score is only a reasonable metric if one is working with a balanced dataset. For imbalanced data one encounters the *accuracy paradox* in which our baseline model performs increasingly well the more imbalanced the data. Be very wary of any study that reports the accuracy score and check the imbalance of the dataset to get an idea of the baseline accuracy.

8.12.4.1 Baseline corrected accuracy score

When using the accuracy score, in order to focus purely on model performance it may be convenient to discard the baseline contribution altogether, leading to the baseline corrected accuracy score (BCAS)

Sample code

(gist)

```
import numpy as np

def BCAS(y_validation, y_pred):
    label, count = np.unique(y_validation, return_counts=True)
    most_frequent_class = label[np.argmax(count)]
    y_baseline = np.full(len(y_validation), most_frequent_class)
    as_baseline = np.mean(y_validation == y_baseline)
    as_predicted = np.mean(y_validation == y_pred)
    return (as_predicted - as_baseline)
```

8.12.5 Precision and recall

The precision metric favours few false positives. A use case for precision could be in classifying whether a student text is a case of plagiarism or not; we would rather not falsely accuse someone, so we would like as few false positives as possible.

$$\text{precision} := \frac{TP}{TP+FP} \qquad \in [0,1] \tag{8.35}$$

The recall metric favours few false negatives

$$\text{recall} := \frac{TP}{TP+FN} \qquad \in [0,1] \tag{8.36}$$

A use case of recall could be in initial cancer screening tests; we would rather err on the side of caution and try to catch all of the subjects that may have cancer, thus we would rather have false positives than let one false negative slip through.

However, both of these metrics can be trivially gamed to achieve perfect scores; the precision by predicting `0` for everything and a `1` for the single most probable example, and the recall simply by always predicting `1`, thus these metrics are of little use when reported alone.

8.12.6 F_1 score

The F_1 score is the harmonic mean of the precision and recall metrics:

$$F_1 := 2\frac{\text{precision} \times \text{recall}}{\text{precision} + \text{recall}} = \frac{2TP}{2TP+FP+FN} \qquad \in [0,1] \tag{8.37}$$

It is worth observing that the F_1 score does not take into account the number of true negatives (TN). This metric is available in scikit-learn via `from sklearn.metrics import f1_score` or as part of a `classification_report`. (Note: The F_1 score is a special case of the F_β score where $\beta = 1$).

8.12.7 Negative rates

The precision and recall can be considered to be positive rates, and there are also two negative rates:

$$\text{specificity} := \frac{TN}{TN+FP} \qquad \in [0,1] \tag{8.38}$$

and

$$\text{negative predictive value} := \frac{TN}{TN+FN} \qquad \in [0,1] \tag{8.39}$$

8.12.8 Matthews correlation coefficient (MCC)

The Matthews correlation coefficient (MCC), created in 1912 by George Udny Yule,[15] ranges form -1 to 1, where 1 is a perfect prediction.

$$\text{MCC} := \frac{TP \times TN - FP \times FN}{\sqrt{(TP+FP)(TP+FN)(TN+FP)(TN+FN)}} \qquad \in [-1,1] \tag{8.40}$$

The baseline score, where we predict the negative class for everything so there are neither any TP nor FP, the numerator then becomes zero and hence we have MCC$=0$. The MCC is arguably one of the best metrics for assessing binary classification performance[16] as it takes into account not only both of the positive rates but also both of the negative rates.

8.13 Multiclass classification

8.13.1 One-vs-rest

Say instead of binary classification ($\{0,1\}$) we now have three classes: $\{0,1,2\}$. The *one-vs-rest* technique involves training as many binary classifiers as there are classes, where we decompose the data as follows:

- classifier 1: treat class 0 now as class 1, and both classes 1 and 2 as class 0
- classifier 2: treat class 1 as class 1, and both classes 0 and 2 as class 0
- classifier 3: treat class 2 now as class 1, and both classes 0 and 1 as class 0

The final classification result is given by that of the classifier with the highest probability score.

> Example If the kind reader will permit the anthropomorphization, say we have a row of test data whose ground truth value corresponds to class 2. We show this row to classifier 1, which was specifically trained to detect class 0 as the positive class, and it says "My prediction for this row is 0.325 thus it is not an example of class 0". We then show this row to classifier 2, which was trained specifically to detect class 1, and it says "My prediction for this row is 0.221 thus it is not an example of class 1". Finally, we show this row to classifier 3, which was specifically trained to detect class 2, and it says "My prediction for this row is 0.827, I really think what we are seeing here is an example of class 2".

8.13.2 Multinomial logistic regression

The general form of logistic regression for N mutually independent classes is given by

$$p(y_i = \text{class } n|X_i) = \frac{e^{\kappa^n X}}{\sum_{m=0}^{N-1} e^{\kappa^m X}} \tag{8.41}$$

where the RHS is the normalized exponential, often known as the softmax function. In the case of binary logistic regression, where $N=2$, we have

$$p(y_i = \text{class } 1|X_i) = \frac{e^{\kappa^1 X}}{e^{\kappa^0 X} + e^{\kappa^1 X}}$$

and

$$p(y_i = \text{class } 0|X_i) = \frac{e^{\kappa^0 X}}{e^{\kappa^0 X} + e^{\kappa^1 X}}$$

[15] G. Udny Yule *"On the Methods of Measuring Association Between Two Attributes"*, Journal of the Royal Statistical Society **75** 579-652 (1912)

[16] Davide Chicco, Giuseppe Jurman *"The Matthews correlation coefficient (MCC) should replace the ROC AUC as the standard metric for assessing binary classification"*, BioData Mining **16** 4 (2023)

Given the condition that the sum of all of the probabilities is 1, leading to

$$p(y_i = \text{class } 0|X_i) = 1 - p(y_i = \text{class } 1|X_i)$$

we can do away with overspecification by arbitrarily choosing to set $\kappa^0 = 0$, thus recovering the familiar logistic function

$$p(y_i = \text{class } 1|X_i) = \frac{e^{\kappa^1 X}}{1 + e^{\kappa^1 X}} = \frac{1}{1 + e^{-(\kappa^1 X)}}$$

In view of the similarity between the softmax function and the Boltzmann distribution from statistical mechanics κ has become associated with the inverse temperature.

```
def logits_to_softmax(logits, temperature=1):
    return np.exp(logits/temperature)/np.sum(np.exp(logits/temperature))
```

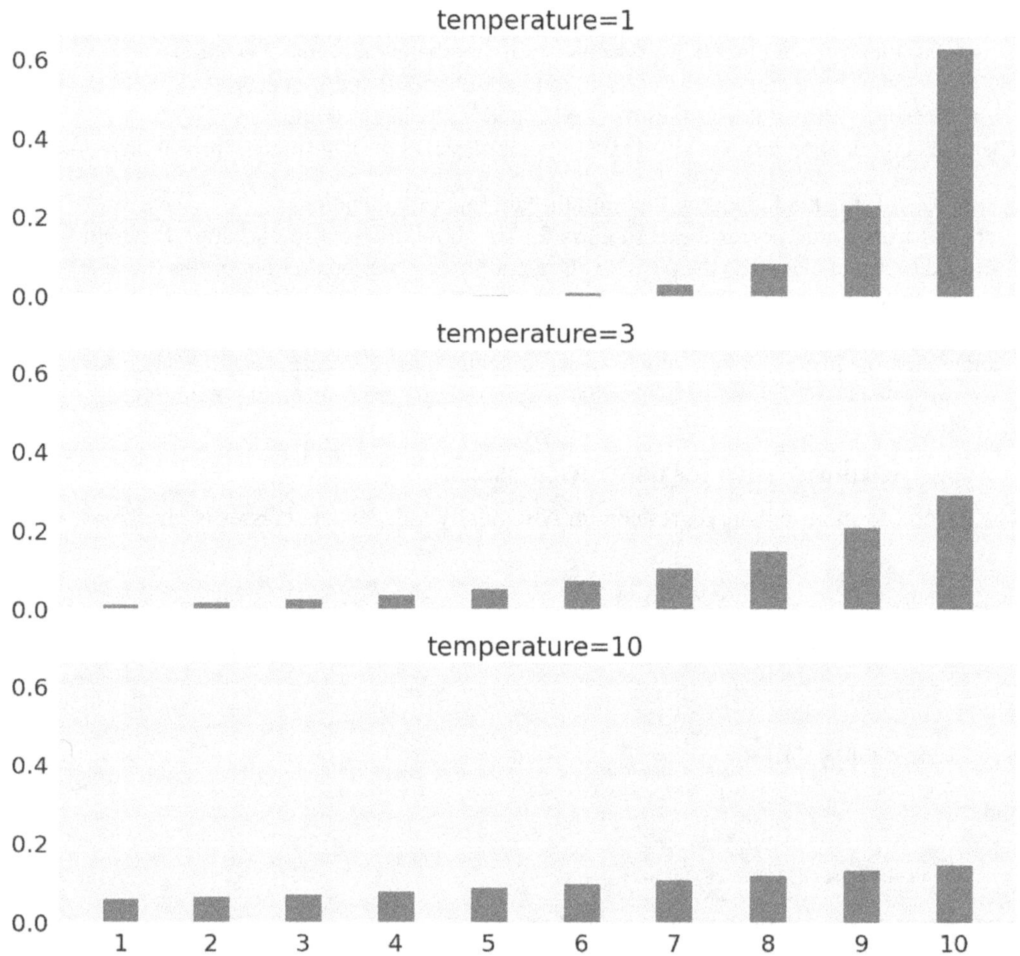

Figure 8.24: The effect of softmax normalization at various temperatures on a vector of logits.

8.13.3 Multiclass metrics

Binary metrics can be easily extended for multiclass classification[17]. For example for n classes:

$$\text{precision} = \frac{\sum_{i=1}^{n} TP_i}{\sum_{i=1}^{n}(TP_i + FP_i)} \tag{8.42}$$

$$\text{recall} = \frac{\sum_{i=1}^{n} TP_i}{\sum_{i=1}^{n}(TP_i + FN_i)} \tag{8.43}$$

Scikit-learn can produce a class-wise `classification_report`

```
              precision    recall  f1-score   support

           0       0.66      0.77      0.71      1000
           1       0.73      0.86      0.79      1000
           2       0.58      0.52      0.55      1000
           3       0.49      0.44      0.46      1000
           4       0.60      0.61      0.61      1000
           5       0.55      0.57      0.56      1000
           6       0.68      0.80      0.73      1000
           7       0.84      0.56      0.67      1000
           8       0.80      0.71      0.75      1000
           9       0.70      0.77      0.74      1000

    accuracy                           0.66     10000
   macro avg       0.66      0.66      0.66     10000
weighted avg       0.66      0.66      0.66     10000
```

Figure 8.25: Example of a scikit-learn `classification_report`. Here we have ten classes ($\{0,...,9\}$).

where `support` is the number of ground truth samples seen for each class, and is used in calculating the weighted average.

8.14 Imbalanced classification

Imbalanced data is, in the binary case, when the number of examples of the majority class in the training data far outweighs the minority class, as represented in Figure 8.26.

[17] Marina Sokolova, Guy Lapalme "*A systematic analysis of performance measures for classification tasks*", Information Processing & Management **45** pp. 427-437 (2009)

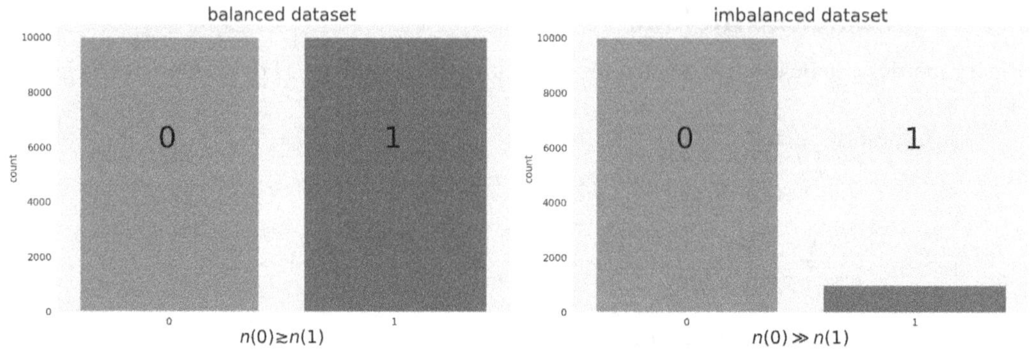

Figure 8.26: Countplots for a balanced and an imbalanced training dataset

There have been rivers of ink dedicated to the so-called problem of imbalanced classification, and I would suggest the only reason for this is that if there is very little data associated with the minority class most classification metrics behave badly as seen in Figure 8.27. I say so-called because quite frankly modern estimators do not have any particular problem with performing imbalanced classification at all as long as there is a respectable quantity of minority class data.

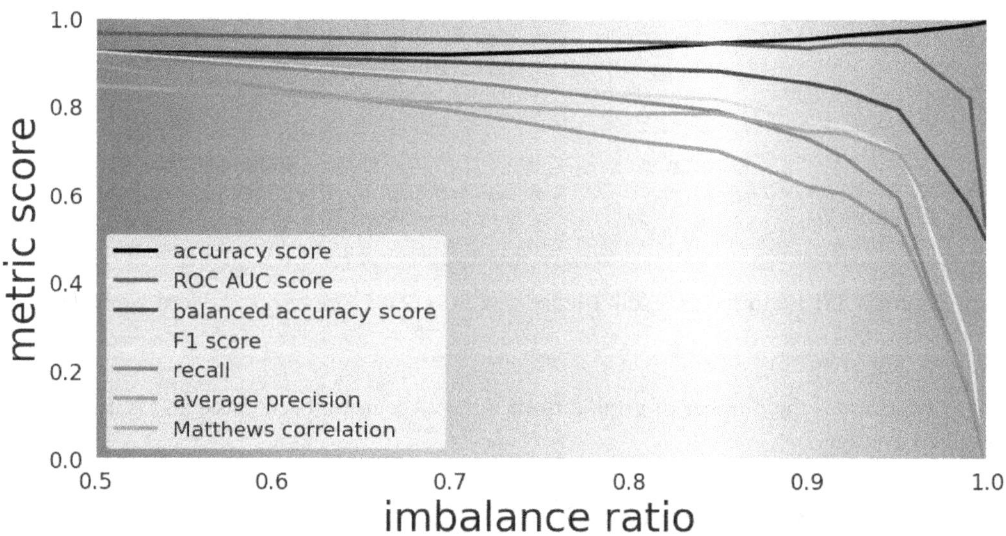

Figure 8.27: The deleterious effect of a paucity of minority class data on common classification metrics.

N Jupyter Notebook: Classification: How imbalanced is "imbalanced"?

8.14.1 The things you see people do to imbalanced data

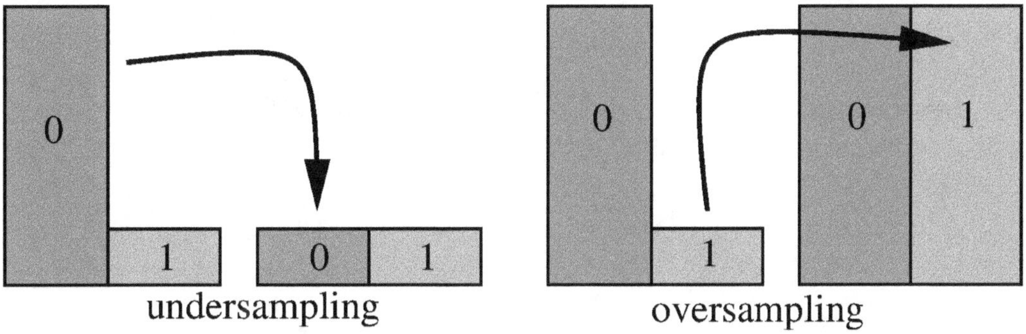

Figure 8.28: Undersampling and oversampling to rebalance binary data.

When it comes the imbalanced data one often encounters several potential approaches:

Undersampling

This is the wasteful practice of throwing away perfectly good data from the majority class (0) so that there become equal numbers of samples of each class in the misguided belief that ones data should for some reason be balanced. However, if one really needs to create a class balanced set from an imbalanced dataset one can use the following code (`gist`).

```
def undersample_df(df, target, seed=42):
    label, count = np.unique(df[target], return_counts=True)
    most_frequent_class = label[np.argmax(count)]
    # sample ALL of the minority class data
    df_class_1 = df.loc[df[target] != most_frequent_class]
    # randomly sample the majority class data
    df_class_0=df.loc[df[target]==most_frequent_class].sample(
                                n=len(df_class_1), random_state=seed)
    # now randomly shuffle the new dataset
    X = pd.concat([df_class_0, df_class_1]).sample(
                  frac=1, random_state=seed).reset_index(drop=True)
    y = X.pop(target)

    return X, y
```

Oversampling

Regarding oversampling: this is the method of bulking up the minority class with synthetic data but has a fundamental flaw; if one can readily classify the minority class examples that one wishes to synthesize more of, then there is actually no need to create any more new data in the first place. And if one cannot readily classify the minority class, then one simply ends up producing yet more noisy hard to classify points. Either way it really is a pointless exercise.

Remark: Whatever you do, do not use SMOTE or variants thereof to create synthetic data (see the excellent paper: "To SMOTE, or not to SMOTE?").

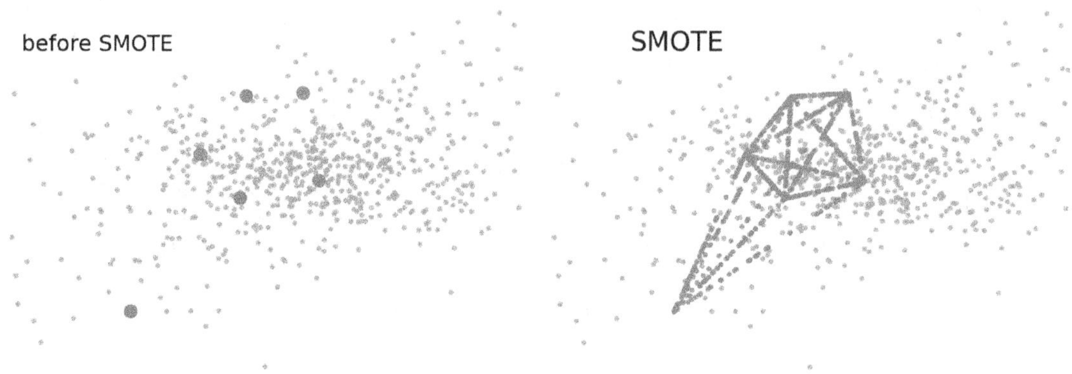

Figure 8.29: Example of how SMOTE creates new minority class datapoints from the 6 original points.

Weight the loss function

The scikit-learn classifiers have the option `class_weight` where if one specifies `balanced` then weights are assigned that are inversely proportional to class frequencies. Adding an extra weight, n, to the calculation of the loss for a minority class data point is the numerical equivalent to having duplicated n more examples of said datapoint, so we see we are back to the same paradox as we have with oversampling. For completeness we should mention that XGBoost, LightGBM, and CatBoost all have the `scale_pos_weight` option. The LightGBM manual states *"...while enabling this should increase the overall performance metric of your model, it will also result in poor estimates of the individual class probabilities"*.

8.14.2 A question of i.i.d. datasets

Just as in regression, the train, validation, and test sets should also be i.i.d. samples of our expected production data. Exactly the same philosophy applies to classification; for the metrics to be transferable the imbalance should be the same in each of the aforementioned sets (hence the stratification of the class labels when performing the train test split). For example, here using the accuracy score, if we have differing dataset sizes (α and β, where $\alpha \neq \beta$) we see our performance metric is perfectly transferable

$$\frac{\alpha TN + \alpha TP}{\alpha TN + \alpha FP + \alpha FN + \alpha TP} = \frac{\beta TN + \beta TP}{\beta TN + \beta FP + \beta FN + \beta TP} \tag{8.44}$$

In other words, the accuracy score is independent of the overall number of samples in the dataset. On the other hand in general

$$\frac{TN + \gamma TP}{TN + FP + \gamma FN + \gamma TP} \neq \frac{TN + \delta TP}{TN + FP + \delta FN + \delta TP} \tag{8.45}$$

thus the application of `scale_pos_weight` will influence the value reported by our metric (the balanced accuracy score was designed in order to mitigate this situation, and is the average of the recall and specificity scores).

At no point have we seen any requirement that that majority and minority class samples should be balanced. Indeed, we see from Eq. 8.45 that if we are going to monitor the performance of our model during production it would be most reasonable the the imbalance of the train, validation, and test sets should reflect the imbalance of the production data we expect to receive (*i.e.* we should have no training-serving skew). A number of studies have corroborated that rebalancing classification data has no advantages whatsoever.[18, 19]

8.15 Overfitting

Visual examples of under and overfitting for a parametric classifier

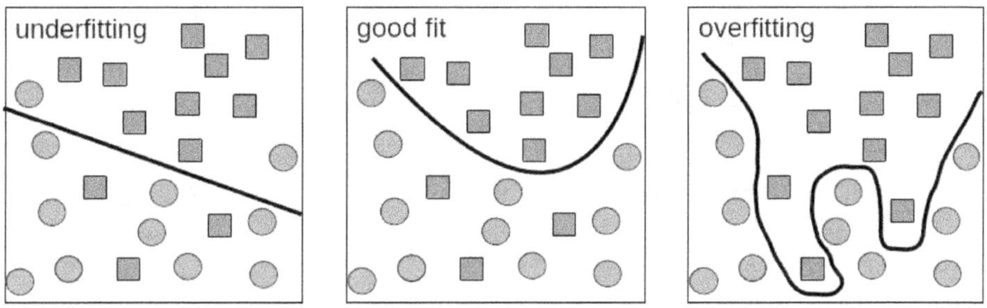

Figure 8.30: Underfitting and overfitting for a parametric classifier.

and for a non-parametric classifier

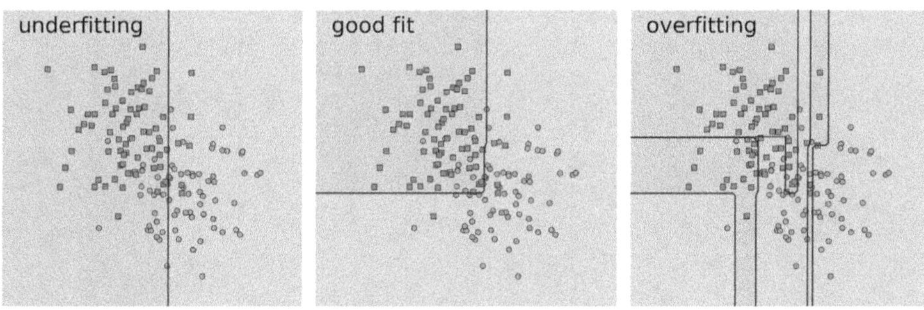

Figure 8.31: Underfitting and overfitting for a Decision Tree classifier

In classification, just as in regression, one can reduce overfitting in parametric models (such as logistic regression) by using regularization ($L1$, $L2$, $L1+L2$), and in tree based estimators by increasing the `min_samples_leaf` hyperparameter.

[18] van den Goorbergh, van Smeden, Timmerman, Van Calster *"The harm of class imbalance corrections for risk prediction models: illustration and simulation using logistic regression"*, Journal of the American Medical Informatics Association **29** pp. 1525-1534 (2022)

[19] Alex Carriero, Kim Luijken, Anne de Hond, Karel GM Moons, Ben van Calster, Maarten van Smeden "*The harms of class imbalance corrections for machine learning based prediction models: a simulation study*", arXiv:2404.19494 (2024)

8.16 No free lunch theorem

Which is the best estimator? Well that depends on the dataset: *a priori* one does not know which estimator is the best for your dataset. For some datasets maybe a parametric linear model will work best, and for others maybe a Decision Tree will work best. Suffice to say that a model trained on a specific dataset is not transferable to a different dataset. This goes by the rather fanciful name of the *'No free lunch theorem'*[20].

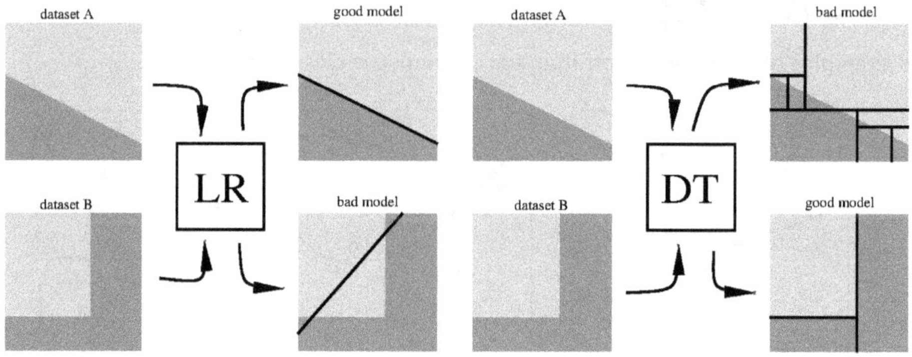

Figure 8.32: Different estimators for different datasets; there is no one model that will always perform the best on all possible datasets.

[20] David Wolpert *"The Lack of A Priori Distinctions Between Learning Algorithms"*, Neural Computation **8** pp. 1341-1390. (1996)

Recommended reading

Papers

- Kartik Waghmare, Johanna Ziegel *"Proper scoring rules for estimation and forecast evaluation"*, arXiv:2504.01781 (2025)
- Tom Fawcett *"An introduction to ROC analysis"*, Pattern Recognition Letters **27** pp. 861-874 (2006)
- Yotam Elor, Hadar Averbuch-Elor *"To SMOTE, or not to SMOTE?"*, arXiv:2201.08528 (2022)
- Telmo Silva Filho, Hao Song, Miquel Perello-Nieto, Raul Santos-Rodriguez, Meelis Kull, Peter Flach *"Classifier calibration: a survey on how to assess and improve predicted class probabilities"*, Machine Learning **112** pp. 3211-3260 (2023)
- Dimitriadis, Gneiting, Jordan, Vogel "*Evaluating probabilistic classifiers: The triptych*", International Journal of Forecasting **40** pp. 1101-1122 (2024)
- Juri Opitz *"A Closer Look at Classification Evaluation Metrics and a Critical Reflection of Common Evaluation Practice"*, arXiv:2404.16958 (2024)

Books

- Kumar Abhishek, Mounir Abdelaziz "*Machine Learning for Imbalanced Data*", Packt Publishing Limited (2023)
- Valery Manokhin "*Practical Guide to Applied Conformal Prediction in Python*", Packt Publishing Limited (2023) (Chapter 6)

Packages

- scoringrules
- imbalanced-learn
- `betacal` - Beta calibration
- Venn-ABERS calibration by Ivan Petej

9. GLM and GAM

All analytics models do well at what they are biased to look for.

Matthew Schneider

9.1 Generalized linear models (GLM)

In Chapter 7 on regression we saw the linear model, and in Chapter 8 on classification we saw the probit and logistic models. It was in 1972 that John Nelder and Robert Wedderburn provided a unified perspective of statistical models whose distributions pertain to the exponential family into a class known as the generalized linear models (GLM). The linear regression model (section 7.2) is given by

$$\begin{aligned}\hat{\mathbf{y}} &= \hat{\beta}_n \mathbf{x}_n + \ldots + \hat{\beta}_1 \mathbf{x}_1 + \hat{\beta}_0 \mathbf{x}_0 \\ &= 1.\left(\sum_{i=0}^{n} \hat{\beta}_i \mathbf{x}_i\right)\end{aligned}$$

where $\mathbf{x}_0 = \mathbf{1}$. The logistic regression model (section 8.2.3) has the form

$$\hat{y} = \sigma\left(\sum_{i=0}^{n} \hat{\beta}_i \mathbf{x}_i\right)$$

where σ is the logistic function

$$\sigma := \frac{1}{1+e^{-x}} \equiv \frac{e^x}{1+e^x}$$

and the probit regression model (section 8.2.2) has the form

$$\hat{y} = \Phi\left(\sum_{i=0}^{n} \hat{\beta}_i \mathbf{x}_i\right)$$

where Φ is the Gaussian cumulative distribution function (see Eq. 8.1). A model that we did not see, but shall mention here, is Poisson regression used for count data

$$\hat{y} = \exp\left(\sum_{i=0}^{n} \hat{\beta}_i \mathbf{x}_i\right)$$

and is implemented in the `sklearn.linear_model.PoissonRegressor`, or via the more general `sklearn.linear_model.TweedieRegressor` by setting the parameter `power=1`.

Here the identity (1), σ, Φ, and exp are all examples of what are known as *inverse link functions* (g^{-1}), or in neural network parlance *activation functions* (A).

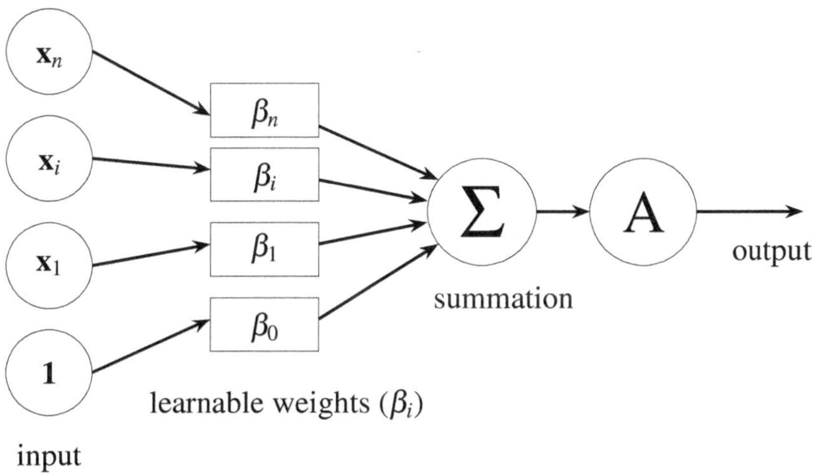

Figure 9.1: Graphical representation of a generalized linear model (GLM).

Activation functions

The nomenclature activation function stems from the extremely tenuous relation to the activation of biological neurons. Despite this gross reductionism, networks with nodes constructed from artificial neurons have proved to be stunningly successful in the fields of computer vision (CV) in the form of convolutional neural networks, and in natural language processing (NLP) in the form of recurrent neural networks.

Of particular historical note is the perceptron model

$$\hat{y} = H\left(\sum_{i=0}^{n} \hat{\beta}_i \mathbf{x}_i\right) \equiv H(\boldsymbol{\beta}^{\mathsf{T}}\mathbf{X})$$

where H is the Heaviside function, which is known as the binary activation function. This does, however, have the disadvantage of having a differential of zero for all points other than at the discontinuity at zero, making it unsuitable for gradient based training algorithms that use, for example, gradient descent. Another extremely important activation function is the rectified linear unit (ReLU), proposed in 1969 by Kunihiko Fukushima[1]

$$\hat{y} = \text{ReLU}(\boldsymbol{\beta}^\top \mathbf{X})$$

where the ReLU function is given by $\max(0,x)$. The above model frequently constitutes the artificial neuron found in artificial neural networks (ANN).

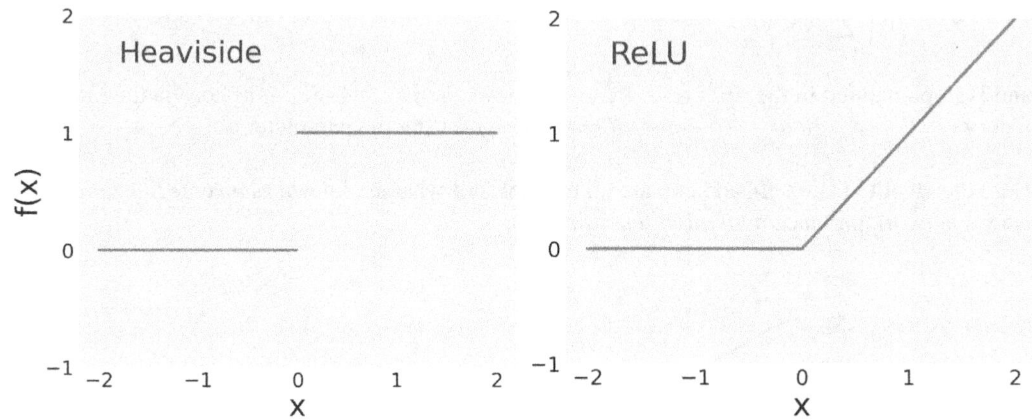

Figure 9.2: The Heaviside and ReLU functions.

It is worth mentioning that

$$\frac{\partial \text{ ReLU}[\mathbf{x}]}{\partial \mathbf{x}} = H(\mathbf{x}) \tag{9.1}$$

Note that activation functions are in general bereft of the probabilistic properties associated with the inverse link functions. Over the years over 400 different activation functions have been explored.[2]

9.2 Kolmogorov-Arnold superposition theorem

The Kolmogorov-Arnold superposition theorem posits that any multivariate continuous function can be represented by a linear combination of continuous univariate functions.

$$y(\mathbf{x}) = f(x_n, \ldots, x_1, x_0) = \sum_{j=0}^{2n+1} A_j \left(\sum_{i=0}^{n} B_{i,j}(x_i) \right) \tag{9.2}$$

i.e. $2n+1$ 'outer' univariate functions composed of n 'inner' univariate functions, where n is the number of features in our dataset. A simple example would be

$$f(x_1, x_2) = x_1 x_2 \equiv \exp(\log(x_1) + \log(x_2))$$

for positive values of x.

[1]K. Fukushima *"Visual Feature Extraction by a Multilayered Network of Analog Threshold Elements"*, IEEE Transactions on Systems Science and Cybernetics **5**, pp. 322-333 (1969)

[2]Vladimír Kunc, Jiří Kléma *"Three Decades of Activations: A Comprehensive Survey of 400 Activation Functions for Neural Networks"*, arXiv:2402.09092 (2024)

9.3 Generalized additive models (GAM)

Generalized additive models were proposed by Trevor Hastie and Robert Tibshirani in 1986. In the linear model there is one parameter, β_i, associated with each feature $\mathbf{x}_i$. Generalized additive models introduce substantial flexibility by instead now fitting a function, B_i, to each feature $\mathbf{x}_i$. This can be seen as an approximation to the Kolmogorov-Arnold equation; now having a fixed outer function and a learnable inner function

$$\begin{aligned} y(\mathbf{x}) &= A(B_n(x_n) + \dots + B_1(x_1) + B_0(1)) \\ &= A\left(\sum_{i=0}^{n} B_i(x_i)\right) \end{aligned} \tag{9.3}$$

The $2n+1$ outer functions are represented by a single smooth monotonic activation function (A), and for the inner univariate functions (B) one could fit basis functions such as local polynomial representations in the form of B-splines. The practicalities of fitting GAM models can be achieved, for example, by using the python `pyGAM` package.

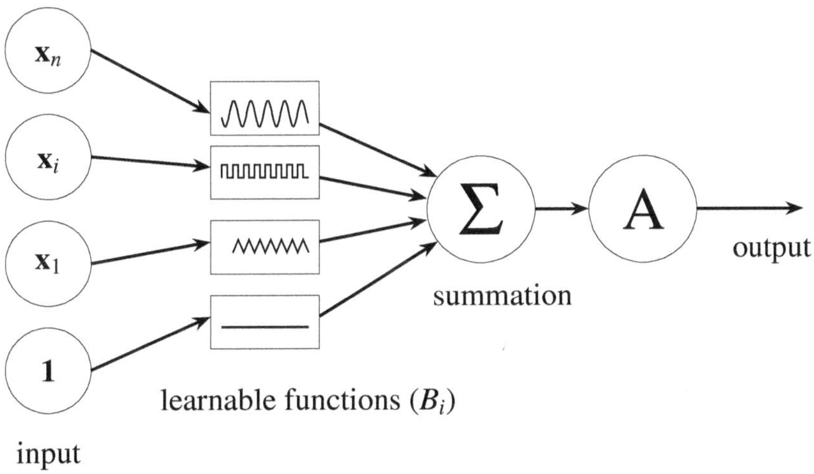

Figure 9.3: Graphical representation of a generalized additive model (GAM).

N Jupyter Notebook: Regression using Generalized Additive Models and Classification using Generalized Additive Models, which demonstrate the `pyGAM` package.

Recommended reading

Papers

- J. A. Nelder, R. W. M. Wedderburn *"Generalized Linear Models"*, Royal Statistical Society. Journal. Series A **135** pp. 370-384 (1972)
- T. J. Hastie, R. J. Tibshirani *"Generalized Additive Models"*, Statistical Science **1** pp. 297-310 (1986)

Books

- P. McCullagh and J. A. Nelder *"Generalized Linear Models"*, Chapman and Hall (1989)
- Annette J. Dobson, Adrian G. Barnett *"An Introduction to Generalized Linear Models"*, Chapman and Hall/CRC 4th Edition (2018)
- Trevor Hastie and Robert Tibshirani *"Generalized Additive Models"*, Routledge (1990)
- Simon N. Wood *"Generalized Additive Models: An Introduction with R"*, Chapman and Hall/CRC 2nd Edition (2017)

Packages

- `pyGAM`

10. Ensemble estimators

> ...while the individual man is an insoluble puzzle, in the aggregate he becomes a mathematical certainty.
>
> *Arthur Conan Doyle*

Thus far we have seen individual estimators in action, namely linear regression, the decision tree regressor, logistic regression, and the decision tree classifier. However, by carefully aggregating individual estimators into an ensemble much better predictive performance can be achieved.

10.1 Random Forest

Random Forests, described by Leo Breiman in 2001, is an example of a 'bagging' (bootstrap + aggregating) ensemble estimator. In order to reduce the amount of noise that we fit to (*i.e.* overfitting) as seen with the Decision Tree estimator we average the results of a collection of trees *i.e.* a forest!

- new hyperparameter: `n_estimators` (default = 100)

Suffice to say simply creating 100 trees, each exactly the same (perfectly correlated), is pointless; we have to mix things up a bit.

10.1.1 Bootstrapping: row subsampling with replacement

The first step is bootstrap sampling[1] to create `n_estimators` datasets, each of the datasets having exactly the same number of rows as the original training dataset. This is done by random sampling *with replacement*, where rows can be sampled multiple times:

```
sample = df.sample(frac=1, replace=True)
```

(creating subsets without replacement is known as *pasting*). On average each of these bootstrap datasets

[1] B. Efron, R. J. Tibshirani "*An Introduction to the Bootstrap*", Chapman and Hall/CRC (1994)

will contain $\approx 1-e^{-1}= 63.2\%$ of the rows form the original dataset.

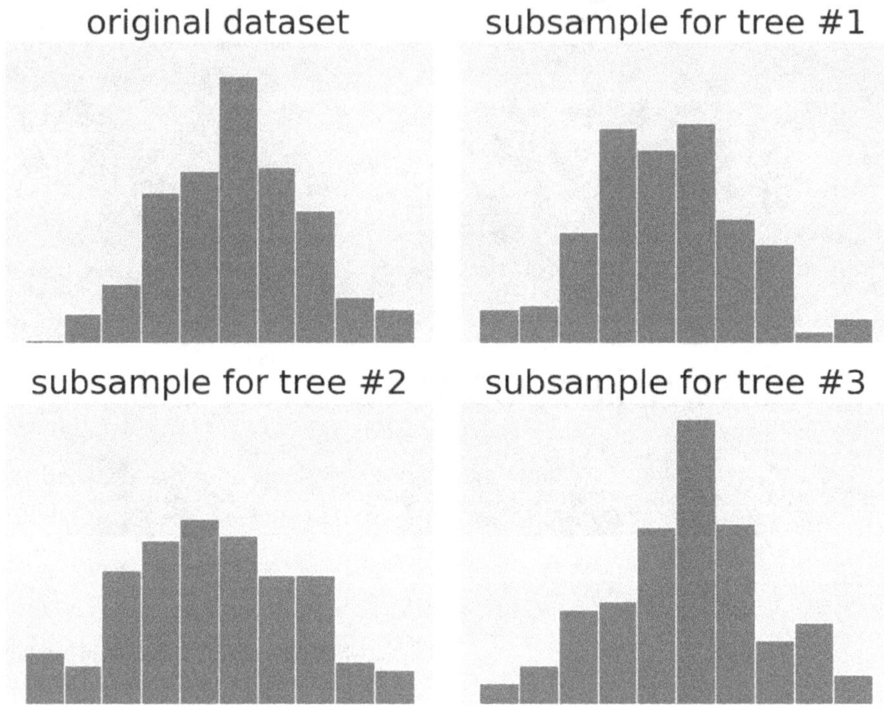

Figure 10.1: Bootstrap sampling with replacement.

out-of-bag samples

Clever use can be made of the unchosen 37% of the rows for each tree; these can be used as a validation set to monitor the generalization performance by setting the parameter `oob_score=True`. Each row of the training data is fed to each tree that did not use said row of data, and the score is recorded and the average result becomes the `oob_score_`. By default `regressor.oob_score_` returns the R^2 metric and the `classifier.oob_score_` returns the accuracy score (both of which I would suggest are perhaps unfortunate choices).

10.1.2 Feature subsampling

Feature subsampling, using the random subspace method proposed by Tin Kam Ho in 1995, can further decorrelate trees by randomly using different subsets of the features (subspaces of the feature vectors) when fitting each tree. In this way each tree thus effectively fits to a slightly different dataset.

> Remark: By default the scikit-learn `RandomForestClassifier` can use up to $\sqrt{\texttt{n\_features}}$. However, their `RandomForestRegressor` can use all of the features, so strictly speaking is not actually Random Forest but rather bagged trees. This can be changed by setting the `max_features` hyperparameter to a value less than 1.

Figure 10.2: Due to row and feature subsampling each individual tree in the Random Forest is slightly different.

Figure 10.3: Random Forest: each individual Decision Tree is fitted to $\approx 63\%$ of the rows and, if using a typical feature subsample fraction of 0.8, thus to a total of $\approx 50\%$ of the data points, which we see here as a collection of random patches.

Sample code

The following is a didactic implementation of the Random Forest regressor (gist)

```
from sklearn.tree import DecisionTreeRegressor

def random_forest_regressor(X_train, y_train, X_test,
                            max_depth    = None,
                            n_estimators =  100,
```

```
                              max_features = 1.0):

    # convert X into a pandas dataframe
    X_train = pd.DataFrame(X_train)
    X_test  = pd.DataFrame(X_test)
    # somewhere to store the results of each tree
    y_preds = []

    # single decision tree
    DT = DecisionTreeRegressor(max_depth=max_depth)

    for _ in range(n_estimators):
        # bootstrap sample rows (with replacement)
        X_sample = X_train.sample(frac=1, replace=True)
        y_sample = y_train[X_sample.index].copy()

        # random subspace method: randomly sample columns
        X_sample_RSM = X_sample.sample(frac=max_features, axis='columns')
        # now select the very same columns from X_test
        X_sample_RSM_columns = X_sample_RSM.columns.values.tolist()
        X_test_RSM = X_test.iloc[:, X_sample_RSM_columns]

        # fit and predict the tree
        y_pred_DT = DT.fit(X_sample_RSM, y_sample).predict(X_test_RSM)
        # store the predictions of this tree
        y_preds.append(y_pred_DT)

    # now average over the n_estimators trees
    y_pred = np.mean(y_preds, axis=0)

    return y_pred
```

10.1.3 Results

When making a prediction for a new feature vector the data is given to each of the trees, and the final result is the average of the prediction returned for each tree. In classification the final result can be obtained via the majority vote for each of the trees, or (as in scikit-learn) by averaging the probabilities.

Why does the Random Forest work so well? A simple intuition is that each individual decision tree fits to both the signal and to the random noise. Averaged over many trees the random noise component, having $\mathbb{E}(\varepsilon) = 0$, becomes cancelled out, leaving just the signal. (See the interesting paper *"Why do Random Forests Work? Understanding Tree Ensembles as Self-Regularizing Adaptive Smoothers"*).

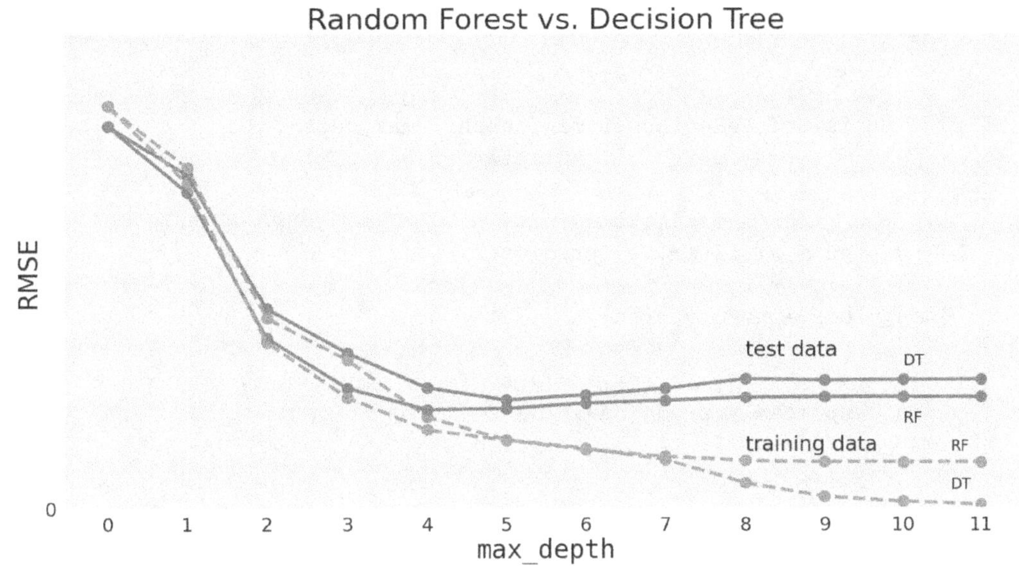

Figure 10.4: Occam curves: Random Forest vs. the decision tree

Explainability

With the `RandomForest` we gain in performance, but now we cannot draw our prediction process as a single tree as there are now many of them. We have sacrificed our ability to easily explain the output of our model.

> Remark: XGBoost has Random Forest and is significantly faster than the scikit-learn implementation. In LightGBM one can set `boosting="random_forest"`.

10.2 Extremely Randomized Trees

Extremely Randomized Trees, or 'Extra-Trees', constructs an ensemble of decision trees where the cut-point of the split for each feature is performed completely randomly. Amazingly this chaotic approach to individual tree building can sometimes perform even better than the more contemplative Random Forest, and runs much faster.

Sample code

Here is some code that mimics the scikit-learn `ExtraTreesRegressor`. Notice that Extra-Trees, unlike Random Forests, by default does not create bootstrap samples but rather uses all of the training data so as to minimize the bias.

```
from sklearn.tree import DecisionTreeRegressor

def extra_trees_regressor(X, y,
                          max_depth=None,
                          n_estimators=100):

    # somewhere to store the results of each tree
```

```
    y_preds = []

    # single decision tree
    DT = DecisionTreeRegressor(max_depth = max_depth,
                               splitter = 'random')

    for _ in range(n_estimators):
        y_pred = DT.fit(X, y).predict(X)
        # store the predictions of this tree
        y_preds.append(y_pred)

    # average over the n_estimators trees
    y_fit = np.mean(y_preds, axis=0)

    return y_fit
```

10.3 Weak learners and boosting

In 1989 the question was asked whether a collection of weak learners, which do just a little better than random guessing, could constitute a strong learner and a year later Robert Schapire in the paper *"The strength of weak learnability"* showed that this was indeed the case leading to AdaBoost.

10.3.1 AdaBoost (Adaptive Boosting)

Freund and Schapire invented AdaBoost[2] in 1995 and it led to them winning the prestigious Gödel Prize for 2003. Bagging works in parallel, creating many independent trees, and the final prediction is the average of the predictions of each of the component trees. On the other hand boosting is sequential, performing various iterations, each new fit is based on the results of the fit before. In AdaBoost the base estimator is, just like in Random Forest, a decision tree. However in this case the tree is only of depth 1 (also known as a *decision stump*) (by default the scikit-learn `AdaBoostRegressor` uses trees of depth 3 as the base estimator). AdaBoost (regression) proceeds as roughly as follows:

1. Assign weights to each individual feature vector (initially all equal)
   a. subsample (with replacement) the training data with a probability calculated as a function of a weight assigned to each feature vector
   b. fit the weak learner to this subsample
   c. calculate the loss for each feature vector and use this to update (adapt) the weights so that the worst preforming 'difficult' predictions are more likely to be sampled in the next iteration
   d. save the predictions and an overall weight for each feature vector
2. the final prediction is obtained from a weighted median of the predictions

(see the paper by Harris Drucker for precise details).

> **Remark:** The scikit-learn implementations of AdaBoost has a `learning_rate` hyperparameter, which does not form part of the original AdaBoost algorithm.

A problem with the AdaBoost algorithm is that it will eventually specifically hone in on trying to fit to any

[2] Yoav Freund, Robert E. Schapire *"A decision-theoretic generalization of on-line learning and an application to boosting"*, Computational Learning Theory pp 23-37 (1995)

bad outlier points, to the detriment of the overall fit. AdaBoost, although now no longer widely used, paved the way for what is the state of the art technique in tabular data; gradient boosted decision trees.

10.4 Gradient boosted decision trees (GBDT)

Gradient boosted decision trees (sometimes known as Multiple Additive Regression Trees (MART)), along with foundation models (TFM), constitute the *state of the art* (SoTA) in tabular machine learning. In gradient boosting each iteration fits a tree to the negative gradient of the loss function (see gradient descent) this time w.r.t the predictions rather than the parameters. For regression using the $L2$ loss function, where the loss for each individual point (i) is given by $(y_i - \hat{y}_i)^2$ we proceed as follows

1. First we fit an initial baseline estimator ($\hat{y}_0$) to the target column (y_i). For regression this is the optimal constant model, *i.e.* simply the mean of the targets ($\bar{y}_i$) (for classification we use the probabilistic baseline model and use the corresponding loss function). This is estimator $j = 0$. This first contribution can be thought of as being the overall bias term, and the subsequent trees introduce the variance.
2. Then, for $j = 1$ to `n_estimators`:
   a. calculate a (new) column of pseudo-residuals (y_j) which is given by the negative gradient of the loss function

$$\begin{aligned} y_j &= -\left(\frac{\mathrm{d}L(y_i, \hat{y}_{j-1})}{\mathrm{d}\hat{y}_{j-1}}\right) \\ &= -\left(2\left(y_i - \hat{y}_{j-1}\right) \cdot (-1)\right) \\ &= 2(y_i - \hat{y}_{j-1}) \end{aligned}$$

   b. we drop the factor of 2 (think of it as becoming absorbed into η) and fit a decision tree to this new pseudo-residual target column y_j
   c. multiply the predictions of this fitted tree by the learning rate η and add this prediction, $\eta\hat{y}_j$, to the previous predictions
   d. the next pseudo-residual column is given by subtracting the sum of our previous predictions from the target column (y_i)
   e. repeat until reaching either `n_estimators`, or an early stopping condition is met.

Thus our final prediction is given by

$$\hat{y} = \text{baseline} + \eta\hat{y}_1 + \eta\hat{y}_2 + \ldots + \eta\hat{y}_n \tag{10.1}$$

This is somewhat akin to a predictor-corrector method. Rather than fitting directly to the target GBDT iteratively fits to a new target column which is the error of the current predictions w.r.t. the target, starting from a simple baseline model. The first trees grown learn the overall bias of the dataset, and subsequent trees fine tune to deviations from the initial bias trees.

Sample code

Sample code for a GBDT for the $L2$ loss (`gist`)

```
from sklearn.tree import DecisionTreeRegressor

def gradient_boosting_regressor(X, y,
                                n_estimators = 100,
                                learning_rate = 0.1):

    y_train = y
    # create the baseline model
```

```
    y_train_mean = np.ones(len(y_train)) * np.mean(y_train)
    # save this baseline fit
    y_fit = y_train_mean

    # shallow decision tree
    regressor = DecisionTreeRegressor(max_depth=3)

    for j in range(n_estimators):
        y_pred = regressor.fit(X, y_train).predict(X)
        # add this prediction to the fit
        y_fit += learning_rate * y_pred
        # calculate the residual
        y_train = y - y_fit
    return y_fit
```

10.4.1 The 'big four' GBDT

The *big four* GBDT implementations are:

- XGBoost - 'eXtreme Gradient Boosting' (2014)
- LightGBM - 'Light Gradient Boosting Machine' (2016)
- CatBoost - 'Categorical Boosting' (2017)
- HistGradientBoostingRegressor or the HistGradientBoostingClassifier from scikit-learn

The hyperparameters provided in each of these examples represent the default values. XGBoost has a version that uses the Scikit-Learn API:

```
import xgboost as xgb

regressor = xgb.XGBRegressor(max_depth= 6,
                             min_child_weight= 1,
                             n_estimators= 100,
                             learning_rate= 0.3,)
regressor.fit(X_train, y_train)
```

One of the ways that XGBoost improves upon standard gradient boosting is to also use the second order derivative for the loss function, *i.e.* using both the gradient (∇) and the Hessian (H), thus performing Newton descent rather than gradient descent.

Equation: The Taylor expansion is given by

$$f(\mathbf{x}) = f(\mathbf{a}) + \frac{(\mathbf{x}-\mathbf{a})^T}{1!}\nabla f(\mathbf{a}) + \frac{(\mathbf{x}-\mathbf{a})^T}{2!}Hf(\mathbf{a})(\mathbf{x}-\mathbf{a}) + \ldots \tag{10.2}$$

```
from lightgbm import LGBMRegressor

regressor = LGBMRegressor(max_depth= -1, # no limit
                          min_child_samples= 20,
```

```
                                n_estimators= 100,
                                learning_rate= 0.1,
                                verbose= -1 )
regressor.fit(X_train, y_train)
```

```
from catboost import CatBoostRegressor

regressor = CatBoostRegressor(depth= 6,
                              grow_policy='SymmetricTree',
                              #min_data_in_leaf= 1, # not used
                              iterations= 1000,
                              #learning_rate is automatic
                              silent= True)
regressor.fit(X_train, y_train)
```

Remark: If you increase the number of iterations, you should decrease the learning rate, η.

Suffice to say each of these estimators has much more functionality and many more parameters to tune, and can be used with GPU's to speed up training, especially if one has a very large dataset. Much has been written as to which is the *best of the best*. Personally I would suggest simply trying all four out on ones particular dataset, and choosing based of performance, as per the 'No free lunch' theorem.

N Jupyter Notebook: An introduction to XGBoost regression

10.4.2 Feature quantization: histogram gradient boosting

As we saw earlier, for a feature having n data points finding the optimal split in a decision tree involves making $n-1$ evaluations. For large dataset, with many features, this becomes very computationally expensive. Histogram gradient boosting bins continuous features into histograms. This significantly speeds up the tree building process and reduces memory. In LightGBM the default parameter is `max_bin=255`. In XGBoost one can set the parameter `tree_method="hist"` and by default has `max_bin=256`, and for CatBoost one has `border_count=254` when running on a CPU. In scikit learn the default value is 255 bins (bin number 256 is reserved for `NaN` values)

```
from sklearn.ensemble import HistGradientBoostingRegressor

regressor = HistGradientBoostingRegressor(max_depth= None,
                                          min_samples_leaf= 20,
                                          max_iter= 100,
                                          learning_rate= 0.1,
                                          max_bins=255,)
regressor.fit(X_train, y_train)
```

10.4.3 Tree growth strategy

When growing a Decision Tree it is usual to grow downwards by performing recursive binary splitting of each node until stopping when either `max_depth` is reached or the node is pure. In XGBoost and CatBoost this standard depth-first growth policy is known as depthwise. However, an alternative is best-first growth in which the nodes that will result in the greatest loss reduction are grown first which is the default strategy used by LightGBM (and can be chosen in XGBoost and CatBoost by via grow_policy="lossguide") Either growth strategy should result in the same fully grown tree, and only the order in which the tree grows changes. In CatBoost the default strategy is SymmetricTree which is essentially a computationally efficient form of growing depthwise trees.

Remark: For CatBoost the min_data_in_leaf hyperparameter is only used in conjunction with the lossguide and depthwise growth strategies.

10.4.4 Dropout: DART

The DART technique uses a concept borrowed from the area of training deep neural networks, namely dropout. However here, instead of dropping neurons (and rescaling the weights of the remaining neurons so as to pick up the slack) it randomly temporarily drops k trees from the current ensemble before computing the next tree in the ensemble, it then scales this new tree by $1/k$ and then also rescales the new tree as well as all the temporarily dropped trees by $k/(k+1)$ before appending the new tree to the ensemble. This scaling is done to compensate for all the trees that were dropped when the contribution of the new tree was computed. Both XGBoost and LightGBM incorporate DART via the options:

```
# XGBoost
booster = "dart"
rate_drop = 0.0 # default value (i.e. no DART!)

# LightGBM
boosting = "dart"
drop_rate = 0.1 # default value
```

Remark: Using DART in XGBoost can incur significant slowdown in model training times; in benchmark tests it has been found to be $\times 40$ slower. On the other hand for LightGBM the slowdown is negligible.

10.4.5 Categorical features: native support

As mentioned in Chapter 4 our dataframe should be entirely numerical in nature, and categorical features should be encoded. That said, the big three have native support of such features. It is often sufficient to simply identify said features as being categorical and leave the encoding to the estimator, for example via

```
categorical_features_list = ['has_car', 'has_house', 'has_yacht']

for feature in categorical_features_list:
    for df in [train, test]:
        df[feature] = df[feature].astype('category')
```

LightGBM will then automatically pick up on the categorical features from the dataframe dtypes. In CatBoost the relevant parameters are

```
# CatBoost parameters
cat_features = categorical_features_list,
one_hot_max_size = 2 # CPU default
```

where categorical_features_list is a list of the categorical column names. For CatBoost, below a certain number of categories in a feature (one_hot_max_size, having a default value of 2) one-hot encoding is used, otherwise for higher cardinality features a bespoke CatBoost target encoder is used. LightGBM also basically dispenses with one-hot encoding (default max_cat_to_onehot=4) and Fisher grouping is used to partition such features into two subsets based on the loss function. Indeed, if one were to provide LightGBM with one-hot encoded data its inbuilt *exclusive feature bundling* (EFB) would collapse these mutually exclusive features back into the original feature. XGBoost also has native support for categorical features which is (still) experimental

```
# XGBoost parameters
enable_categorical = True,
max_cat_to_onehot = None # default
```

> Remark: We can see from the XGBoost default value that Fisher grouping is not actually used, and everything is one-hot encoded. However, this one-hot encoding schema is not guaranteed to apply to the test or production data you provide at prediction time, so if you use XGBoost native encoding be absolutely sure to set the max_cat_to_onehot parameter.

10.4.6 Missing values: native support

The 'big four' also handle missing values (NaN) obviating the need for imputation. The NaN values are simply treated as a new value or a new category (the scikit HistGradientBoosting has a bin specifically reserved for missing values). For example XGBoost (see §3.4 of the XGBoost paper) when happening upon a missing value sends it down both splits of the decision tree and learns which of the two paths leads to the best reduction in the loss. When a missing value is then seen at the time of predicting the test data it refers to this learnt optimal path. As mentioned before such treatment of missing values outperforms any of the traditional techniques for handling missing data[3].

10.5 Extrapolation

As we have seen earlier in Section 7.6 extrapolation is something we wish to avoid. It is worth mentioning that even the mighty gradient boosted decision tree estimators have problems with extrapolation. In Figure 10.5 we fit to the function $y = x$. In this case, given the linear nature of the data unsurprisingly a linear regressor fits the data perfectly, and intuitively we see that it also extrapolates as expected. However, XGBoost does not fare so well.

[3] Perez-Lebel, Varoquaux, Le Morvan, Josse, Poline *"Benchmarking missing-values approaches for predictive models on health databases"*, GigaScience **11** giac013 (2022)

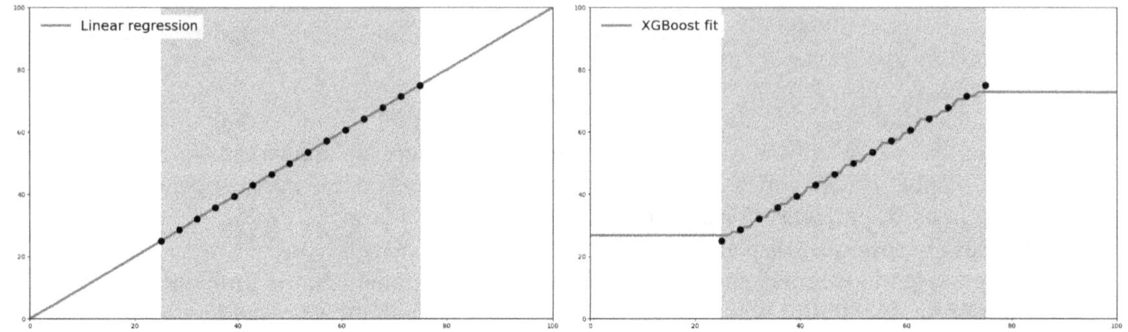

Figure 10.5: Extrapolation with linear regression (LHS) and XGBoost (RHS)

This can be understood in terms of our very first experience with the Decision Tree Regressor (the building blocks of gradient boosting decision trees); the extremal plateaux remain constant regardless of how far we travel either side from the region they were fitted on. With Random Forests, composed of an ensemble of n Decision Trees, for regression our prediction is given by

$$\hat{y}(X) = \sum_{i=1}^{n} \omega \hat{y}_i(X) \tag{10.3}$$

where $\omega = 1/n$. In other words our prediction for a vector X is the average of the predictions of each individual tree (i) for said vector. This convex combination is bounded by the maximum and minimum values of $\hat{y}_i(X)$.

So-called out-of-distribution generalization[4] is a complex issue and beyond the scope of this book.

N Jupyter Notebook: Extrapolation: Do not stray out of the forest!

10.5.1 Linear tree

In an effort to overcome this extrapolation limitation associated with tree-based estimators, especially in the context of forecasting which, by its very nature, will frequently have production data that lies outside the convex hull of the original training data one can combine trees with linear (LASSO) regression[5]. First one fits the training data with the LASSO, then a Random Forest is fit to the errors made by LASSO. Our predictions are then given by

$$\hat{y}(X) = \underbrace{\hat{\beta} X}_{LASSO} + \underbrace{\sum_{i=1}^{n} \omega \cdot \underbrace{\hat{y}_i(X)}_{DecisionTree}}_{RandomForest} \tag{10.4}$$

where the $\hat{\beta}$ are the estimated LASSO coefficients for each feature. This is akin to our gradient boosting model; the first term is the bias (here the LASSO rather than the optimal constant model), and the subsequent terms model the variance w.r.t. the overall bias. This technique is available in the magnificent package `linear-tree` written by Marco Cerliani.

[4] Liu, Shen, He, Zhang, Xu, Yu, Cui "*Towards Out-Of-Distribution Generalization: A Survey*", arXiv:2108.13624 (2023)

[5] Zhang, Nettleton, Zhu "*Regression-Enhanced Random Forests*", arXiv:1904.10416 (2019)

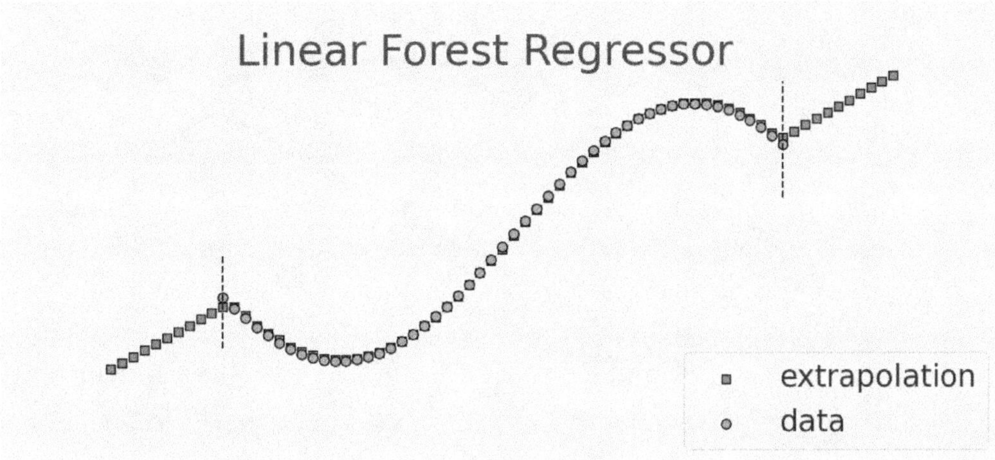

Figure 10.6: Extrapolation with the `linear-tree` `LinearForestRegressor`.

In the example in Fig. 10.6 we can see the linear extrapolation having a global slope $\hat{\beta}$.
In LightGBM one has the option

```
linear_tree=True
```

where, rather than each leaf fitting the standard horizontal optimal constant model, a linear fit is performed to the samples contained in the leaf (thus making the `min_child_samples` parameter especially important).

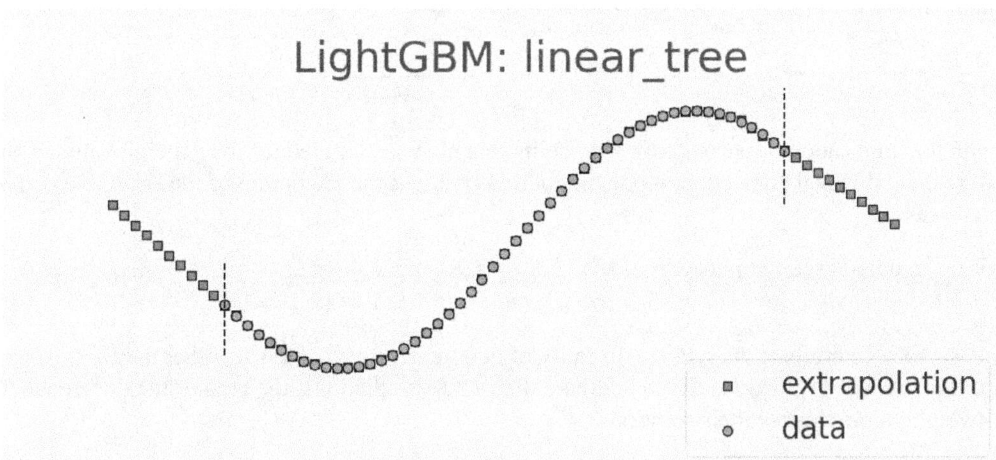

Figure 10.7: Extrapolation with the LightGBM `linear_tree`.

In Fig. 10.7 we see that the linear extrapolations are now local in nature. In XGBoost one has the

```
booster="gblinear"
```

which, by default, performs boosted linear regression. One can introduce regularization by setting the `lambda` hyperparameter to perform Ridge regression, and `alpha` to perform LASSO.

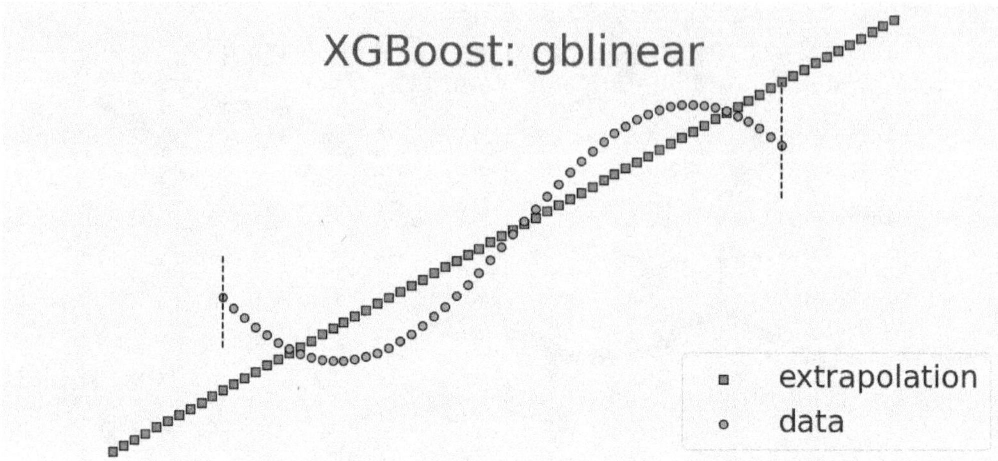

Figure 10.8: Using XGBoost `gblinear` to perform boosted linear regression.

10.6 Bias-variance-diversity decomposition and tradeoff

For individual models we saw earlier the bias-variance decomposition for the MSE. When it comes to ensembling the diversity of the estimators plays a rôle

Equation:

$$\underbrace{\frac{1}{n}\sum_{i=1}^{n}(y_i-\hat{e}_i)^2}_{\text{MSE}} = \overline{\text{bias}(\hat{y})^2} + \overline{\text{variance}(\hat{y})} - \underbrace{\overline{\frac{1}{m}\sum_{j=1}^{m}(\hat{e}-\hat{y}_j)^2}}_{\text{diversity}} \tag{10.5}$$

with the implication of the negative sign being that diversity can reduce the generalization error. Notation: $\hat{y}$ are the individual component model predictions and $\hat{e}$ is the prediction of the ensemble composed of all m models.

For more details see the paper Wood, Mu, Webb, Reeve, Luján, Brown "*A unified theory of diversity in ensemble learning*", Journal of Machine Learning Research **24** pp. 17302-17350 (2023).

Remark: To evaluate the relative diversity of two models one could use either the Kolmogorov-Smirnov or the Cramér-von Mises tests to compare their OOF predictions; the greater the difference between the two, the more diverse their solutions.

10.7 Convex combination of model predictions (CCMP)

A trick that sometimes results in an, albeit often small, performance boost is to ensemble diverse estimators, such as a parametric model with a non-parametric model. A simple method for regression is to create a new set of predictions from a convex combination of the predictions of the constituent models:

$$\hat{y} = a_1 \times \hat{y}\ (model\ 1) + a_2 \times \hat{y}\ (model\ 2)\ +\ \ldots\ +\ a_n \times \hat{y}\ (model\ n) \tag{10.6}$$

where $\sum a_i = 1$ and $a_i \geq 0 \, \forall \, a_i$.

In Figure 10.9 and Table 10.1 we can see the results of combining 50% of the output value of a linear regression with 50% of the decision tree regression.

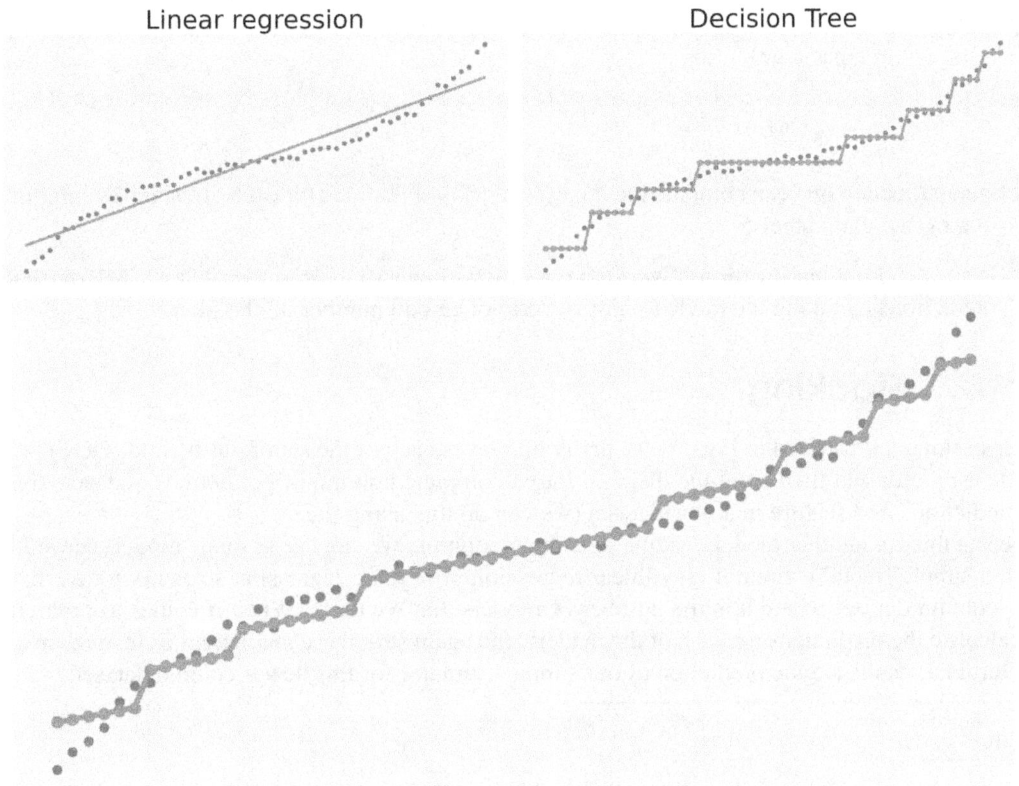

Figure 10.9: Ensembling of a linear regression and a decision tree

Model	RMSE
Linear regression	3.96
Decision tree	2.59
CCMP ensemble	2.36

Table 10.1: Ensemble results

Visually we can see where the performance boost came from; the linear regressor added inclination to the horizontal plateaus of the decision tree, leading to a better overall fit to the data. Indeed, it has been shown[6] that, when using a metric based on the squared loss, an ensemble using the arithmetic mean is guaranteed to perform as well as, if not better, than the average of the individual estimators. When working with the absolute error one should use the median.

[6]Krogh, Vedelsby *"Neural Network Ensembles, Cross Validation, and Active Learning"*, NIPS 7 (1994)

Sample code

```
df["y_pred"] = 0.5*df["y_pred_LR"] + 0.5*df["y_pred_DT"]
```

The optimal weights can be found by fitting either to a hold-out dataset or to the out-of-fold (OOF) predictions obtained from cross-validation by using the hill climbing optimization technique (see the `hillclimbers` package).

N Jupyter Notebook: Ensembling: Convex combination of model predictions (CCMP) and the hillclimbers package

For classification one can combine the the calibrated probabilities for each classifier by minimizing the log loss w.r.t. the class labels.

Remark: For classification if working directly with class labels, rather than CCMP one can combine predictions by taking the mode (majority vote) of an odd number of classifiers.

10.8 Stacking

In stacking[7], illustrated in Fig. 10.10, firstly one saves each of the set of out-of-fold (OOF) predictions for the estimator and then combine them all into a complete column of predictions and save this column of predictions as a feature in a new dataset (we can do this using the code provided in Chapter 5). We then repeat this for another model, leading to another column. We can use as many models as we like. Next we fit a simple 'meta' estimator (say linear regression or logistic regression so as not to overfit) to this new n-column dataset where n is the number of models that we used. When it comes to prediction time we calculate the predictions for each of the models, and again save these predictions as features in a new dataset. Our final results are the prediction of our simple estimator for this new n-column dataset.

[7] David H. Wolpert "*Stacked generalization*", Neural Networks **5** pp. 241-259 (1992)

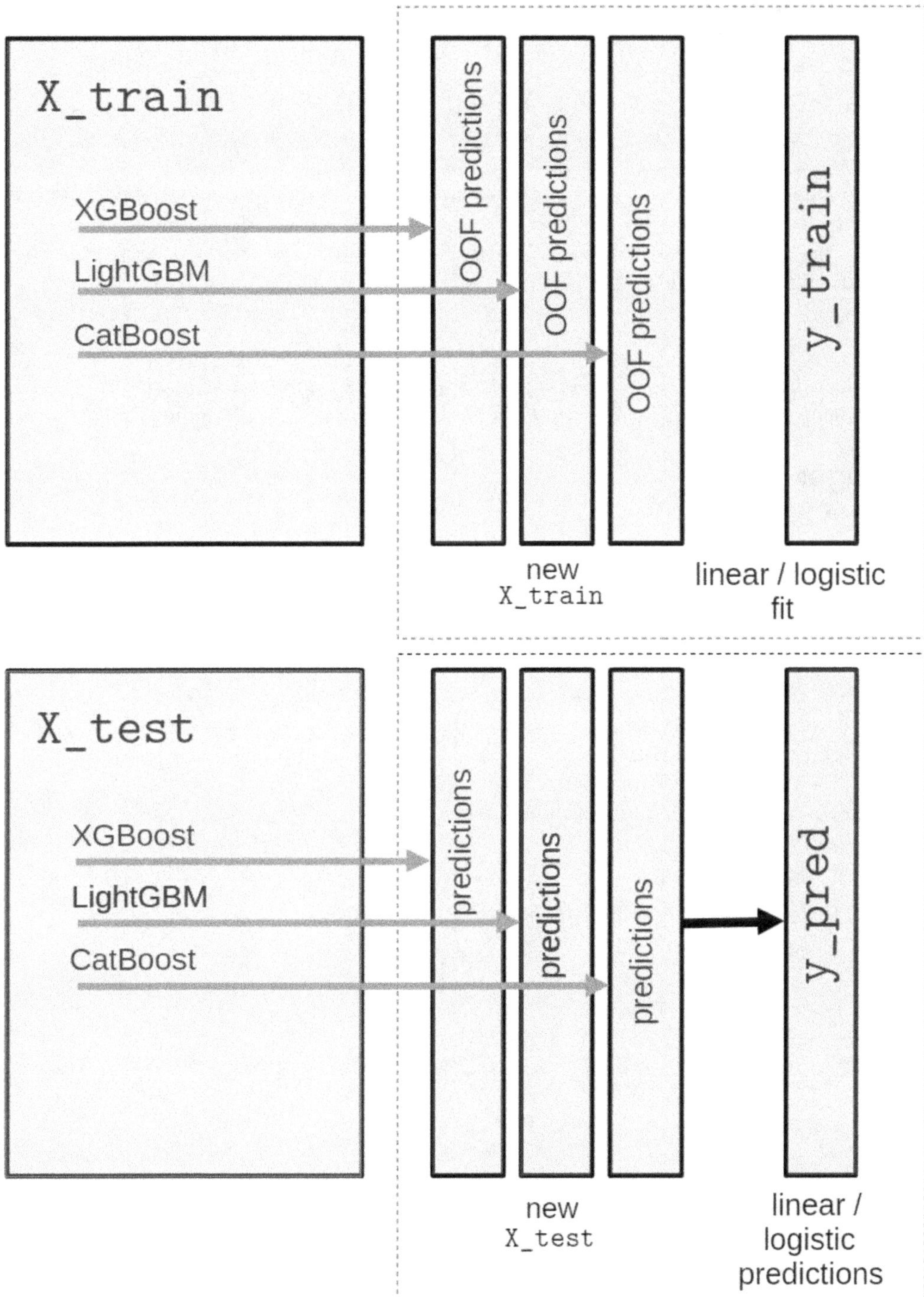

Figure 10.10: Stacking

Recommended reading

Papers

- Leo Breiman *"Random Forests"*, Machine Learning **45** pp. 5-32 (2001)
- Robert E. Schapire *"The Boosting Approach to Machine Learning: An Overview"*, Nonlinear Estimation and Classification **171** pp. 149-171 (2003)
- Jerome H. Friedman *"Greedy function approximation: A gradient boosting machine"*, The Annals of Statistics **29** pp. 1189-1232 (2001)
- R. Caruana, A. Niculescu-Mizil, G. Crew, A. Ksikes *"Ensemble selection from libraries of models"*, Proceedings of ICML'04 (2004)

Books

- Robert E. Schapire, and Yoav Freund *"Boosting: Foundations and Algorithms"*, MIT Press (2012)
- Gautam Kunapuli *"Ensemble Methods for Machine Learning"*, Manning Publications (2023)

Packages

- XGBoost
  - *"XGBoost: A Scalable Tree Boosting System"*, arXiv:1603.02754
- LightGBM
  - *"LightGBM: A Highly Efficient Gradient Boosting Decision Tree"*, NIPS 2017
- CatBoost
  - *"CatBoost: gradient boosting with categorical features support"*, arXiv:1810.11363
  - *"CatBoost: unbiased boosting with categorical features"*, arXiv:1706.09516
- linear-tree by Marco Cerliani
- hillclimbers by Matt Hill
- YDF - Yggdrasil Decision Forests (paper, GitHub)
- cuML - a GPU-accelerated machine learning library

Other

- MLWave *"Kaggle Ensembling Guide"*

11. Hyperparameter optimization (HPO)

"knobs to twiddle"

Brad Efron

What are hyperparameters? We have seen an example of a continuous hyperparameter in the form of λ for Ridge and LASSO regularization, and a discrete hyperparameter in the form of the depth of a tree (`max_depth`). The parameters are the values found by the model whilst fitting to the training data, for example the β in linear regression. On the other hand hyperparameters help to define the model one will fit, and are chosen before the fitting process begins; these are not parameters that change during the learning process. The objective of machine learning is to find the model that fits to as much signal as possible, but does not fit to the noise. Such model is located at the minimum of the n-dimensional Occam curve *i.e.* the model with the smallest estimated generalization error, where n is the number of hyperparameters.

11.1 The Optimizer's Curse: optimistic bias

Imagine the hypothetical situation that our Occam surface has a constant value regardless of the hyperparameters chosen, *i.e.* the ideal value of the generalization error is always exactly the same. Given that our validation dataset is a sample of finite size, and said data has an aleatoric noise component, then there will be both random statistical fluctuations in our estimates of the generalization error, and there will be errors due to epistemic uncertainty as we are making predictions for points that were never seen in training. Since our task is to find the set of hyperparameters that give the very best results, our final choice will be the set that returns (for regression) the lowest metric score. As we can see in this case that, by design, our results will always be overly optimistic.

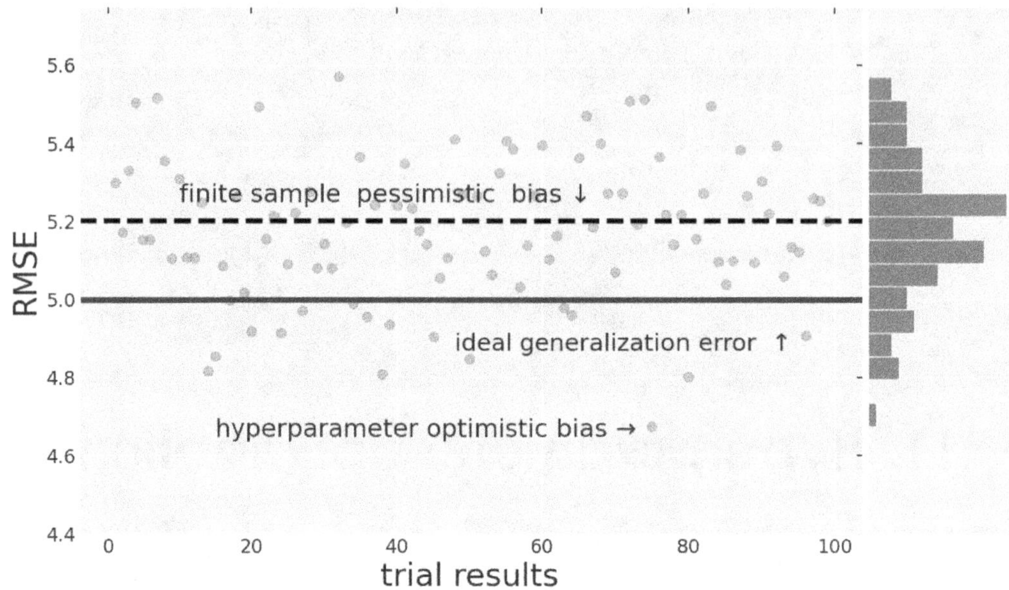

Figure 11.1: Optimizer's curse. In this figure 100 runs were performed for the very same set of hyperparameters. We see the 'best' result is actually spurious and overoptimistic.

This goes by the rather fanciful name of 'The Optimizer's Curse. Indeed somewhat paradoxically, the greater the number of hyperparameter sets that are evaluated, the more overoptimistic our estimate is likely to be. This phenomena is perfectly highlighted in the paper "`torch.manual seed(3407)` is all you need" where, as an experiment, the authors try out 10,000 different random seed values (where evidently the seed value is not a true hyperparameter) and find a 'black swan' seed that does inordinately well.

It is for this reason we made a three-way split of our dataset into train, validation and a hold-out test set; we find our best hyperparameters for the validation set and then obtain a more realistic estimate of the true generalization error by refitting our model, now with said hyperparameters, to the combined train + validation data, and perform a final evaluation on the never seen before hold-out test set. Even so, this is just one single estimate for a finite size test set, so one should not be surprised if, when putting ones model into production, the results are not quite as good as one hoped for. It is a sensible idea to take ones 'best' hyperparameter set and perform a series of additional runs, this time only changing the seed of the `random_state` to make sure we were not simply looking at a spuriously good result.

> Remark: In summary: with enough hyperparameter trials you will most certainly overfit to the validation set.

11.2 Linear and logistic regression: `None`

The linear and logistic models are essentially bereft of hyperparameters. However, if one performs regularization then `alpha` (λ) becomes a tuneable hyperparameter, representing $L2$ in Ridge or $L1$ in LASSO regression. Given the one-dimensional nature of the hyperparameter space one could locate the optimal value via a simple `for` loop.

Sample code

(gist)

```
from sklearn.linear_model import Ridge
from sklearn.model_selection import cross_val_score

alphas = np.linspace(start=50, stop=300, num=10)
RMSE_results = []

for alpha in alphas:
    regressor = Ridge(alpha=alpha)
    CV_scores = cross_val_score(regressor, X, y, cv=5,
                                scoring="neg_mean_squared_error")
    RMSE = np.sqrt(np.mean(-CV_scores))
    RMSE_results.append([alpha, RMSE])

results = np.array(RMSE_results)
print("Best alpha:", results[np.argmin(results, axis=0)[1]][0])
print("Best score:", results[np.argmin(results, axis=0)[1]][1])
```

11.3 Decision trees: max_depth and min_samples_leaf

The primary hyperparameter is the depth (max_depth) and a reasonable initial setting for this parameter would be $\approx \lfloor \log_2(n_{rows}) \rfloor - 1$. For example, for a training dataset of 5,000 rows a suggested max_depth would be 11 and one could start exploring the generalization error either side of this value.

> Remark: To know just how deep a fully-grown decision tree model can go (which is guaranteed to overfit) for your particular dataset one can set max_depth=None and then, after fitting:
> print(model.tree_.max_depth)

To regulate overfitting one can use min_samples_leaf. In scikit-learn min_samples_leaf has a default value of 1 but I would suggest never setting a value below 3.

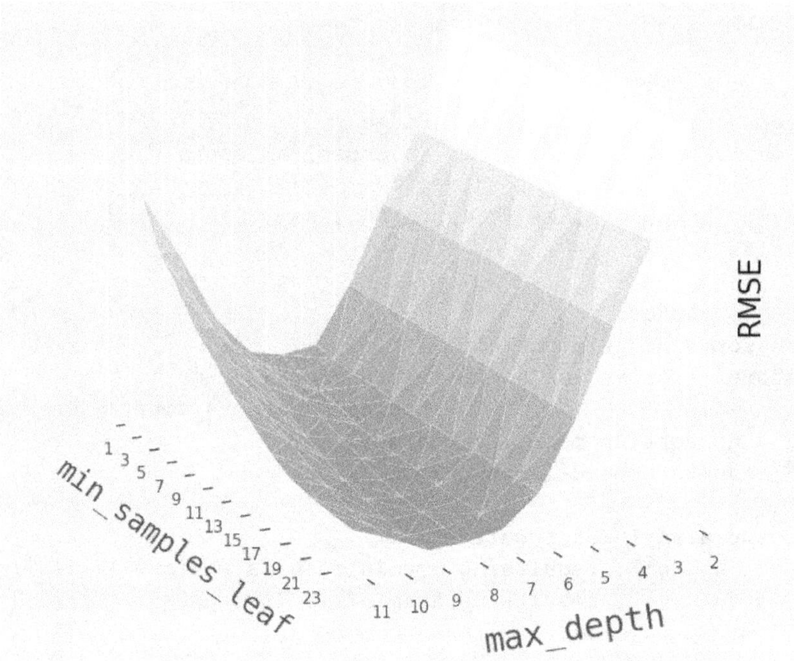

Figure 11.2: Example of a Decision Tree hyperparameter hypersurface.

However, at the end of the day, given how fast one can fit a Random Forest model, I personally would suggest not bothering with using a single decision tree as ones model. Another drawback to working with a single decision tree is their sensitivity to the very first split; a small variation in the input data could lead to growing radically different trees. On the other hand this variability is actually used to good effect with the Random Forest estimator.

11.4 Random Forest: `n_estimators` (?)

Building upon the decision tree estimator one would be inclined to think that most important hyperparameter for the Random Forest after `max_depth` and `min_samples_leaf` would be `n_estimators`. However a beautiful design feature of Random Forest is that one cannot overfit by increasing the number of trees, as seen empirically in Figure 11.3. This can be intuitively understood from the law of large numbers; imagine each decision tree were overfitted to both the signal and the random noise in the dataset. If one averages over a large enough set of diverse trees the noise will become cancelled out, leaving only the signal. Tree diversity is vitally important in such an ensemble and, in conjunction with bootstrapping, is controlled by `max_features`.

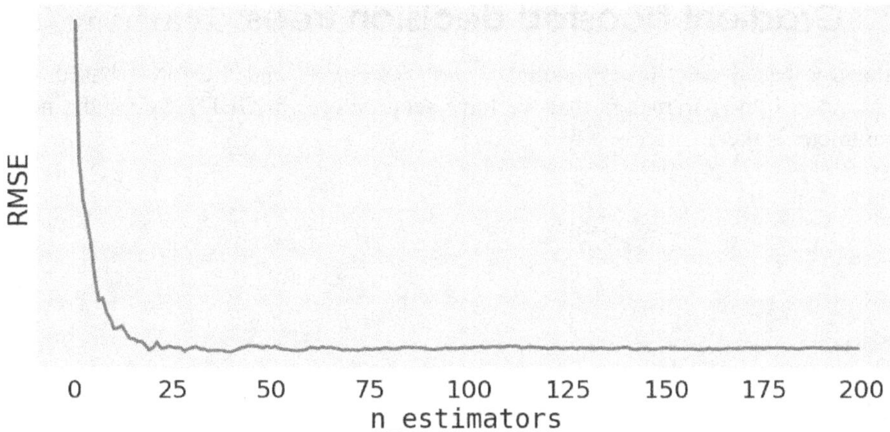

Figure 11.3: Random Forest does not overfit w.r.t. n_estimators.

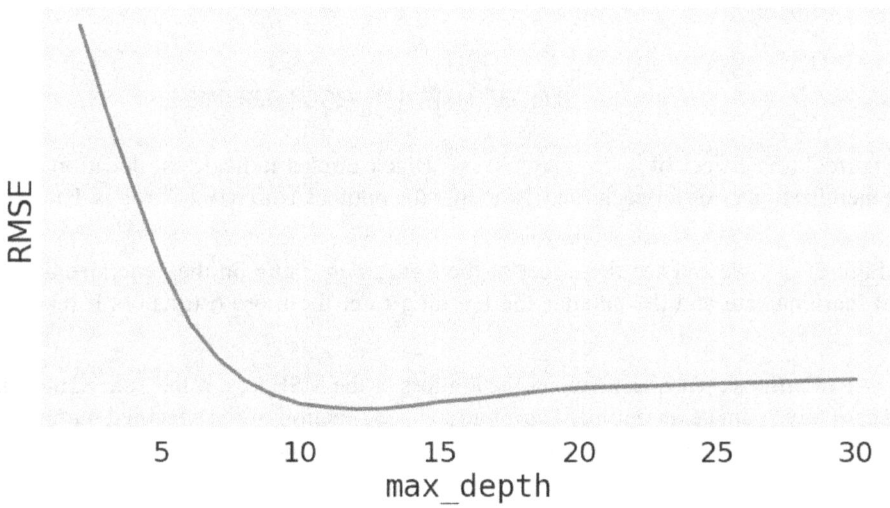

Figure 11.4: Random Forest is robust with regards to max_depth (here **n_estimators** was fixed at 100).

Given this, a suggestion is to set n_estimators to a large value (for example average over 100 trees), and then tune the two parameters associated with the decision tree, namely max_depth and min_samples_leaf, along with the max_features hyperparameter. Once one has found the optimal values for these parameters, then gradually reduce n_estimators until performance starts to degrade.

> Remark: In RandomForest the max_depth hyperparameter can be slightly deeper than the optimal value for a corresponding decision tree model since the process of averaging over multiple trees reduces this added variance.

11.5 Gradient boosted decision trees: learning_rate

After the tree based max_depth and min_samples_leaf, and the forest based max_features and n_estimators hyperparameters that we have seen before, in GBDT by far the next most influential hyperparameter is the learning_rate

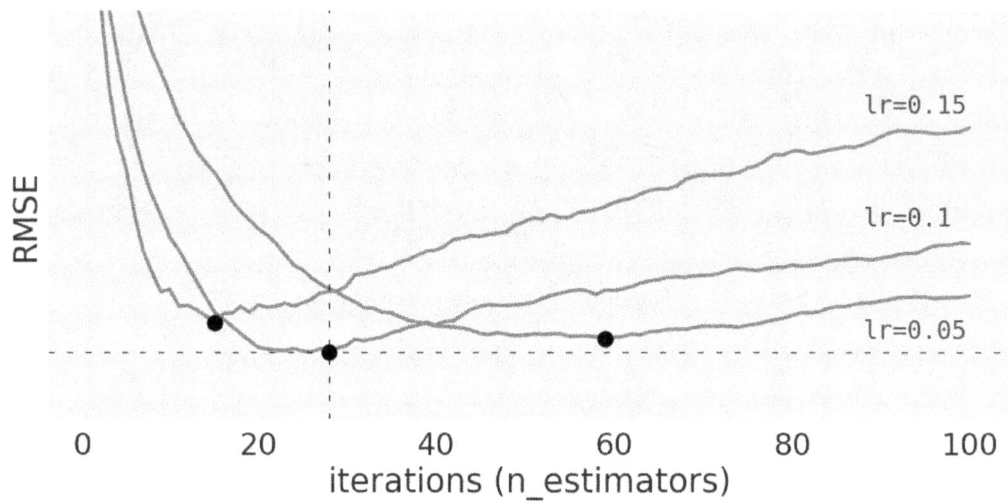

Figure 11.5: Effect of learning_rate. Black circles indicate the location of the optimal generalization error for each run. (Note that the optimal learning_rate is dataset dependant).

In Figure 11.5 we can see the effect of the learning_rate on the generalization error; there is an optimal learning rate and the smaller the learning rate, the more estimators it takes to reach the minima.

> Remark: CatBoost, when using either the log loss or the MSE loss, if the learning_rate is unset will automatically estimate an optimal learning rate as a function of the specified number of iterations and the number of rows in the dataset (otherwise the default value is 0.03).

11.5.1 Overfitting: early stopping

One can set a very large value for n_estimators and then during the training, if no improvement is seen within the specified number of early_stopping_rounds (sometimes known as the patience) then training will automatically be stopped. Here are some examples of implementing early stopping

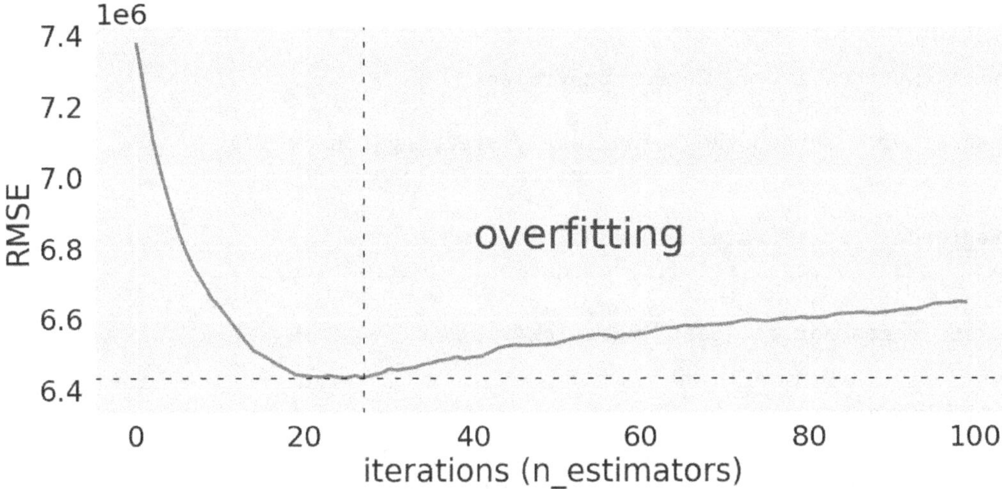

Figure 11.6: GBDT will overfit with too many estimators

XGBoost

```
import xgboost as xgb

regressor = xgb.XGBRegressor(early_stopping_rounds=10)

regressor.fit(X_train, y_train,
              eval_set=[(X_validation, y_validation)],
              verbose=False)

print(regressor.best_iteration)
print(regressor.best_score)
```

LightGBM

```
from lightgbm import LGBMRegressor
from lightgbm.callback import early_stopping

regressor = LGBMRegressor()

regressor.fit(X_train, y_train,
                  eval_set=[(X_validation, y_validation)],
                  callbacks=[early_stopping(10)], )

print(regressor.best_iteration_)
```

CatBoost

```
from catboost import CatBoostRegressor

regressor = CatBoostRegressor(early_stopping_rounds=10,
                              silent= True)

regressor.fit(X_train, y_train,
              eval_set=[(X_validation, y_validation)] )

print(regressor.get_best_iteration())
```

Scikit-learn

By default, for datasets having more than 10K rows, the scikit HistGradientBoosting routines automatically apply early stopping, setting aside 10% of the training data for validation, and will stop if there is no improvement after 10 iterations.

```
# report the number of iterations performed
print(regressor.n_iter_)
```

11.5.1.1 Early stopping and cross-validation

If ones motivation for using cross-validation is to find a good set of hyperparameters (number of iterations being one of them) with a view to creating ones final model by fitting to all of the available data then one should not use early stopping since the number of iterations will almost certainly differ for each of the folds. On the other hand if one is using CV to find the most faithful estimate of the generalization error, for example via nested CV, then one should indeed use early stopping.

11.5.1.2 Early stopping and refinement

It has recently been suggested that, when performing probabilistic classification, rather than stopping based on the proper loss (*i.e.* the log loss or Brier score) provided that post hoc calibration is performed it is optimal to stop based on the refinement error. For details see the paper *"Rethinking Early Stopping: Refine, Then Calibrate"*.

11.5.2 Some other GBDT hyperparameters

The big three have many more hyperparameters, many of which are regularization parameters like the following:

hyperparameter	**XGBoost**	**LightGBM**	**CatBoost**
$L1$	alpha	lambda_l1	–
$L2$	lambda	lambda_l2	l2_leaf_reg
min_samples_leaf	min_child_weight	min_data_in_leaf	min_data_in_leaf
max_features	colsample_bytree	feature_fraction	rsm

Table 11.1: Hyperparameter name lookup table.

11.6 Automated search routines

In practice how does one find this optimal set of hyperparameters? One can perform a manual search, but that can be rather tedious. Scikit-learn provides the following three routines:

- sklearn.model_selection.GridSearchCV
- sklearn.model_selection.RandomizedSearchCV
- sklearn.model_selection.HalvingGridSearchCV

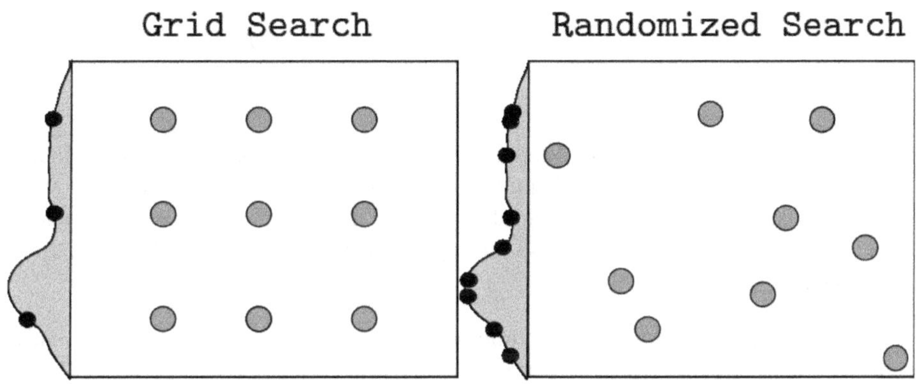

Figure 11.7: Grid search vs. randomized search: for continuous hyperparameters a randomized search better explores space. (Image based on the work of James A. Bergstra, Yoshua Bengio *"Random search for hyper-parameter optimization"*, The Journal of Machine Learning Research **13** pp. 281-305 (2012))

Perhaps the best suited of the three routines for a tree estimator, many of whose most important hyperparameters such as max_depth and min_samples_leaf are integers, is the uninformed exhaustive grid search. Meanwhile the RandomizedSearch randomly selects only n_iter of the possible hyperparameter combinations. For a neural network model, where important hyperparameters like learning_rate and batch_size have continuous values, a random (perhaps Bayesian) search is better. The halving grid search initially evaluates all of the parameter combinations, just as with the exhaustive grid search, however, using only a very small subset of the training data, thus is much faster. Informed by the results of this initial exploration, it then selects the, say, top 30% best performing parameter sets, and recalculates the results, now using more rows from the training data, and so on.

Sample code

```
%%time

from sklearn.model_selection import GridSearchCV, KFold

kf = KFold(n_splits=5, random_state=42, shuffle=True)

param_grid = { "max_depth": [4, 5, 6], # DT
               "min_samples_leaf": [10, 15, 20], # DT
               "max_features": [0.7, 0.8, 0.9], # RF
```

```
            "n_estimators": [100, 200, 300], # GBDT
            "learning_rate": [0.02, 0.015, 0.01]} # GBDT

search = GridSearchCV(regressor,
                      cv=kf,
                      param_grid,
                      scoring="neg_root_mean_squared_error",
                      n_jobs=-1).fit(X_train,y_train)

print("Best hyperparameters: ",search.best_params_)
```

> Remark: The above grid search will run a total of $(3\times3\times3\times3\times3)\times5=1215$ fits, so if for example a single fold calculation takes just 1 minute to run be aware that this grid search would take over 20 hours to complete! That said, both the grid search and the randomized search are independent, and thus is an embarrassingly parallel problem, so it is a good idea to set `n_jobs=-1` so as to run in parallel using all available processors.

Notice that here the regression scoring function has the prefix `neg_`. This is because the scikit-learn convention is the higher the score the better (which is the typical case for classification metrics). We can tabulate all of the results of this search via

```
search_results = pd.DataFrame(search.cv_results_)
columns = [col for col in search_results if col.startswith('param_')]
columns.extend(["mean_test_score","rank_test_score"])
search_results[columns].sort_values(by='rank_test_score')
```

giving

param_learning_rate	param_max_depth	param_n_estimators	mean_test_score	rank_test_score
0.015	4	200	-30197.520902	1
0.015	5	200	-30372.950429	2
0.01	5	200	-33367.680344	3
0.01	4	200	-33595.134238	4
0.015	5	100	-37251.033265	5
0.015	4	100	-37594.748265	6
0.01	5	100	-44158.702251	7
0.01	4	100	-44597.319138	8

Figure 11.8: Example of tabulated grid search results.

An appealing aspect of undertaking a grid search is that it naturally lends itself to reproducibility, thus allowing a trivial comparison of the time and metric performance of different routines.

11.6.1 Specialized packages

There are specialized packages that are dedicated to the process of hyperparameter optimization, perhaps two of the most well known being Hyperopt and Optuna. They include Bayesian optimization routines that work by fitting, and updating, a surrogate model to the hyperparameter hypersurface such as the Tree-Structured Parzen Estimator, Gaussian process, or SMAC which uses a Random Forest (turtles all the way down!). Note however that one is now fitting said surrogate models to what is a small noisy n-dimensional dataset (where n is the number of hyperparameters) having fewer than 1000 datapoints (and quite potentially less than 100).

11.7 ...now change the `random_state`

Once you have found the optimal set of hyperparameters for your estimator + dataset, try out 10 different seed values of the `KFold random_state` and check the expected variance, and also compare the results with those obtained when using the estimator default settings.

Recommended reading

Papers

- James A. Bergstra, Yoshua Bengio *"Random search for hyper-parameter optimization"*, The Journal of Machine Learning Research **13** pp. 281-305 (2012)
- Tong Yu, Hong Zhu *"Hyper-Parameter Optimization: A Review of Algorithms and Applications"*, arXiv:2003.05689 (2020)
- Li Yang, Abdallah Shami *"On Hyperparameter Optimization of Machine Learning Algorithms: Theory and Practice"*, arXiv:2007.15745 (2020)
- Franceschi *et al.* *"Hyperparameter Optimization in Machine Learning"*, arXiv:2410.22854 (2024)

Books

- Louis Owen *"Hyperparameter Tuning with Python"*, Packt Publishing Limited (2022)
- *"Hyperparameter Tuning for Machine and Deep Learning with R: A Practical Guide"*, Springer (2023)

Packages

- Optuna: A hyperparameter optimization framework
- Hyperopt: Distributed Hyperparameter Optimization
- scikit-optimize (`skopt`): `BayesSearchCV`
- HEBO - Heteroscedastic Evolutionary Bayesian Optimisation
- ConfOpt - optimization performance through conformal uncertainty quantification

Other

- scikit-learn "Tuning the hyper-parameters of an estimator"

12. Feature engineering and selection

> The greatest value of a picture is when it forces us to notice what we never expected to see.
>
> *John Tukey*

If one has ever had the pleasure of seeing an armillary sphere based on the geocentric model (there is a magnificent example in the library of the Real Monasterio de San Lorenzo de El Escorial I would be happy to show if you are passing through Madrid) and compares it to an orrery based on the heliocentric model one will appreciate the relative simplicity of calculations in the Copernican system. When it comes to feature engineering we need be like Copernicus, we need to create features that help the estimator to find simplicity in the data. Feature engineering is about creating new, more predictive features out of either the features we have been given, or by adding features from an external or secondary data source.

On the other hand feature selection is about dropping either irrelevant, overly noisy, or generally low value features, leading to a simpler more robust model. Deleting features also leads to more memory efficient model with faster predictions. This can also result in cost savings, as some features may be very expensive to obtain. Such ablation involves contrasting the difference between the performance of a model trained with the feature and a model trained without the feature; if the performance between models remains relatively unchanged (or even improves) then, in the name of parsimony[1], said feature is deleted.

12.1 Feature engineering

Feature engineering can work wonders for model performance, and is perhaps the aspect of machine learning that requires the most craftsmanship, with 'domain knowledge' often playing a large role. We have already seen magnificent examples of feature engineering in Section 7.5 where we created the x^2 feature form the x term, which immediately led to a much better fit, and in Section 8.7 for the XOR problem where we created

[1] George E. P. Box *"Robustness in the Strategy of Scientific Model Building"*, Robustness in Statistics pp. 201-236 (1979)

the feature $x_1 \times x_2$ from the features x_1 and x_2.

12.1.1 Interaction and cross features

Linear regression learns from linear combinations of features, *i.e.*

$$\hat{y}(x_1, x_2) = \hat{\beta}_1 x_1 + \hat{\beta}_2 x_2 + \hat{\beta}_0 \tag{12.1}$$

They can learn non-linear behavior by explicitly incorporating appropriate basis functions, for example to learn multiplication:

$$\hat{y}(x_1, x_2) = \hat{\beta}_1 x_1 + \hat{\beta}_2 x_2 + \hat{\beta}_3 (x_1 \cdot x_2) + \hat{\beta}_0 \tag{12.2}$$

Due to the piece-wise inductive bias decision trees, built by way of a multitude of feature comparisons, then can naturally learn about non-linear feature interactions, indeed they are universal function approximators having the capacity to fit the training data exactly. However, explicitly creating interaction features is a good idea, especially when it comes to feature importance analysis where in general only the unary features are presented in said analysis.
In view of this, worth exploring are

- power features *i.e.* x^2, $x^{1/n}$,...
- interactions between features *i.e.* $(x_1 + x_2)$, $(x_1 \times x_2)$,...
- difference features, such as $(x_1 - x_2)$
- ratio features, such as (x_1/x_2)

If one has n features one can create as many as $(n^2 - n)/2$ binary additive and multiplicative features, and as many as $n^2 - n$ binary difference and ratio features. For example:

```
df["area"] = df["length"] * df["breadth"]
df["disposable_income"] = df["income"] - df["taxes"]
```

One can use the scikit-learn `PolynomialFeatures` to help with this process but if one has many features in ones dataset this could easily get out of hand and even accidentally create spuriously effective features, so I would suggest creating bespoke interaction features based on common sense and domain knowledge.

12.1.2 Bucketing of continuous features

One can perform discretization or *bucketing* of continuous features prior to modeling, for example via the scikit-learn `sklearn.preprocessing.KBinsDiscretizer`, which has options such as 'uniform', 'quantile', or 'kmeans'. However, I would strongly suggest this process is actually best left in the hands of ones tree model. Indeed converting continuous features into histograms forms an integral part of histogram gradient boosting.

12.1.3 Power transforms: Yeo-Johnson

Variance-stabilizing transformations, or power transforms[2], can potentially be useful for parametric models. For example converting a feature having the positive skewed Galton distribution into a Gaussian distribution: `df["log_x1"] = np.log(df["x1"])` (note that $\ln(0) = -\infty$, so watch out for zero-inflated features, where one could perhaps take the liberty of converting the zeros into ones before transforming, or use `np.log(df["x1"] +1)`). A Yeo-Johnson transform can be used to correct skewness or kurtosis (for example by using the scikit `power_transform`). Such a transform may help in interpreting linear models that assume a Gaussian distribution of errors. However, feature transformations probably will not enhance the predictive performance of a linear model, and certainly will not help tree based estimators.

[2] Jonathan T. Barron *"A Power Transform"*, arXiv:2502.10647 (2025)

12.1.4 User defined transform

If one wishes to apply a bespoke transformation an option is to do so using a function

```
def fn(x):
    # y=f(x) here
    return y

df["new_feature"] = df["old_feature"].apply(fn)
```

For example, one may have origin-destination data in terms of latitude and longitude features, but in some cases converting these into relative distances may be more informative (see the `vincenty` package).

12.1.5 Temporal features

If one has a datetime column this can easily be decomposed into potentially informative features, for example

```
df['year']  = df['datetime'].dt.year
df['month'] = df['datetime'].dt.month
df['day']   = df['datetime'].dt.day
df['DoW']   = df['datetime'].dt.day_of_week
df['hour']  = df['datetime'].dt.hour
```

Such cyclic month, day, and day of the week features can be excellent at capturing what is known as seasonality. However, be wary of the year feature; new data will quite potentially have a value for the year that was not seen in the training data, and thus will force your model to extrapolate, something that tree-based estimators do not do well.

Circle transform

A saw-tooth wave, such as the time of day, can be transformed into Cartesian positions on a unit circle so as to make, for example, 23:00 closer to 00:00 than 12:00 is

```
period = 24
df["hour_sin"] = np.sin(df["hour"] / period * 2 * np.pi)
df["hour_cos"] = np.cos(df["hour"] / period * 2 * np.pi)
```

12.1.6 External secondary features

Adding external data can also lead to a significant improvement in model performance. An example could be in modeling taxi usage; maybe adding a feature based on the weather could be informative as people may be more inclined to make use of a taxi service if it is raining, and less inclined if it is sunny. This data could be scraped from a meteorological service. Another useful feature could be to add a categorical column that indicates if the day was a weekday, and weekend, or a local or national holiday (one could use `dateutil.easter` for adding the Easter holidays to ones feature).

12.2 Feature selection

Feature selection is the removal of weak features from the model, leading to a more robust model with less potential for overfitting and faster to train. The very first thing to do is to drop features that have zero variance, and also perfectly (or very highly) correlated features.

12.2.1 Correlation

Remark: Some statistical texts recommend dropping features that are uncorrelated with the target variable based on the linear parametric Pearson correlation coefficient. However, if one is using a non-linear/non-parametric model I would advise against doing this as we have seen that seemingly uncorrelated features can indeed contain mutually useful information.

12.2.2 Permutation importance

Permutation importance[3] is performed as follows:

1. fit a model to the training data
2. calculate model metric score for a test dataset, which becomes our point of reference
3. randomly reorder the values of a single column (feature) in the test data (*i.e.* `df['feature_n'] = df['feature_n'].sample(frac=1).values`)
4. re-predict, and re-calculate the metric score for this new test `df`
5. the importance of the feature is proportional to how much the metric score degrades (*i.e.* if the feature was unimportant the metric score would not degrade at all)
6. reset the column and repeat for each of the columns in the dataset
7. produce an importance ranking based of relative score degradation

	feature_1	feature_2	feature_3	feature_4	feature_5	feature_6	feature_7	feature_8	feature_9	Target
0	0	0	8	0	0	0	0	0	0	0
1	1	1	1	1	1	1	1	1	1	1
2	2	2	5	2	2	2	2	2	2	2
3	3	3	0	3	3	3	3	3	3	3
4	4	4	7	4	4	4	4	4	4	4
5	5	5	2	5	5	5	5	5	5	5
6	6	6	9	6	6	6	6	6	6	6
7	7	7	4	7	7	7	7	7	7	7
8	8	8	3	8	8	8	8	8	8	8
9	9	9	6	9	9	9	9	9	9	9

Figure 12.1: Permutation importance: a test `df` with a randomly shuffled column.

This is an inexpensive technique, only requiring as many evaluations as there are features, along with the unperturbed reference calculation.

Remark: There is a caveat that should be mentioned in that, especially if there are highly correlated features, the act of random permutation on such features will create a dataset that has points outside of the convex hull of data that the model was trained on, *i.e.* we end up extrapolating which leads to

[3] Leo Breiman "*Random Forests*", Machine Learning **45** 5-32 (2001) §10

unreliable results especially for tree models[a], and this should be borne in mind if using permutation importance as a model interpretability tool.

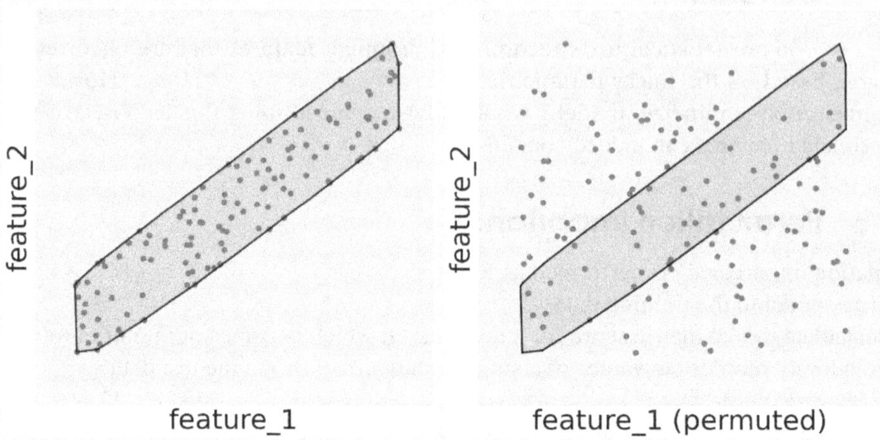

Figure 12.2: Permuted points can lie outside the convex hull of the training data. Point predictions outside of the hull will be the result of extrapolation, and as such are highly unreliable.

[a] Giles Hooker, Lucas Mentch, Siyu Zhou "*Unrestricted Permutation forces Extrapolation: Variable Importance Requires at least One More Model*", arXiv:1905.03151 (2021)

N Jupyter Notebook: House Prices: Permutation Importance example.

Sample code

Example of performing permutation importance on a test set using ELI5

```
import eli5
from eli5.sklearn import PermutationImportance

# first fit the regressor on the training data
model = regressor().fit(X_train, y_train)
feature_names = X_train.columns.tolist()

# calculate the permutation importance using the test set
perm_import = PermutationImportance(model,
              random_state= 42).fit(X_test, y_test)
eli5.show_weights(perm_import, top=None,
              feature_names = feature_names)
```

Weight	Feature
1.1113 ± 0.0215	m2_edificados
0.3970 ± 0.0121	precio_zona
0.0194 ± 0.0013	precio_alquiler
0.0065 ± 0.0006	ascensor
0.0019 ± 0.0004	exterior
0.0007 ± 0.0001	aparcamiento
0.0004 ± 0.0001	n_habitaciones
0.0003 ± 0.0002	m2_útiles
0.0002 ± 0.0001	orientación_este
0.0002 ± 0.0002	precio_aparcamiento
0.0002 ± 0.0001	nueva_construcción
0.0001 ± 0.0001	orientación_oeste
0.0001 ± 0.0000	orientación_norte
0.0001 ± 0.0000	planta
0.0001 ± 0.0001	n_baños
0.0000 ± 0.0000	orientación_sur
0.0000 ± 0.0000	año_construción
0.0000 ± 0.0000	necesita_reforma

Figure 12.3: Permutation importance output from ELI5.

Remark: The relative importance of the features will vary between estimators.

12.2.3 SHAP exact explainer

The Exact explainer from the SHAP package calculates the mean Shapley value[4] for each feature. There is also a Permutation explainer which implements a faster approximate method and is more suitable for datasets that have a large number of features.

[4] Rozemberczki *at al.* *"The Shapley Value in Machine Learning"*, arXiv:2202.05594 (2022)

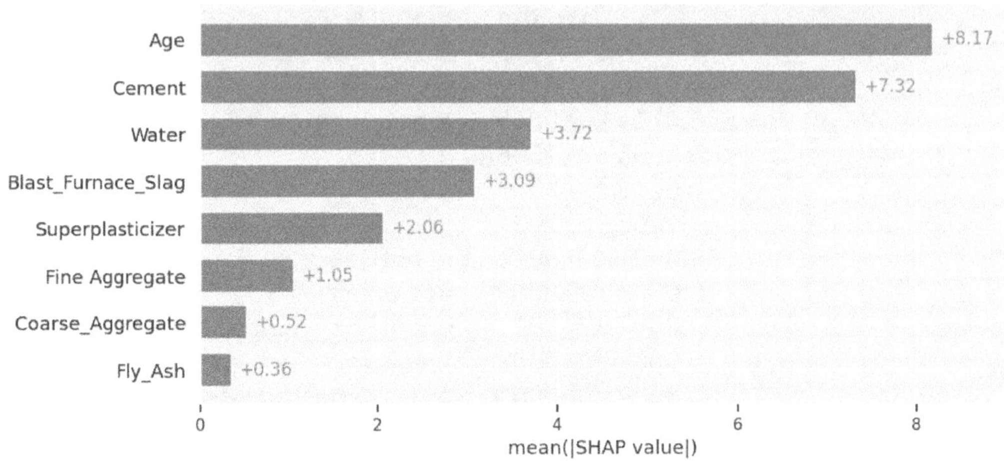

Figure 12.4: Example of the SHAP Exact explainer output.

Sample code

```
import shap

explainer = shap.explainers.Exact(model.predict, X)
shap_values = explainer(X)
shap.plots.bar(shap_values, max_display = X.shape[1])
```

12.2.4 Stepwise regression

Stepwise regression techniques either go forward by starting from no features and accreting new features until no improvement is seen. Or they can go backward, deleting features whose removal do not degrade the model (ablation). Choosing the features based on statistical significance has long been known to be problematic[5] and stepwise regression should be based on out-of-fold or out-of-sample results, *i.e.* by monitoring the effect on the validation set. However, one should still be wary, due to the potentially large number of test performed, of overfitting to the validation set.

Recursive feature elimination (RFE)

Choose the number of features one wishes to select (n) then:

1. calculate the importance of each feature,
   for example via the RandomForest `feature_importances_`
2. eliminate the weakest feature
3. repeat until n features remain

I would suggest setting `n_features_to_select` parameter to be 1 to produce a ranking, then remove the weakest features one by one by hand, all the while monitoring validation performance. Scikit-learn also has the `RFECV` routine that performs RFE in conjunction with cross-validation.

N Jupyter Notebook: "Recursive Feature Elimination (RFE) example"

[5] Gary Smith *"Step away from stepwise"*, Journal of Big Data **5** 32 (2018)

12.2.5 LASSO

The LASSO regularization can be used to eliminate weak features. Unlike Ridge regression, as the regularization strength is increased the LASSO can effectively reduce coefficients to become zero (see Fig 7.35), at which point they no longer form part of the model.

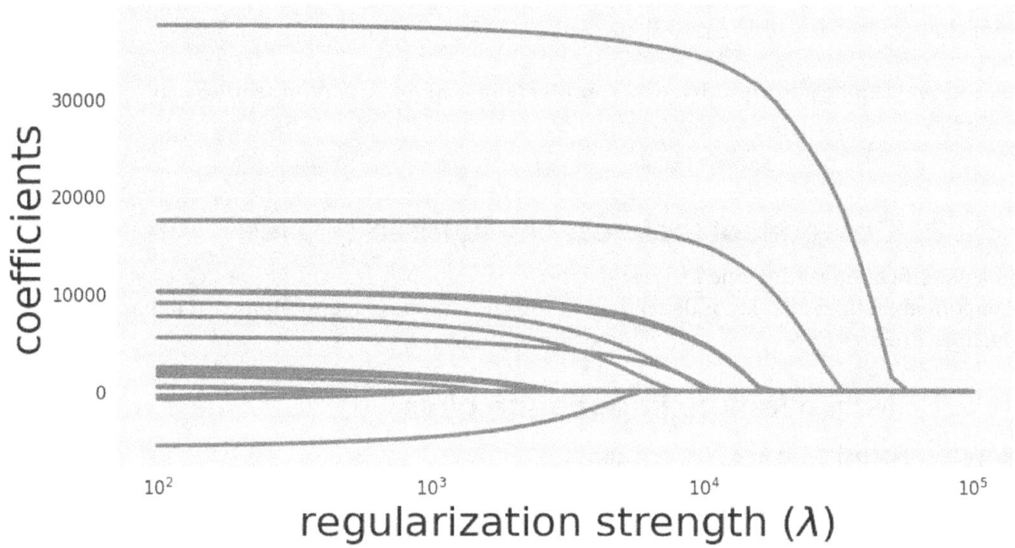

Figure 12.5: The effect of increasing the LASSO λ parameter on the feature coefficient paths.

N Jupyter Notebook: Feature importance using the LASSO

12.2.6 Maximum relevance minimum redundancy (mRMR)

The mRMR feature selection method[6], rather than trying to identify the top n most important features, seeks to create the best set of n features, which is not necessarily the same thing as some of the top n features may be somewhat correlated, and hence potentially redundant. Correlation between the features is calculated for example by using the mutual information. A python implementation can be found in the `mrmr_selection` package, which comes with both a classifier and a regressor and returns a list of the n selected features:

```
from mrmr import mrmr_regression

# select 10 features
selected_features = mrmr_regression(X= X_train, y= y_train, K=10)
```

12.2.7 Boruta trick

The 'Boruta' trick[7] consists of (temporarily) inserting a number of random noise features into ones training dataset. Any feature whose importance is lower than any one of these nose features is, by extension, also

[6] Zhao, Anand, Wang *"Maximum Relevance and Minimum Redundancy Feature Selection Methods for a Marketing Machine Learning Platform"*, arXiv:1908.05376 (2019)

[7] Stoppiglia, Dreyfus, Dubois, Oussar *"Ranking a random feature for variable and feature selection"*, Journal of Machine Learning Research **3** pp. 1399-1414 (2003)

essentially insignificant noise, and can be dropped.

Sample code

```
df['RANDOM_1'] = np.random.normal(size=len(df))
df['RANDOM_2'] = np.random.normal(size=len(df))
df['RANDOM_n'] = np.random.normal(size=len(df))
```

Indeed one can be surprised by how spuriously important a random feature can sometimes be in a small dataset.

N Jupyter Notebook: "Feature selection using the Boruta-SHAP package"

12.2.8 Categorical features: chi-squared (χ^2) test

In a classification setting one can use the `sklearn.feature_selection.chi2` statistical test to identify categorical features that are independent of the target. One can apply this test to continuous features too if the have previously been bucketed into discrete values.

12.2.9 Native feature importance plots

RandomForest `feature_importances_`

The scikit-learn RandomForest estimators upon fitting can provide `feature_importances_` based on the mean decrease in impurity.

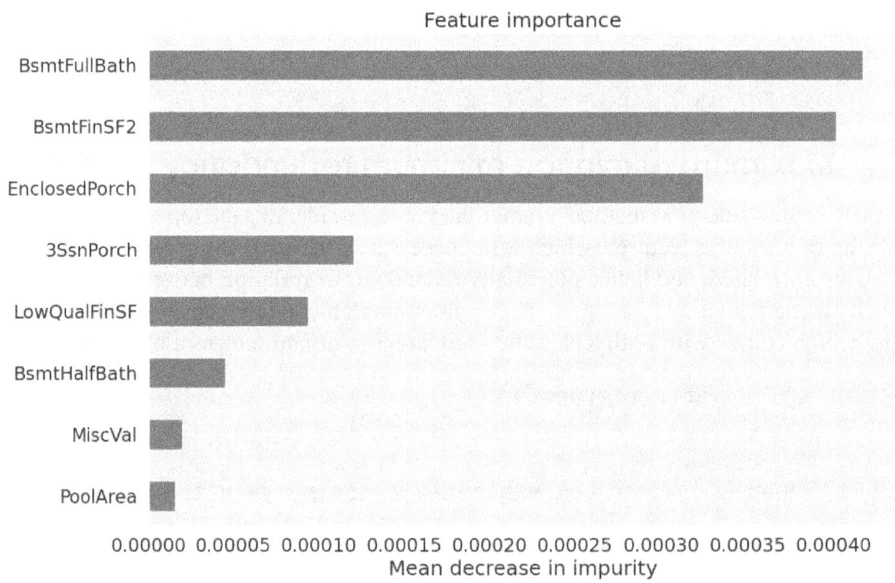

Figure 12.6: RandomForest feature importance plot

Remark: **Warning**: The mean decrease in impurity can be untrustworthy as it assigns high importance to noisy features.[a] For example a random noise feature would be incorrectly ranked as one of the most

> important features in the model!
>
> [a]Li, Wang, Basu, Kumbier, Yu *"A Debiased MDI Feature Importance Measure for Random Forests"*, arXiv:1906.10845 (2019)

Sample code

```
feature_importances = RF_regressor.feature_importances_
feature_names = X_train.columns.tolist()
importances = pd.Series(feature_importances, index=feature_names)
sorted_importances = importances.sort_values(ascending=Fasle)

fig, ax = plt.subplots()
sorted_importances.plot.barh()
ax.set_title("Feature importance")
ax.set_xlabel("Mean decrease in impurity")
plt.show()
```

XGBoost feature importance

XGBoost provides a similar plot via `plot_importance` method, this time reporting something called the 'F score' which is *"...based on the number of times that variable was selected for splitting in the tree weighted by the squared improvement to the model as a result of each of those splits*[8]". The great thing about both of these plots is that they require no extra computation, although they are not as trustworthy as out-of-sample methods.

Sample code

Here is the code to plot the 8 most important features for our `XGB_regressor`:

```
from xgboost import plot_importance

fig, ax = plt.subplots(figsize=(12,8))
plot_importance(model,
                max_num_features=10, # show top 10 features
                importance_type='weight',
                ax=ax)
plt.show();
```

Jupyter Notebook: An introduction to XGBoost regression

LightGBM feature importance

LightGBM has `plot_importance`. One can plot the importances by either `gain` or `split`.

```
import lightgbm

lightgbm.plot_importance(model,
                         max_num_features=10, # show top 10 features
```

[8]Jerome H. Friedman, Jacqueline J. Meulman *"Multiple additive regression trees with application in epidemiology"*, Statistics in Medicine **22** pp. 1365-1381 (2003)

```
                                importance_type='gain')
plt.show()
```

CatBoost feature importance

CatBoost has the `get_feature_importance` method.

```
from catboost import CatBoostRegressor

model = CatBoostRegressor()
model.fit(X,y)

feature_importances = model.get_feature_importance()
feature_names = X.columns

# save in a dataframe
importance_df = pd.DataFrame(feature_names, columns=['feature'])
importance_df["importance"] = feature_importances

# display the dataframe
importance_df.sort_values(by=["importance"], ascending=False)
```

12.3 Principal component analysis (PCA)

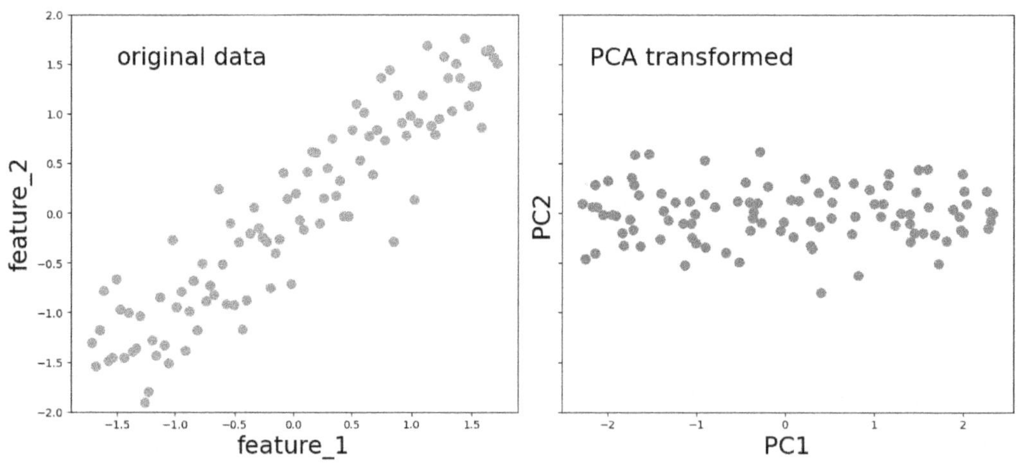

Figure 12.7: PCA using SVD in action.

Principal component analysis (PCA) is a venerable technique, going back to Karl Pearson in 1901 and Harold Hotelling in 1933. PCA is an an affine transformation, specifically a linear mapping, which calculates the eigenvalues and eigenvectors of the covariance matrix, the eigenvectors becoming the new features. The variance of each new feature is known as the *explained variance*. Given that we are essentially rotating our dataset one needs to standardize the data, thus removing the mean of each feature (an operation sometimes known as *centering*), before performing the PCA transformation (note this will make PCA very sensitive to the presence of outliers). It is interesting in that it is a technique that both creates new features, and at the same time can be used to reduce the number of features (dimensionality reduction) that we use in our model. For example, one could have an n-dimensional dataset, having n features, and reduce the dataset all the way down to 1-dimension by dropping all new features other than the first principal component. However, when it comes to making predictions one still need access to all of the original features so as to re-create the same principal component(s) to feed into the trained model. So, although PCA can be used to reduce the number of dimensions, it is not to be considered a feature elimination technique. PCA can also be used as an unsupervised technique for anomaly detection, or for outlier removal.

```
from sklearn.preprocessing import StandardScaler
scaler = StandardScaler()
scaler.fit(dataset)
dataset = scaler.transform(dataset)

# using scikit-learn:
from sklearn.decomposition import PCA
pca = PCA()
pca.fit(dataset)
dataset_transformed = pca.transform(dataset)

# using numpy:
# compute the covariance matrix (CM)
CM = np.cov(dataset, rowvar=False)

# calculate the eigenvalues and eigenvectors
eigenvalues_CM, eigenvectors_CM = np.linalg.eigh(CM)

idx = eigenvalues_CM.argsort()[::-1]  # descending sort
eigenvalues_CM = eigenvalues_CM[idx]
eigenvectors_CM = eigenvectors_CM[:,idx]

dataset_transformed = np.dot(dataset, eigenvectors_CM)
```

It should be mentioned that PCA has notable limitations; the feature-mixtures in the components created by PCA become uninterpretable (see Figure **??**). Furthermore a recent study has found[9]:

> ...*we carried out extensive analyses on twelve PCA applications, using model- and real-populations to evaluate the reliability, robustness, and reproducibility of PCA. We found that PCA failed in all criteria and showed how easily it could generate erroneous, contradictory, and absurd results.*

so use PCA with caution.

[9] Eran Elhaik "*Principal Component Analyses (PCA)-based findings in population genetic studies are highly biased and must be reevaluated*", Scientific Reports **12** 14683 (2022)

Recommended reading

Papers

- Isabelle Guyon, André Elisseeff *"An Introduction to Variable and Feature Selection"*, Journal of Machine Learning Research **3** pp. 1157-1182 (2003)
- A. Jović, K. Brkić, N. Bogunović *"A review of feature selection methods with applications"*, MIPRO pp. 1200-1205 (2015)
- Loren Nuyts, Jesse Davis *"The When and How of Target Variable Transformations"*, arXiv:2504.20821 (2025)

Books

- Alice Zheng, Amanda Casari "*Feature Engineering for Machine Learning*", O'Reilly Media, Inc. (2018)
- Max Kuhn, Kjell Johnson "*Feature Engineering and Selection: A Practical Approach for Predictive Models*", CRC Press (2019)
- Pablo Duboue *"The Art of Feature Engineering"*, Cambridge University Press (2020)
- Soledad Galli "*Python Feature Engineering Cookbook*" 3rd Edition, Packt Publishing Limited (2024)

Packages

- Boruta-Shap
- Featuretools
- Feature Engine
- LOFO (Leave One Feature Out) Importance by Ahmet Erdem
- mRMR - minimum Redundancy Maximum Relevance by Samuele Mazzanti
- Xgbfir - ranks features as well as feature interactions for XGBoost by Boris Kostenko
- SHAP - SHapley Additive exPlanations

13. Tabular foundation models (TFM)

> There are two kinds of fools: one says, "This is old, therefore it is good"; the other says, "This is new, therefore it is better."
>
> *William Ralph Inge (1931)*

Tabular foundation models; pretrained neural networks using an encoder-only attention based transformer architecture that perform 'in-context' learning, stand shoulder to shoulder with gradient boosted decision trees (GBDT) in terms of predictive performance. In this chapter we look at what went wrong with traditional neural networks, and what is now going right, specifically the paradigm shift form fitting a neural network from scratch to the training data, as per the standard machine learning pipeline we have seen thus far, to pretraining on a corpus of tables followed by in-context learning of the combined train/test dataset.

13.1 Artificial neural networks: simple examples

The following are code snippets to perform linear regression and logistic regression. Here we use the Keras library, where we can see the `fit` and `predict` methods, just as with scikit-learn. We create a sequential model having a simple linear topology which is populated with a `list` of the layers; here having an input layer, followed by a final dense (fully connected) output layer. We use the SGD (stochastic gradient descent) optimizer, having the `learning_rate` hyperparameter.

```
import keras
from keras.models import Sequential
from keras import layers
from keras import optimizers
```

> Remark: Just as with the statistical linear and logistic regression routines for neural networks the data should be scaled beforehand.

```
from sklearn.preprocessing import RobustScaler

scaler = RobustScaler()
X_scaled = scaler.fit_transform(x.values.reshape(-1, 1))
```

or perhaps using the recently developed SquashingScaler available in the skrub library, very much designed with neural networks in mind.

Linear regression

For linear regression we use the mean_squared_error loss, no hidden layers, and with no (*i.e.* linear) activation function[1] on the output node:

```
n_features = 1 # one input feature
n_neurons = 1 # one output neuron

model = keras.Sequential([
    # input layer
    layers.Input(shape = (n_features,)),
     # linear output layer
    layers.Dense(units =  n_neurons, activation = None),
])

optimizer = keras.optimizers.SGD(learning_rate=0.3)
model.compile(loss = 'mean_squared_error',
              optimizer = optimizer)

model.fit(X_scaled.reshape(-1, 1), y,
          epochs = 200, verbose = 0)

y_pred  = model.predict(X_scaled.reshape(-1, 1))

# get the weights and bias of the output layer
beta_1 = model.layers[-1].get_weights()[0]
beta_0 = model.layers[-1].get_weights()[1]
```

In Figure 13.1 we depict a fully connected feed-forward network having a two neuron hidden layer.

[1] Kunc, Kléma *"Three Decades of Activations: A Comprehensive Survey of 400 Activation Functions for Neural Networks"*, arXiv:2402.09092 (2024)

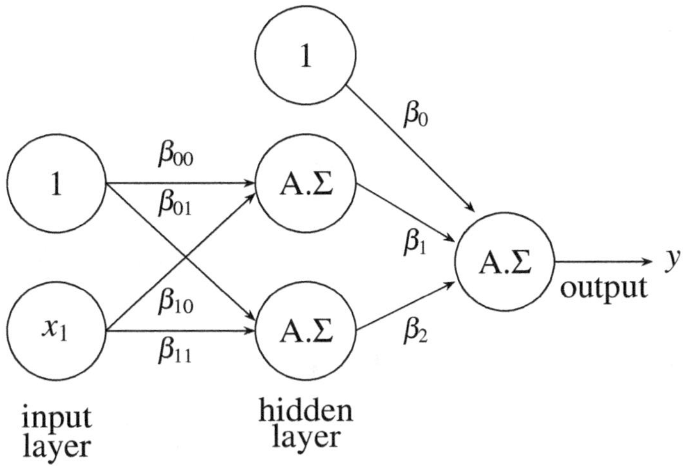

Figure 13.1: Graphical representation of a fully-connected feed forward network.

If the activation function is always linear ($A = 1$) we have

$$\begin{aligned} y &= \beta_2(\beta_{11}x_1 + \beta_{01}) + \beta_1(\beta_{10}x_1 + \beta_{00}) + \beta_0 \\ &= (\beta_2\beta_{11} + \beta_1\beta_{10})x_1 + (\beta_2\beta_{01} + \beta_1\beta_{00}) + \beta_0 \\ &\equiv \alpha_1 x_1 + \alpha_0 \end{aligned}$$

i.e. any number of hidden layer neurons can be represented by a single equivalent output neuron. We see from this that for a neural network to be non-trivial, the activation functions must be non-linear.

Logistic regression

Here we use the binary_crossentropy loss in conjunction with the non-linear sigmoid activation function to perform Bernoulli regression. Note that we use an order of magnitude more epochs (iterations) than with linear regression to reach convergence.

```
n_features = 1 # one input feature
n_neurons = 1 # one output neuron

model = keras.Sequential([
     # input layer
    layers.Input(shape = (n_features,)),
     # output layer
    layers.Dense(units =  n_neurons, activation = 'sigmoid'),
])

optimizer = keras.optimizers.SGD(learning_rate=0.3)
model.compile(loss = 'binary_crossentropy',
              optimizer = optimizer)

model.fit(X_scaled.reshape(-1, 1), y,
          epochs = 2000, verbose = 0)
```

```
y_pred  = model.predict(X_scaled.reshape(-1, 1))

# get the weights and bias of the output layer
kappa_1 = model.layers[-1].get_weights()[0]
kappa_0 = model.layers[-1].get_weights()[1]
```

For a network of such non-linear activation functions other than on the output node it has been shown that, for sufficient neurons in the hidden layer, in principle it is capable of approximating any continuous function.[2,3,4]

13.2 Why no traditional ANN?

When it comes to tabular data it has been found that traditional artificial neural networks (ANN), also known as multilayer perceptrons (MLP) are, quite literally, a waste of time.

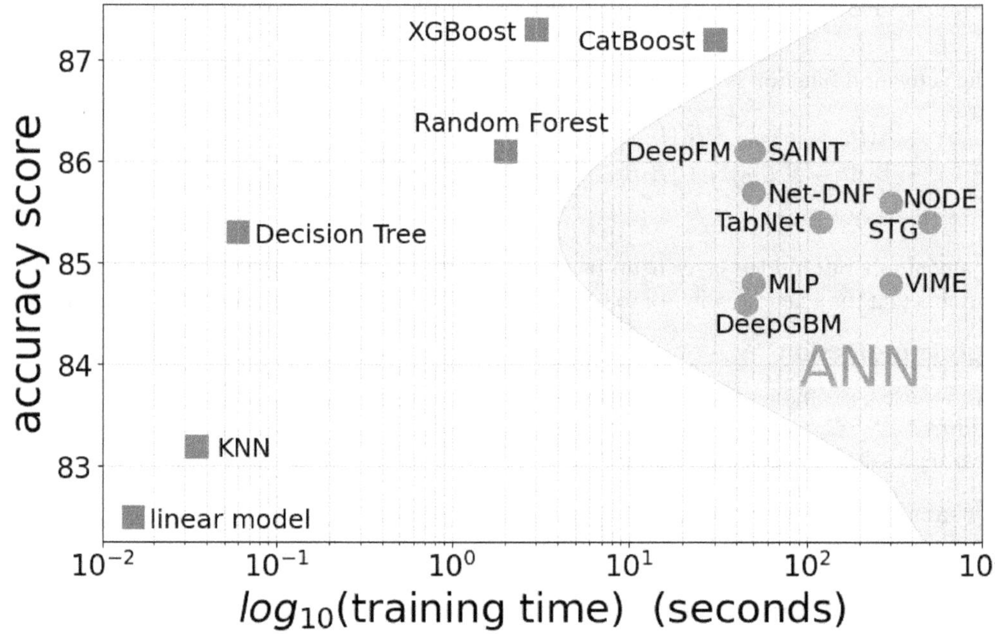

Figure 13.2: Benchmark performance comparison of ANN models based on the traditional fit/predict paradigm. (Data taken from: Borisov, Leemann, Seßler, Haug, Pawelczyk, Kasneci, *"Deep Neural Networks and Tabular Data: A Survey"*, IEEE Transactions on Neural Networks and Learning Systems **35** pp. 7499-7519 (2024)).

In Figure 13.2, taken from a study published in 2024 which plots performance against time (on a

[2] George V. Cybenko *"Approximation by superpositions of a sigmoidal function"*, Mathematics of Control, Signals, and Systems **2** pp. 303-314 (1989)

[3] Ken-Ichi Funahashi *"On the approximate realization of continuous mappings by neural networks"* Neural Networks **2** pp. 183-192 (1989)

[4] Kurt Hornik, Maxwell Stinchcombe, Halbert White *"Multilayer feedforward networks are universal approximators"*, Neural Networks **2** pp. 359-366 (1989)

logarithmic scale), to the left we can see our linear and decision tree models and on the RHS are neural network estimators which at best are on par with the Random Forest, and none achieving the performance of XGBoost or CatBoost seen at the very top of the plot. This is curious because neural networks in the form of MLP, just like decision trees, have been shown to be universal approximators.[5] A potential reason is because tabular data does not form a smooth continuous hypersurface due to noisy data, missing values, categorical features (for example see Fig. 13.3), and features with disparate ranges (for example `salary` and `age`, *etc.*) all working against the manifold hypothesis which neural networks make use of.

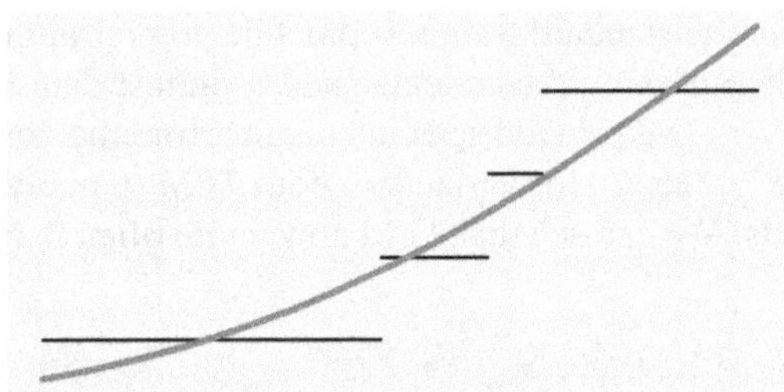

Figure 13.3: Example fit of an MLP (green curve) to a step function representing categorical data; despite being universal approximators it is not an easy task to fit a smooth function to a piecewise continuous function.

In the paper *"Why do tree-based models still outperform deep learning on tabular data?"* three reasons are suggested:

- MLP have spectral bias; they tend to prioritize learning low frequency modes, and find it harder to fit to a high-frequency hypersurface such as that of tabular data
- rotational invariance: in a paper by Andrew Ng[6] it is suggested that the MLP is a rotationally invariant algorithm, and that '*rotationally invariant algorithms are unlikely to be effective feature selection algorithms*'
- in the same paper it is stated that decision trees (and by extension GBDT) are a non-rotationally invariant algorithm, and thus are much better at ignoring any uninformative features that are present in the dataset.

For example, principal component analysis is a technique that rotates a dataset; the implication is that a neural network would perform equally well if fed the PCA rotated data, whereas GBDT would be able to achieve improved performance by focusing on the principal components and disregarding the lesser components, which are often associated with noise.

13.3 Foundation models

TabNet, developed in 2019 by Google, was perhaps one of the very first forays into the application of the then nascent attention mechanism, originally designed for text data, which sits at the very heart of transformer models. The specific role of attention is to add a component of situational context to the embedding vectors. The are various implementations of attention, but perhaps the most well known today is that of the scaled dot-product attention by Vaswani *et al.* from the famous "Attention Is All You Need" paper

$$\text{attention}(Q,K,V) = \text{softmax}\left(\frac{QK^T}{\sqrt{d_K}}\right)V \tag{13.1}$$

[5] Davis, Motamed *"Approximation Power of Deep Neural Networks: an explanatory mathematical survey", arXiv:2207.09511 (2024)*

[6] Ng *"Feature selection, L_1 vs. L_2 regularization, and rotational invariance"*, ICML '04: Proceedings pp. 78 (2004)

where Q is the query, K is the key, and V is the value (nomenclature inherited from database terminology). The dot product QK^T calculates a matrix of similarity scores (analogous to the covariance matrix we saw earlier for random vectors) between embedding vectors. These similarity scores are then normalized by the standard deviation ($1/\sqrt{d_K}$, where d is the dimension of K) before passing through the softmax function thus creating a row stochastic matrix, *i.e.* converting the scores into probabilities. This matrix represents the weights that are then applied to the vector V, which adds an attention component to the original (unattentive) embedding vectors. Experience showed, however, as reflected in Fig. 13.2 that the results for TabNet were somewhat underwhelming. The long sought-after performance improvement finally arrived by radically shifting the approach from the standard train/test pipeline, to pretraining a transformer network on a huge corpus of datasets and then passing the concatenated train/test dataset through this tabular 'foundation' model (TFM). In Figure 13.4 we provide selected results from the comprehensive `TabArena` benchmark suite in terms of their the Elo rating for variants of both TFM (namely TabPFN and TabICL) and three of the big four GBDT models. We can see that TFM now, more often than not, outperform GBDT.

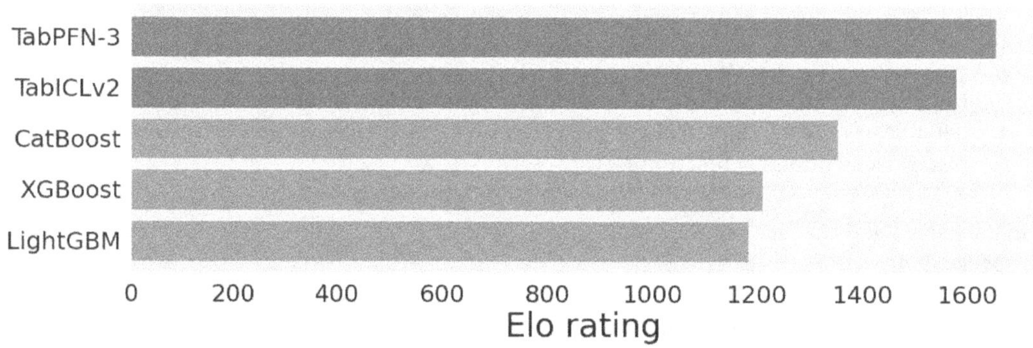

Figure 13.4: Point prediction performance using the default settings in terms of Elo rating (the higher the better) for a selection of models (TFM in green, GBDT in orange) taken from the TabArena leaderboard as of 2026-06-03.

13.3.1 Pretraining corpus

As always the quantity and quality of the training data is absolutely primordial, and this is just as true when it comes to the pretraining data. For TFM each document in the pretraining corpus is a tabular dataset which are either synthetically generated, or the corpus can consist of a mixture of both synthetic and real datasets (for example in the case of training Real-TabPFN 2.5). The underlying data generating process, used to model the inter-feature relationships, features, and targets, along with a noise component, can be

- SCM: structural causal models having differing directed acyclic graphs (DAG) by randomly dropping edges
- BNN: Bayesian neural networks with randomly sampled architectures
- TBE: priors produced from tree-based estimators

Random samples from these data generating algorithms form the pretraining corpus. Given that the encoder architecture always remains the same, *i.e.* the input layer always expects to see the same number of feature columns, any datasets that have fewer than the maximum number of possible columns are zero-padded. To improve pretraining efficiency curriculum learning can be used; initially training on small simple datasets, before then proceeding to train on larger more complex datasets. By randomly masking cells in the synthetic datasets the pretraining corpus also teach TFM how to impute missing (MCAR) values. In the case of training TabPFN-2 130 million such datasets were used, and for TabICLv2 a rather more modest 35 million. The TabPFN-3 model was trained on more than 8 trillion cells of data.

13.3.2 TFM architecture

TFM models follow the encoder-only transformer schema.

Preprocessing and token embedding Each of the features are first preprocessed by way of standardization so as to have zero mean and unit variance, optionally followed by a Yeo-Johnson power transform. Outliers beyond $\pm 12\sigma$ for TabPFN, and $\pm 4\sigma$ for TabICL, are then removed. For tabular data each cell in the dataset is analogous to a token in text data. Each token is individually projected into a d_{model} dimensional latent space via an affine linear transformation. Thus for example a dataset $\mathbf{X} \in \mathbb{R}^{n \times m}$, having n features and m rows, becomes an embedded 'tensor' of dimensions $\mathbf{E} \in \mathbb{R}^{n \times m \times d_{model}}$. This constitutes the initial input embedding of the transformer. (see also the paper "On Embeddings for Numerical Features in Tabular Deep Learning").

Positional encoding In principle, due to the permutation invariance of tabular datasets, positional encodings should not be required. However, if say two different features happen to have the very same distribution then they will have the very same columnar embedding, and something known as representation collapse may occur. To alleviate this TabPFN adds random feature identifier vectors to the column embedding vectors, and TabICL uses the rotary position embedding (RoPE) technique, thus now permitting feature discrimination (however, this comes at the cost of breaking permutation invariance).

Multi-head self-attention Unlike text data, which is 1D in nature, tabular data is 2D, composed of columns (features) and rows (feature vectors). In view of this TabPFN implements two-way self-attention by flipping between vertical column-wise sample and horizontal row-wise feature self-attentions. On the other hand TabICL uses a shared permutation invariant set transformer which learns the statistics associated with each column, such as its mean, skewness, and kurtosis. Schematic depictions of the model architectures are presented for TabPFN and TabICL in Figures 13.5 and 13.6 respectively.

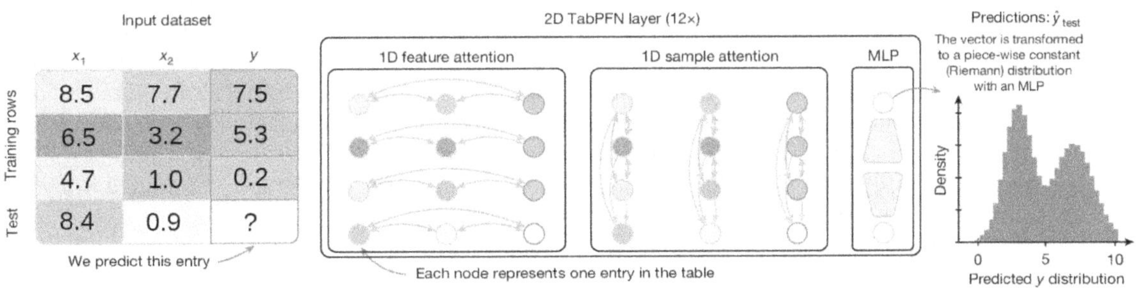

Figure 13.5: Architecture overview of TabPFN-2. (Image adapted from: Noah Hollmann, Samuel Müller, Lennart Purucker, Arjun Krishnakumar, Max Körfer, Shi Bin Hoo, Robin Tibor Schirrmeister, Frank Hutter *"Accurate predictions on small data with a tabular foundation model"*, Nature **637** pp. 319-326 (2025)).

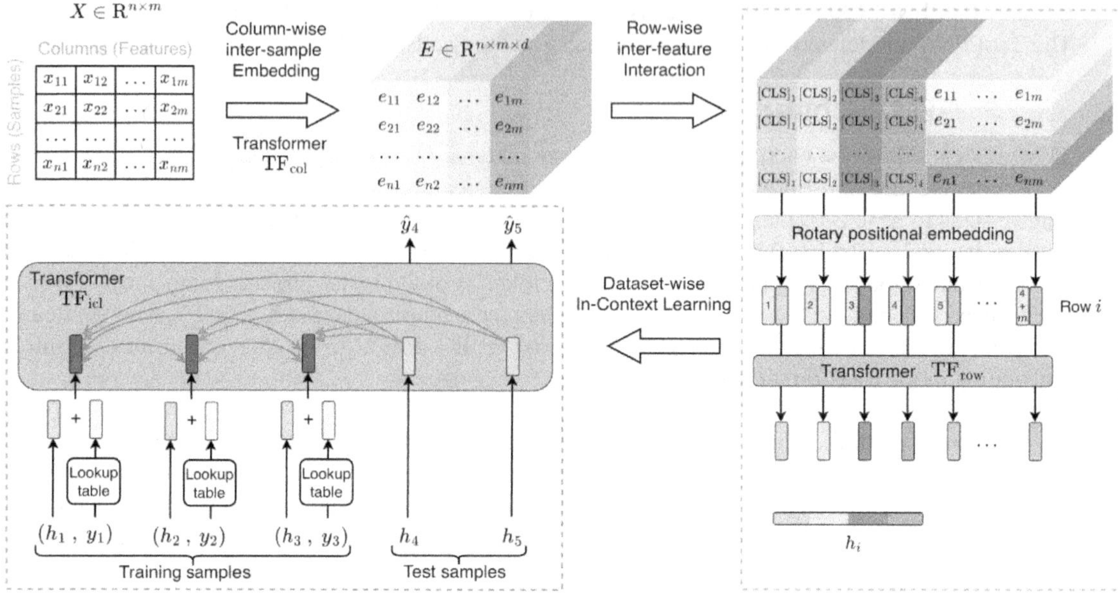

Figure 13.6: Architecture overview of TabICL. (Image credit: Jingang Qu, David Holzmüller, Gaël Varoquaux, Marine Le Morvan *"TabICL: A Tabular Foundation Model for In-Context Learning on Large Data"*, arXiv:2502.05564 (2025)).

Embedding vectors can be chunked into equal sized subspaces known as 'heads', each with their very own self-attention process. This is somewhat reminiscent of the random subspace method used in the Random Forest estimator; here we create an ensemble of heads, each individual head seeing a different subspace. TabPFN uses 4 attention heads, each of dimension $d_{model}/4$, both for the columns and for the rows. The set transformer employed in TabICL uses 8 such heads for the columns to learn distribution awareness, which is then passed to an 8 head transformer to learn the inter-feature interactions. After attention, each of the resulting components are then concatenated back together in order to create the overall modification to be applied to the original embedding vectors.

Both the TabPFN-2 and TabICLv2 transformers have a stack of 12 such attention sub-layers, each interlaced with intervening standardization layers (TabPFN-3 uses a more efficient `RMSNorm` layer which dispenses with mean centering), and capped by a two layer output MLP.

13.3.3 In-context learning (ICL)

When it comes to making predictions `X_train`, `y_train`, and `X_test` are embedded and cross-attention processed; `X_train` and `y_train` provide the context, and `X_test` adopts the role of a query, Q_{test}, that only attends to the K_{train} and V_{train} keys and values, *i.e.* the query is masked from the context, with self-attention taking place only within the train data

$$\text{attention}(Q_{1:n_{train}+n_{test}}, K_{1:n_{train}}, V_{1:n_{train}}) \tag{13.2}$$

leading to conditional predictions for each feature vector in the test data

$$\hat{y} = p(y_{test}|x_{test}, X_{train}, y_{train}) \tag{13.3}$$

Memorization or emergent learning? In the paper "What Can Transformers Learn In-Context? A Case Study of Simple Function Classes" experiments were undertaken where a TFM was provided with context (*i.e.* the `X_train`, `y_train` data) that was disjoint from the pretraining corpus, and the queries (`X_test`) were located in a different orthant from the context, thus forcing extrapolation. In particular they studied linear regression, and the resulting performance for the query predictions (in terms of the squared error) was found to be comparable to that of the optimal ordinary least squares solution. They concluded that

> "...the model cannot be relying on memorization of training prompts or weight vectors, and instead encodes an algorithm capable of in-context learning linear functions that are very different from those seen during training."

It seems that TFM are not using the pretraining data as a glorified lookup table from which to interpolate, but rather they use said data to learn how to learn; "meta-learning". This has huge implications for out-of-distribution performance; a significant failure mode for standard machine learning models. The suggestion is that tabular foundation models are not just a different ML pipeline, but represent a whole new learning paradigm.

13.3.4 Classification and regression

Whether the transformer encoder performs classification or regression is largely predicated on the tooling of the final MLP output (prediction) layer. For classification tasks the last layer of the MLP is a softmax function, returning the probabilities of belonging to each of the (10 by default) classes. If a class prediction is required the probabilities can then be dichotomized via an `argmax` function, which highlights the most probable class. For regression the last layer for TabPFN is again a softmax, returning a discretized probability distribution for $\hat{y}_i$ in the form of (5000) bin borders, which represent positions on the eCDF where by definition

$$\mathrm{CDF}(x) = \int_{-\infty}^{x} \mathrm{PDF}(t)\ \mathrm{d}t \tag{13.4}$$

and quantiles that are desired can be obtained by inverting this cumulative distribution function (see also the paper "Regression using classification algorithms"). On the other hand TabICL last layer is linear, and directly produces (999) equidistant quantiles, *i.e.* for a test feature vector x the prediction is

$$\hat{Q}(\alpha|x) \qquad \text{for } \alpha \in \{0.001, 0.002, ..., 0.998, 0.999\} \tag{13.5}$$

The median point prediction can be trivially obtained from $\hat{Q}(0.5|x)$. The mean, or expectation value, can be obtained from numerical quadrature, for example using the trapezium rule

$$\mathbb{E}(x) = \int_0^1 Q(\alpha)\ \mathrm{d}\alpha \approx \sum \frac{(Q_b + Q_a)(\alpha_b - \alpha_a)}{2} \tag{13.6}$$

Indeed, quantiles have been shown to be optimal point predictors. If $\alpha_b - \alpha_a$ is always equidistant, then for a large number of quantiles by using a Riemann sum the mean point prediction is approximately equal to the mean of the quantiles

$$\hat{y}(x) \approx \overline{Q} \tag{13.7}$$

since here $\alpha_{max} - \alpha_{min} \approx 1$.

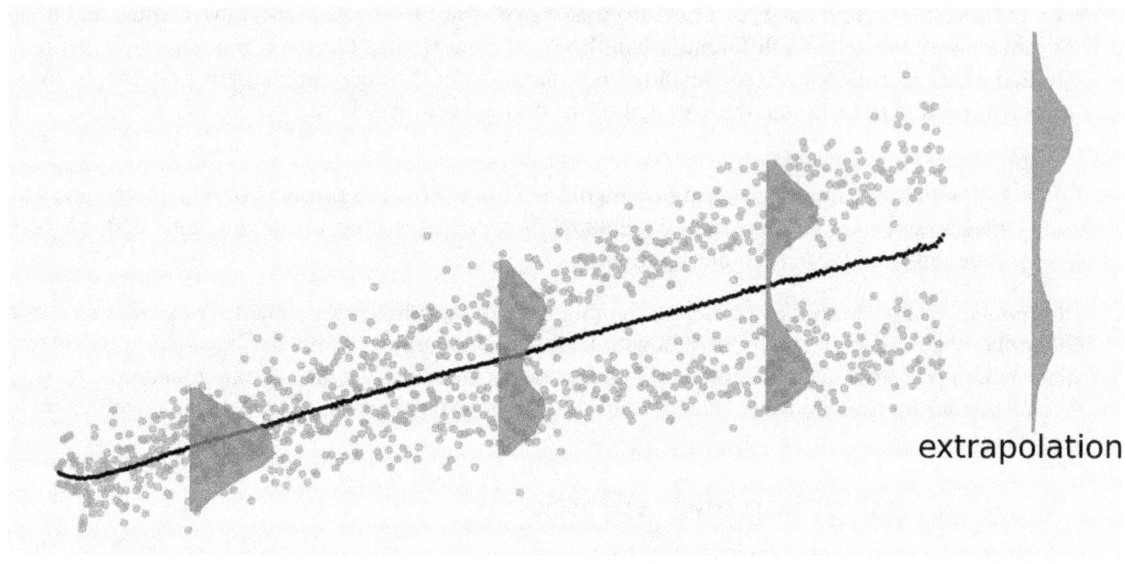

Figure 13.7: Examples of conditional prediction distributions for regression generated from a TFM (here TabPFN) in green. The black line represents point predictions. The rightmost prediction demonstrates a case of extrapolation.

Sample code

Despite the considerable underlying complexity of tabular foundation models, using both TabPFN and TabICL for either regression or classification tasks is the height of simplicity, both following the scikit `fit/predict` API. For probabilistic classification both implement the familiar `.predict_proba()` method. As far as data cleaning is concerned both can natively handle missing data; TabPFN thanks to learning to impute during pretraining (TabPFN-3 also creates a binary indicator column), and TabICL via mean imputation and the creation of a separate category for missing categorical values. Any categorical features are one-hot encoded in TabPFN, and ordinally encoded in TabICL.

TabPFN

```
!pip install -q tabpfn

from tabpfn import TabPFNRegressor
#from tabpfn import TabPFNClassifier

# point prediction
model = TabPFNRegressor()
model.fit(X, y)
y_pred = model.predict(X_test)

# quantile regression
quantiles = [0.05, 0.5, 0.95] # median and 90% coverage
q_pred = model.predict(X_test, output_type = "quantiles",
                       quantiles = quantiles)
```

(Note that the latest versions of TabPFN require license acceptance in order to download the model weights.)

TabICL

```
!pip install -q tabicl

from tabicl import TabICLRegressor
#from tabicl import TabICLClassifier

# point prediction
model = TabICLRegressor()
model.fit(X, y)
y_pred = model.predict(X_test)

# quantile regression
quantiles = [0.05, 0.5, 0.95] # median and 90% coverage
q_pred = model.predict(X_test, output_type = "quantiles",
                       alphas = quantiles)
```

Jupyter Notebook: Examples: [Prior Labs] Binary classification with TabPFN and House Prices using TabICL (v2)

Recommended reading

Papers

- Ravid Shwartz-Ziv, Amitai Armon *"Tabular Data: Deep Learning is Not All You Need"*, arXiv:2106.03253 (2021)
- Müller, Hollmann, Pineda Arango, Grabocka, Hutter *"Transformers Can Do Bayesian Inference"*, arXiv:2112.10510 (2021)
- Grinsztajn, Oyallon, Varoquaux *"Why do tree-based models still outperform deep learning on typical tabular data?"*, arXiv:2207.08815 (2022)
- Borisov, Leemann, Seßler, Haug, Pawelczyk, Kasneci, *"Deep Neural Networks and Tabular Data: A Survey"*, IEEE Transactions on Neural Networks and Learning Systems **35** pp. 7499-7519 (2024)
- Holzmüller, Grinsztajn, Steinwart *"Better by Default: Strong Pre-Tuned MLPs and Boosted Trees on Tabular Data"*, arXiv:2407.04491 (2025)

Books

- Ian Goodfellow, Yoshua Bengio and Aaron Courville *"Deep Learning"*, The MIT Press (2016)
- Christopher M. Bishop, Hugh Bishop *"Deep Learning: Foundations and Concepts"*, Springer (2024)
- Simon J. D. Prince *"Understanding Deep Learning"*, (2025)
- Charles H. Martin, Christopher Hinrichs *"SETOL: A Semi-Empirical Theory of (Deep) Learning"*, arXiv:2507.17912 (2025)

Packages

- PyTorch Tabular - written by Manu Joseph
- `TabNet` (paper, GitHub) - implementation by Sebastien Fischman
- `GrowNet` (paper, GitHub) - Gradient Boosting Neural Networks
- `SAINT` (paper, GitHub) - Self-Attention and Intersample Attention Transformer
- `XTab` (paper) - Cross-table Pretraining for Tabular Transformers
- `TabR` (paper, GitHub) - retrieval-augmented tabular DL model
- `TabM` (paper, GitHub) - Tabular Multiple predictions
- `CARTE` (paper) - Context Aware Representation of Table Entries
- `TabDPT` (paper, GitHub) - Tabular Discriminative Pre-trained Transformer
- `TabSTAR` (paper, GitHub) - Tabular Semantically Target-Aware Representations
- `PyTabKit` (paper, GitHub) - includes the RealMLP model.
- `xRFM` (paper, GitHub) - tabular Recursive Feature Machine.
- `TabPFN` (paper, GitHub) - Tabular Prior-Data Fitted Network
  - `TabPFN-3` (technical report, GitHub)
- `nanoTabPFN` (paper, GitHub) - an educational lightweight re-implementation of the TabPFN classifier
- `Mitra` (paper) - Mixed Synthetic Priors for Enhancing Tabular Foundation Models
- `TabICL` (paper, GitHub) - Tabular In-Context Learning classifier
  - `TabICLv2` (paper, GitHub) - Tabular In-Context Learning, version 2
- `NanoTabICL` (GitHub) - a lightweight re-implementation of TabICL
- `LimiX` (paper, GitHub) - Structured-Data Modeling Capability for Generalist Intelligence

Further reading

Books

- Trevor Hastie, Robert Tibshirani, Jerome Friedman *"The Elements of Statistical Learning"*, Springer (2017)
- Gareth James, Daniela Witten, Trevor Hastie, Robert Tibshirani, Jonathan Taylor *"An Introduction to Statistical Learning"*, Springer (2023)
- Christopher M. Bishop *"Pattern Recognition and Machine Learning"*, Springer (2006)
- Kevin Patrick Murphy *"Probabilistic Machine Learning: An Introduction"*, MIT Press (2022)
- Bradley Efron, Trevor Hastie *"Computer Age Statistical Inference: Algorithms, Evidence and Data Science"*, Cambridge University Press (2016)
- Lindholm, Wahlström, Lindsten, Schön *"Machine Learning - A First Course for Engineers and Scientists"*, Cambridge University Press (2022)

Articles

- Ulrike von Luxburg, Bernhard Schoelkopf *"Statistical Learning Theory: Models, Concepts, and Results"*, arXiv:0810.4752 (2008)
- Sebastian Raschka *"Model Evaluation, Model Selection, and Algorithm Selection in Machine Learning"*, arXiv:1811.12808 (2020)

For many more excellent texts visit the compendium of free ML reading resources.

See also

- Carl McBride Ellis *"A selection of my Kaggle notebooks"*

www.ingramcontent.com/pod-product-compliance
Lightning Source LLC
LaVergne TN
LVHW060033210926
848481LV00013B/3855